Public Relations in the Digital Era

Public Relations in the Digital Era

K.M. Shrivastava

PILGRIMS PUBLISHING
◆ Varanasi ◆

Public Relations in the Digital Era
K.M. Shrivastava

Published by
PILGRIMS PUBLISHING

An imprint of
PILGRIMS BOOK HOUSE
B 27/98 A-8 Nawabganj Road
Durga Kund, Varanasi 221010
Phone: 91-542-2314060
Fax: 91-542-2312456
e-mail: pilgrims@satyam.net.in
Website: www.pilgrimsbooks.com

ISBN 81-7769-478-2
ISBN 81-7769-523-1 (pbk)

Cover design
Dushyant Parasher
Layout and typesetting by
Astricks, New Delhi 110070, www.astricks.com
Printed in India at
Pilgrims Press Private Limited, Laipur, Varanasi 221005

To
My Guru
H.Y. Sharda Prasad
Information Adviser to Prime Ministers
Indira Gandhi and Rajiv Gandhi

Preface

When I was heading the Eastern India Campus of Indian Institute of Mass Communication at Dhenkanal (Orissa), I always took my students to Dhauli, near Bhubaneswar. It is here that Emperor Ashoka fought the famous Battle of Kalinga (261 BC) and where today we find a rock edict, representing an early exercise in public relations. Ashoka used the available communication medium of his time to reach out to his people and officials. However it is Edward L. Bernays (1891–1995) also known as the 'father of spin' — who used persuasive communication mainly through the print media in the early part of the twentieth century in the United States — who is called the 'father of public relations'. This is because of two books written by him, *Crystallizing Public Opinion* (1923) and *Propaganda* (1928). The communication revolution in the later part of the twentieth century resulting from the convergence of communication technologies and the emergence of the Internet has changed all professions, particularly those that depend on communication. Public Relations (PR) is one of them.

When information travelled as fast as the telegraph, Mark Twain said, 'A lie can travel halfway around the world while the truth is putting on its shoes.' Today we have to think in terms of real-time responses to bad information. Not in terms of the next news cycle, but *right now* as news cycles do not exist any more. Besides this, economic upheavals, demographic shifts, political winds, everything is in a flux. It has widened the responsibility of PR professionals to anticipate changes, analyse their potential impact on clients and corporations from the standpoint of public perception, and design and implement programmes to help them meet these challenges.

The process of change in PR is a continuing one, as it is with other fields, with the advent of new communication technologies. There is a need to look at the current state of the art. This book is an effort in that direction covering important aspects of theory and practice. It will be useful for managers, PR professionals working in the corporate sector as well as in the government, and students of management and public relations.

K.M. Shrivastava
New Delhi, October 2006

Acknowledgements

I was introduced to Public Relations in 1976, while studying for a Postgraduate Diploma in Journalism at the Indian Institute of Mass Communication (IIMC). Later as a journalist working for various media organizations I became a target of public relations from different organizations, companies and governments. I learnt from all those interactions and am therefore indebted to all those PR professionals who have come in contact with me over the years.

I am particularly indebted to a group of students led by Gurtej Pal Singh who forced me to teach PR to their class in Punjabi University, Patiala in 1987, when I was heading the Department of Journalism and Mass Communication. This situation forced me to critically look at the wealth of PR experience accumulated over the years, as a recipient of corporate and government communications. From 2003 to 2005 as Professor-in-Charge of the Eastern India Campus of IIMC in Dhenkanal (Orissa), I again taught PR thus updating myself on the subject. These students deserve my thanks as the content of this book was put together to satisfy their requirements. Credit has been given in the text wherever possible, but where information about the source is not specific regarding organizations or companies, it may be treated as being from their official websites, visited in many cases several times from July 2003 to May 2006.

I am grateful to Dr O.P. Kejariwal, Member, Central Information Commission who encouraged me to convert the collected material for students into a book. Hartej Baksh Singh has done a good job to make it fit to print. Thanks are also due to Rama Nand who readily agreed to publish it, which will ensure its availability to a wider audience.

Feedback from professionals and students is welcome at kmsiimc@yahoo.com.

Contents

Public Relations
Concept and Scope

Public Relations (PR) as we know it today is believed to have evolved in the early twentieth century in the United States of America. However it has been practiced over the years in varied forms in different civilizations. Rock edicts[1] of the Indian Emperor Ashoka[2] of the third century BC are in fact

1. Ashoka's edicts are to be found scattered in more than thirty places throughout India, Nepal, Pakistan and Afghanistan. Most of them are written in the Brahmi script from which all Indian scripts and many of those used in Southeast Asia later developed. The language used in the edicts found in the eastern part of the sub-continent is a type of Magadhi, probably the official language of Ashoka's court. The language used in the edicts found in the western part of India is closer to Sanskrit although one bilingual edict in Afghanistan is written in Aramaic and Greek.

2. Although the exact dates of Ashoka's life are a matter of dispute among scholars, he was born in about 304 BC and became the third king of the Mauryan dynasty after the death of his father, Bindusara. His given name was Ashoka but he assumed the title Devanampiya Piyadasi which means 'Beloved-of-the-Gods, He Who Looks On With Affection.' In 262 BC, eight years after his coronation, Ashoka's armies attacked and conquered Kalinga, a country that roughly corresponds to the modern state of Orissa. The loss of life caused by battle, reprisals, deportations and the turmoil that always exists in the aftermath of war so horrified Ashoka that it brought about a complete change in his personality. Ashoka died in 232 BC in the thirty-eighth year of his reign.

what amounts to government information or public relations or what is more recently termed as public affairs activity. Here is the content of an Ashokan edict:[3]

> *Beloved-of-the-Gods, King Piyadasi, has caused this Dhamma edict to be written. Here (in my domain) no living beings are to be slaughtered or offered in sacrifice. Nor should festivals be held, for Beloved-of-the-Gods, King Piyadasi, sees much to object to in such festivals, although there are some festivals that Beloved-of-the-Gods, King Piyadasi, does approve of.*
>
> *Formerly, in the kitchen of Beloved-of-the-Gods, King Piyadasi, hundreds of thousands of animals were killed every day to make curry. But now with the writing of this Dhamma edict only three creatures, two peacocks and a deer are killed, and the deer not always. And in time, not even these three creatures will be killed.*

Here is the content of another edict:[4]

> *Everywhere within Beloved-of-the-Gods, King Piyadasi's domain, and among the people beyond the borders, the Cholas, the Pandyas, the Satiyaputras, the Keralaputras, as far as Tamraparni and where the Greek king Antiochos rules, and among the kings who are neighbours of Antiochos, everywhere has Beloved-of-the-Gods, King Piyadasi, made provision for two types of medical treatment: medical treatment for humans and medical treatment for animals. Wherever medical herbs suitable for humans or animals are not available, I have had them imported and grown. Wherever medical roots or fruits are not available, I have had them imported and grown. Along roads I have had wells dug and trees planted for the benefit of humans and animals.*

Modern PR has been around for almost a 100 years. Public relations evolved from individual press agents and publicists,

3. The first of the 14 Rock Edicts.
4. The second of the 14 Rock Edicts.

to counselling firms that offered their services as experts in the field. George V.S. Michaelis, Herbert Small, and Thomas O. Marvin founded the first publicity firm in the USA, The Publicity Bureau, in Boston in 1900. The bureau came into prominence in 1906 when it was hired by the railroads to oppose adverse regulatory legislation that was then before Congress. The firm failed in its efforts, but soon after, the majority of railroads established their own public relations departments.

While many believe that Edward Bernays[5] created the profession of public relations in the 1920s, others point to Ivy Lee,[6] who opened a 'counselling office' in 1904 and described himself as a 'physician to corporate bodies'. In 1906, he invented the 'press release' — to distribute the company's 'news' about an accident before reporters received other versions of the story. In 1915, Lee became John D. Rockefeller's publicity counsel. He advised Rockefeller to hand out dimes to poor children as a way of showing his philanthropy.

Bernays tried to put public relations on a scientific footing, often applying lessons he had learned from his uncle, Sigmund Freud.[7] He applied his uncle's concept of 'mass psychology' to sell bacon, cigarettes and soap. He also staged 'overt acts', or

5. Edward L. Bernays (1891–1995) is called the 'father of public relations.' A nephew of Sigmund Freud he was born in Austria and brought up in New York. In organizing endorsements for a play on the taboo subject of venereal disease, he found his calling as a publicist. His clients included the U.S. War Department, the Lithuanian government and General Motors (GM). He edited *The Engineering of Consent*, Norman: University of Oklahoma Press, 1955, whose title is his often-quoted definition of PR.

6. Ivy Ledbetter Lee worked as a newspaper reporter before becoming 'press representative' for a group of coal miners in 1906. He worked for the Pennsylvania Railroad Co. in 1912. His success in improving their public images brought him many powerful clients, including the Rockefeller interests.

7. Bernays was actually the double nephew of Sigmund Freud. (His

what would now be called 'media events' to awaken apparently subconscious feelings. For example, George Washington Hill, president of the American Tobacco Company, hired Bernays in 1928 to solve a problem: Women weren't smoking cigarettes in public. Hill recognized that changing public opinion could expand his market for Lucky Strike cigarettes. Bernays consulted a psychoanalyst, Dr A.A. Brill, who suggested that smoking in public, which men did openly, be linked to the freedom to vote, a right that women had just won. With the help of his wife, Doris Fleishman, Bernays convinced a group of former suffragettes to march down Fifth Avenue, carrying Lucky Strikes in the air — as if they were 'torches of freedom' — as a gesture to demonstrate their equality with men. It was one of his biggest successes.

Bernays also solidified his reputation as 'the father of spin' by writing books, including *Crystallizing Public Opinion* in 1923 and *Propaganda* in 1928. In fact, Bernays often described what he did as propaganda, and didn't apologize for using the term until after it was adopted in 1933 by Joseph Goebbels, the Minister for Public Enlightenment and Propaganda in Nazi Germany.

In 1939, Germany's effective use of propaganda prompted President Franklin Delano Roosevelt to create a group of 'top men' to start working on an American version of propaganda — just in case it was needed. One of these 'top men' was Harold Lasswell.[8] In 1939, Lasswell was named Director of

8. Lasswell received his Bachelor of Philosophy degree in 1922 and his Ph.D. in 1926 from the University of Chicago. He also studied at the universities of London, Paris, Geneva, and Berlin during those years. In 1927, he wrote 'Propaganda Technique in World War I'. He taught political science at the University of Chicago until 1938, when he went to Yale University to become a visiting lecturer at the Law School. He briefly served at the Washington School of Psychiatry from 1938 to 1939.

War Communications Research at the US Library of Congress. He quickly developed a 'Model of Communication' that was classified 'Top Secret'. Lasswell explained to the other top men working on the project that propaganda — or what the Americans called the communication process — entailed five key elements. He assembled these elements into a model and then turned the model into a simple question: 'Who says what, in which channel, to whom, with what effects?' In his model, 'Who' is the 'Sender', 'What' is the 'Message', the 'Channel' is the 'Medium', the 'Whom' is the 'Receiver', and some of the 'Effects' can be measured by 'Feedback'. If you found the right answers to each of the five elements of the question, then you could create effective propaganda, unless, of course, too much 'noise' — unplanned static or distortion during the communication process — resulted in the receiver receiving a different message than the sender sent.

During World War II, US Federal agencies used Lasswell's secret model to test a variety of propaganda techniques and to create some very powerful propaganda posters, films, and radio broadcasts. For example, it was discovered that 'help win the war' wasn't the most effective slogan to use for selling war bonds. It appealed to men, but not women. This led to the development of a more effective slogan: 'Help win the war and bring the boys home.' This discovery was shared with the US Office of Defense Transportation, who applied it to create a different set of posters urging civilians not to travel unnecessarily, because precious gasoline was needed by the military. Lasswell's model was declassified in 1948, and he published a paper on it in 1949. Both Lasswell's communication model and his question, 'Who says what in which channel to whom with what effects', have been included in standard textbooks of marketing management and communication.

Another pioneer, Arthur W. Page (1883–1960)[9] is credited as being the founder of corporate public relations. As the Vice President of Public Relations for American Telephone and Telegraph Corporation, from 1927 to 1946 he pioneered innovative PR practices that form part of post-modern corporate PR practices and laid the foundation for public relations as a corporate management policy function.

Evolution of Definition

The earliest definitions emphasized the roles of press agencies and publicity since these were major elements from which modern public relations grew. The concept and scope of public relations evolved over the years. Here are some definitions that illustrate it:

1930s

Public relations is the development of cordial, equitable and, therefore, mutually profitable relations between a business, industry or organization and the public it serves. (Thomas W. Parry in an address titled 'Public Relations — First in the Order of Business' to the Advertising Club of St. Louis, 15 June 1937).

1940s

Public relations may be defined as those aspects of our personal and corporate behaviour, which have a social rather than purely private and personal significance. (Harwood L. Childs, *An Introduction to Public Opinion*, 1940).

9. In 1983, the Arthur W. Page Society was founded as a professional organization with a single mission: to strengthen the management policy role of the chief corporate public relations officer.

1950s

'Public relations: The activities of an industry, union, corporation, profession, government, or other organization in building and maintaining sound and productive relations with special publics such as customers, employees, or stockholders, and with the public at large, so as to adapt itself to its environment and interpret itself to society'. (*Webster's New International Dictionary*, 1950).

1960s

'Public relations 1. The activities of a corporation, union, government, or other organization in building and maintaining sound and productive relations with special publics such as customers, employees, or stockholders, and with the public at large, so as to adapt itself to its environment and interpret itself to society'. (*Webster's New Collegiate Dictionary*, 1960).

1970s

'Public relations. *Abbr.* **PR, P.R.** 1. The methods and activities employed by an individual, organization, corporation, or government, to promote a favorable relationship with the public'. (*The American Heritage Dictionary*, 1971).

1980s

'Public relations. The efforts of a corporation to promote goodwill between itself and the public'. (*The Random House Dictionary*, 1980).

'Public Relations is the management function that identifies, establishes, and maintains mutually beneficial relationships between an organization and the various publics on whom its success or failure depends', (S.M. Cutlip, A.H.

Center, and, G.M. Broom, *Effective Public Relations* (Prentice-Hall International, Inc., New Jersey, 6th ed, 1985), p. 1.

'Public relations helps an organization and its publics adapt mutually to each other' — Public Relations Society of America (1988). In this definition, the essential functions of research, planning, communications dialogue and evaluation are implied. Key words are 'organization' rather than the limiting implication of 'company' or 'business', and 'publics' which recognizes that all organizations have multiple publics from which they must earn consent and support.[10]

1990s

'**Public relations**: the business of inducing the public to have understanding for and goodwill toward a person, firm or institution'. (*Webster's Ninth New Collegiate Dictionary*, 1991).

2000s

'An organization's reputation, profitability, and even its continued existence can depend on the degree to which its targeted "publics" support its goals and policies. Public relations specialists serve as advocates for businesses, non-profit associations, universities, hospitals, and other organizations, and build and maintain positive relationships with the public. As managers recognize the growing importance of good public relations to the success of their organizations, they increasingly rely on public relations specialists for advice on the strategy and policy of such programs'. (U.S. Labor Office).

10. The PRSA website has it as its official definition in 2005.

PR: A Working Definition

Dr Rex F. Harlow, public relations scholar and professional leader, undertook the task of collecting such definitions published since 1900, breaking them into major elements, and classifying the basic, central ideas these definitions included. From his analysis of 472 definitions, he produced a working definition that is both conceptual and operational. 'Public relations is a distinctive management function which helps establish and maintain mutual lines of communication, understanding, acceptance and cooperation between an organization and its publics; involves the management of problems or issues; helps management to keep informed on and responsive to public opinion; defines and emphasizes the responsibility of the management to serve the public interest; helps management keep abreast of and effectively utilize change, serving as an early warning system to help anticipate trends; and uses research and sound and ethical communication as its principal tools.'[11]

Related Activities

Public relations involves use of some or all of the following activities depending on various factors and circumstances.

Advertising

Buying space or time in order to relay your message. The upside is you get to choose what is said; the downside is advertising is expensive and not as credible as a third-party relaying your message for you.

11. Rex F. Harlow, 'Building a Public Relations Definition', *Public Relations Review* 2 (Winter 1978), p. 36.

Promotion

Promotion keeps the product in the minds of the customer and helps stimulate demand for the product. Promotion involves ongoing advertising and publicity.

Marketing

Developing a product, for a defined target audience, offered at an appropriate price, that you then promote. Marketing is not just sales and it's not just promotion. Marketing includes all the steps between defining a need and then fulfilling that need. Traditionally, marketing covers the four 'Ps': Product, Positioning, Pricing and Promotion.

Marketing Communications

Communications strategy and tactics that help marketing efforts such as product launches, brand identity and positioning fall under this category.

Sales

Sales involves most or many of the following activities: cultivating prospective buyers (or leads) in a market segment; conveying the features, advantages and benefits of a product or service to the lead and closing the sale (or coming to agreement on pricing and services).

Publicity

Publicity is mention in the media. Organizations usually have little control over the message in the media, at least, not as they do in advertising. Regarding publicity, reporters and writers decide what will be said.

Media Relations

Media relations is, creating an ongoing dialogue between a

news outlet and your spokespeople in an effort to have you or your company discussed in a positive manner, in public, through a publication or broadcast. Without it, no news organization will carry your story unless there is a crisis, which can produce negative publicity.

Scope of PR

The Chartered Institute of Public Relations (CIPR) is the UK's leading public relations industry professional body. Founded in February 1948, it has over 8000 members today. It says: Public relations is about reputation — the result of what you do, what you say and what others say about you. Public relations is the discipline, which looks after reputation, with the aim of earning understanding and support and influencing opinion and behaviour. It is the planned and sustained effort to establish and maintain goodwill and mutual understanding between an organization and its publics.

- Public relations specialists handle organizational functions such as media, community, consumer, and governmental relations; political campaigns; interest-group representation; conflict mediation; or employee and investor relations.
- However, public relations is not only 'telling the organization's story'.
- Understanding the attitudes and concerns of consumers, employees, and various other groups also is a vital part of the job.
- To improve communications, public relations specialists establish and maintain cooperative relationships with representatives of community, consumer,

employee, and public interest groups and with representatives from print and broadcast journalism.

- Informing the general public, interest groups, and stockholders of an organization's policies, activities, and accomplishments is an important part of a public relations specialist's job.
- The work also involves keeping management aware of public attitudes and concerns of the many groups and organizations with which they must deal.
- Public relations specialists prepare press releases and contact people in the media who might print or broadcast their material.
- Many radio or television special reports, newspaper stories, and magazine articles start at the desks of public relations specialist.
- Public relations specialists also arrange and conduct programmes to keep up contact between organization representatives and the public.
- They set up speaking engagements and often prepare speeches for company officials.
- These specialists represent employers at community projects; make films, slides, or other visual presentations at meetings and school assemblies; and plan conventions.
- They are responsible for preparing annual reports and writing proposals for various projects.

PR in Government

In government, public relations specialists — who may be called press secretaries, information officers, public affairs specialists, or communications specialists — keep the public informed about the activities of government agencies and officials. Government departments have designations similar to other official designations — Secretary, Director, Public Relations / Information / Public Affairs Officers, information or media Assistants for official PR positions and may be designated as information or media advisors or specialists for non-cadre (sometimes political) positions.

The Government of India has an Indian Information Service. Officers of this service run the media units of the Ministry of Information and Broadcasting and also serve the media related needs of other ministries through the Press Information Bureau. However, the Prime Minister (or other ministers) may have media advisor's who may not be part of the service. State Governments in India have a department of Public Relations / Information and Publicity and the importance of these departments can be measured from the fact that in most cases these departments are directly under the Chief Minister, who is the political head of the State. These departments have their offices at least up to district level and mainly help the district administrations in their communication needs.

PR in Large Organizations

The key public relations executive, who in large organizations is often a vice-president, may develop overall plans and policies with other executives. In addition, public relations departments employ public relations specialists to write, research, prepare materials, maintain contacts, and respond to inquiries. In the government, PR / information / public affairs has been significant particularly after the Second World War. The corporate world took time to recognize the significance of PR. John Graham of Fleishman-Hillard[12] told a galaxy of PR professionals at the turn of the century, 'Many of us in this

12. Hall of Fame Lecture to Arthur W. Page Society in 2000.

room have worked through periods where public relations people were buried in the corporate hierarchy, reporting to the legal department, human resources, the marketing group, or the executive support organization. Those days are rapidly receding.' PR now has become much more important in the corporate world usually headed by a Vice-President reporting to the Chief Executive Officer.

The strength of the PR department may vary from company to company as well as the budget available for the purpose. Big departments normally handle campaign planning, advertising, media relations, investor relations, government relations, and community relations themselves, and also bring out newsletters or house journals for internal communication and have their own monitoring systems. They may outsource some of the activity in certain specific needs or circumstances. Others may have very few regular members of staff and outsource most of the activities.

PR in Small Organizations

People who handle publicity for an individual or who direct public relations for a small organization may deal with all aspects of the job. They contact people, plan and research, and prepare material for distribution. They also may handle advertising or sales promotion work to support marketing.

What PR Does

The Public Relations Society of America (PRSA), established in 1947, is the world's largest organization for public relations professionals having nearly 20,000 members, organized into 114 chapters, representing business and industry, technology, counselling firms, government, associations, hospitals, schools, professional services firms and non-profit organizations. According to PRSA:

> Public relations helps our complex, pluralistic society to reach decisions and function more effectively by contributing to mutual understanding among groups and institutions. It serves to bring private and public policies into harmony. Public relations serves a wide variety of institutions in society such as businesses, trade unions, government agencies, voluntary associations, foundations, hospitals, schools, colleges, and religious institutions. To achieve their goals, these institutions must develop effective relationships with many different audiences or publics such as employees, members, customers, local communities, shareholders, and other institutions, and with society at large.

The managements of institutions need to understand the attitudes and values of their publics in order to achieve institutional goals. The goals themselves are shaped by the external environment. The public relations practitioner acts as a counsellor to management and as a mediator, helping translate private aims into reasonable, publicly acceptable policy and action. As a management function, public relations encompasses the following:

- Anticipating, analysing and interpreting public opinion, attitudes, and issues that might impact, for good or ill, the operations and plans of the organization.
- Counselling management at all levels in the organization with regard to policy decisions, courses of action, and communications, taking into account their public ramifications and the organization's social or citizenship responsibilities.
- Researching, conducting, and evaluating, on a continuing basis, programmes of action and communication to

achieve the informed public understanding necessary to the success of an organization's aims. These may include marketing, financial, fund raising, employee, community or government relations, and other programmes.

- Planning and implementing the organization's efforts to influence or change public policy. Setting objectives, planning, budgeting, recruiting and training staff, developing facilities — in short, managing the resources needed to perform all of the above.

Examples of the knowledge that may be required in the professional practice of public relations include communication arts, psychology, social psychology, sociology, political science, economics, and the principles of management and ethics. Technical knowledge and skills are required for opinion research, public issues analysis, media relations, direct mail, institutional advertising, publications, film/video productions, special events, speeches, and presentations. In helping to define and implement policy, the public relations practitioner uses a variety of professional communications skills and plays an integrative role both within the organization and between the organization and the external environment.

How PR Can Help

The publicity and promotional aspects pave the way for the sale of products or services, so much so that some companies have placed sales quotas on their product publicity people. Internal motivation is a vital factor that affects the bottom line, by building morale, enhancing productivity and creating a team spirit. It also helps recruit qualified people and retain them.

Public relations provide an early warning system by avoiding disruptions that may occur when a single surprise issue or unplanned-for social/political change arises. It provides an organization with new opportunities because the people involved in public relations interact with more internal and external audiences than anyone else in the organization.

Public relations helps to protect the present position when an organization is under attack. It helps to overcome executive isolation, something that can affect every organization sooner or later. An inescapable assignment of every public relations practitioner is opening the eyes and ears of management to what's really happening 'out there'. Public relations helps organizations manage change, something they must do to stay competitive and efficient. But since change is threatening and often resisted, smooth transition through a necessary change guided by public relations professionals is a real money-saver.

The phrase 'double bottom line' was coined to explain the relationship between an organization and its social responsibility. It's now well understood and accepted that social responsibility does have a traceable effect on the economic success for every type of organization. Public relations staff usually plays the leading role in 'social accountancy'.

The Job and Skills

PR professionals are required to do diverse work assignments:

Writing: News releases, newsletters, correspondence, reports, speeches, booklet texts, radio and television copy, film scripts, trade paper and magazine articles, institutional advertisements, product information and technical materials.

Editing: Special publications, employee newsletters, shareholder reports, and other communications directed to internal and external audiences.

Media Relations: Contacting news media, magazines, weekly supplements, freelance writers, and trade publications with the intent of getting them to publish or broadcast news and features about or originated by the organization. Responding to media requests for information and spokespersons.

Events: Arranging and managing press conferences, conventions, exhibitions, open houses, anniversary celebrations, fund-raising events, special observances, contests and award programmes.

Speaking: Appearing before groups and arranging platforms for others before appropriate audiences by managing speakers' bureau etc.

Production: Creating communications using multi-media knowledge and skills; including art, photography, and layout of brochures, booklets, reports, institutional advertisements, and periodical publications, recording and editing audio and video tapes; and preparations of audio-video presentations.

Research: Gathering intelligence — enabling the organization to plan programmes responsive to its publics and problem situations, monitoring public relations programme effectiveness during implementation and evaluating programme impact.

Programming and Counselling: Determining needs, priorities, goals, publics, objectives, and strategies. Collaborating with management or clients in a problem-solving process.

Training: Working with executives and other organizational representatives to prepare them for dealing with the media, and for making presentations and other public appearances. In-house staff development.

Management: Administering operations of public relations functions — personnel, budget, and programmes.

A PR professional thus should have strong common sense, good command over language, written and spoken, should be multi-skilled in media work, should have good interpersonal skills and should be capable of strategic thinking and management. PR professionals should understand and embrace new communication technology — a very sophisticated and powerful resource. In this era of instant communications, those that understand how such tools can be used will be able to further a bond of trust with external and internal stakeholders, and restore the sense of integrity that stakeholders demand.

Here are thoughts of some senior PR executives on what they are looking for a new hire in PR.

Catherine Bolton, Executive Director, Public Relations Society of America (PRSA): They have to know the basics. They need to be credible PR people with a background and an understanding of the profession. They should have a passion for the profession — they're in PR not because they 'fell' into it, but because they believe in what they do. They can't be afraid to roll up their sleeves and pitch in to get the job done. Business is so hard today; you have to be a team player.

Robbie Vorhaus, President and CEO, Vorhaus & Company Inc. looks for: A passion for the truth (comes from my journalism roots). A drive to make every moment and situation better than how you found it A whoopee cushion sense of humour.

Steve Keeble, CEO, MediaMap: There are so many skills today that a good PR practitioner must possess — the ability to write clearly and creatively, to think strategically, to manage multiple projects at once and to manage their day-to-day operations through the use of technology. A combination of these characteristics along with the insight and experience to drive a client's value and brand into the market is my definition of a great PR hire.

Jeff Hasen, former President, WONGDOODY Communications: This industry calls for passionate professionals who are resourceful, committed, and inclusive. Thomas Edison said genius is one per cent inspiration and ninety-nine per cent perspiration. I believe he was right.

Brenda Clevenger, Proprietor, CornerBarPR: The ability to understand the big picture so he or she can focus on outcomes, not tasks, is critical. Having this big-picture mentality frees supervisors from compiling meaningless 'grocery lists' of things to do to fill the day versus fulfilling the expectations — and needs! — of the client. It's like reaching Nirvana when you find a new hire who truly understands how PR can help an organization achieve its business goals.

Chris Perkett, President and Founder of PerkettPR: For skills and characteristics, they need to be self-motivated and hardworking. Really have a strong work ethic. Being non-egotistical is also really important because the job is about making others shine. Being a team player is important because you can't do this work alone. Also, networking is important — being able to pick up a phone and call strangers is essential. And you have to be passionate about technology. I would also advise that they do internships in both corporate and agency environments so they can decide which works best for them.

Judy Wilks, President, Bite: I'm a great believer in out-thinking rather than out-spending the competition. Creativity cannot be manufactured, only refined, so it's the first thing I look for in potential recruits.

Marika Flatt, Owner, PR by the Book, LLC: They have to be very organized, detail-oriented and thorough. They have to get used to having a lot of balls in the air without dropping any. Being approachable is very important — being someone the media and clients enjoy talking with. Also, clients need to feel that their publicist is there 24/7 for them and cares about their success. Integrity and ethics are very important. All we really have is our reputation. I do feel that if you wrong someone it will come back to haunt you.

Ellen Blattel, Founder and President of Blattel Communications: A college education is very important, perhaps in journalism or English. Taking public speaking, debating, writing — these are all good skills to have. Assertiveness is important in this work, because basically you're in sales, so taking classes or training that foments this is good. You want to do things to enhance self-confidence. Developing critical thinking is very important as is the ability to learn on the job and to know how to make wise assessments.

Adrienne Arieff, Principal, Arieff Communications: You really need to know your product or service before you talk about it. You need to be approachable and flexible. Excellent writing is important. Being able to correct things ASAP. Clear thinking. It's really important to have an excellent boss or mentor somewhere along the line — someone to help you keep your feet on the ground, guide you in a direction where you can stay solid. Lastly, you don't have to live in New York to be in this business. You can be a big fish in a small pond. With today's technology, you can do this job from anywhere.

Mario Almonte, Vice President, Public Relations Group, Herman Associates: Enthusiasm, dedication, intelligence, the willingness to make bold decisions and to pitch a client in a new way. They have to have excellent writing skills, so that they are not falling back on clichés whenever they write press releases. They need to master the art of the e-mail — creating a scintillating subject line that jumps out of the crowd of spam and gets the reporter to click on it — to open it, not delete it! They must also know how to talk on the phone, have a courteous manner that conveys to the reporter a respect for their job; a genuine appreciation for the fact that the reporter is doing them a favour in writing about their product — when they could just as easily be writing about twenty other, similar products. Most important, they must love the challenge of the 'chase'; that is, pitching clients whose products are especially difficult to categorize and consistently getting them media hits.

Brian Solis, Founder and President, FutureWorks Inc.: We try to earn our clients' business everyday. So first and foremost, a new PR hire really needs to understand a particular tech field we work in, such as enterprise storage or digital cameras. And they need to be enthusiastic about that field. We're all tech geeks here. They should also be confident enough to do media and have a solid command of writing — not just AP [Associated Press] style. Lastly, it's important to realize that what has kept us in the PR industry going — ultimately those of us who have worked hard at our craft — has raised the profile of what's needed in PR.

Mark Schannon of Schannon & Associates: The art of persuasion. Good writing, which is becoming a lost art. Asking why. Challenging accepted wisdom. Ability to create sustainable behaviours. And lastly, remembering that behind every negative opinion there's a hurt feeling.

Bob Druckenmiller, co-founder, Porter Novelli International looks for: Characteristics: Inquisitiveness, creativity, conscientiousness, optimism and a good sense of humour. Skills: Good writer — (Hope this doesn't sound more like a personal ad, but we hire for character and train for specific skills).

In sum a PR professional should have the following:

Skills: writing, research, planning, problem solving, publishing, and public speaking;

Knowledge: media, management process, business, economics, finance, business of organization;

Abilities: decision-making, social skills, handling people, assuming responsibility, instilling confidence, listening;

Qualities: stability, common sense, drive, enthusiasm, wide range of interests, intellectual curiosity, tolerance for frustration; style.

There are two streams open to PR professionals. They may work for the PR department of an organization or they may work for a PR agency or PR firm which works for a wide range of clients — corporations, trade associations, governments and even some non-profit advocacy groups. While corporations have fuelled the growth of the industry, in more recent times, governments and political parties have come to rely on PR companies to sell controversial policies and win election campaigns. Most public relations companies have staff or teams of people that specialize in particular skill areas — commonly referred to as practice areas — or groups that support a particular industry sector.

Convergence and Conglomerates

From the middle of 1980s the merger and acquisition activities of communication companies have let to emergence of giant conglomerates. The biggest two are Omnicom Group and WPP.

Omnicom Group Inc.

Omnicom Group Inc. founded in 1986 is a strategic holding company that manages a portfolio of global market leaders.

Omnicom's branded networks and numerous specialty firms provide advertising, strategic media planning and buying, direct and promotional marketing, public relations and other specialty communications services to over 5,000 clients in more than 100 countries. Omnicom Group includes three global advertising brands BBDO Worldwide, DDB Worldwide, and TBWA Worldwide, leading US-based national advertising agencies: Arnell Group; Element 79; Goodby, Silverstein & Partners; GSD&M; Martin/Williams; Merkley + Partners; and Zimmerman Partners Advertising. Its Diversified Agency Services (DAS) consists of a global enterprise of more than 100 companies that provide services in direct marketing/consultancy, public relations, promotional marketing, and specialty communications. Diversified Agency Services (DAS) includes three of the top seven public relations firms in the world, Fleishman-Hillard, Ketchum, and Porter Novelli, as well as specialist agencies including Brodeur Worldwide, Clark & Weinstock, Gavin Anderson & Company, and Cone. Omnicom Media Group (OMG) consists of two full service media companies, OMD Worldwide and PHD Network, as well as several media specialist companies. *Advertising Age* ranked Omnicom as the Number One marketing organization worldwide in 2004 with revenues of $ 9.7 billion. Revenue increased by 8 per cent to $ 10.5 billion in 2005.

WPP

Established as a marketing services group in 1986, WPP built its capabilities *originally* based on 'below-the-line' marketing services with the acquisition of ten marketing services companies in the UK and US. WPP's success story began with Martin Sorrell buying a stake in Wire & Plastic Products PLC, a shopping cart manufacturer in the UK in his search for a public entity through which to build a worldwide marketing services company.

The WPP Group is now the world's second largest media and communications services conglomerate after Omnicom with revenues of $ 9.4 billion in 2004.

Its flagship agency networks, including Grey Worldwide, JWT, Ogilvy & Mather and Young & Rubicam, offer creative campaign development and brand management services. WPP's holdings also include public relations firms, media buying and planning agencies, and many specialized marketing and communications. With three of the world's top ten PR companies — Burson-Marsteller, Hill & Knowlton, Ogilvy Public Relations Worldwide — WPP agencies offer a wide range of general corporate, consumer and brand-building services.

Ketchum

George Ketchum founded Ketchum Communications in 1923, opening his first office in Pittsburgh, Pennsylvania, USA. Even though the agency started off in the advertising business, it quickly expanded to include public relations and, in 1934, the agency launched a public relations department, the first of its kind in a Pittsburgh advertising agency.

Ketchum soon opened additional operations throughout the US, helping to expand the company — now headquartered in New York — into a major national player. Ketchum later expanded globally. During the 1990s, Ketchum expanded their reach to Europe and established operations in Munich, Milan, Paris, London and Madrid. Today Ketchum Europe has professionals and a well-established affiliate network that cover all major European markets.

In 1996, Ketchum and Hong Kong-based Newscan launched Ketchum Newscan, which now serves as the agency's

Asia-Pacific headquarters. With a combination of local talent and international expertise, Ketchum Newscan has expanded with additional offices in Beijing, Shanghai, Guangzhou, Chengdu and Taipei. Ketchum Newscan is one of the top five agencies in Greater China with a staff of multicultural, multilingual professionals and serves as the coordinating office for an Asia Pacific network covering 22 cities across the region.

The year 1996 marked the acquisition of Ketchum by Omnicom Group. Being part of the Omnicom Group enabled Ketchum to grow geographically and also to expand the services and expertise it offers clients. In 1997, Ketchum established its international operations in Latin America, which now includes twelve offices. In 2001, the agency acquired a share of Estratégia Assessoria de Comunição in Brazil.

The agency's acquisitions of such prominent firms as Sheppard Associates (in 1999), The Washington Group (in 2001), Stromberg Consulting (in 2001) and Corporate Technology Communications (in 2001) supplemented Ketchum's strength in its five global practices and portfolio of specialized services.

Eighty years later, the communications company that still carries George Ketchum's name has grown into a world-leading public relations firm with a network of twenty-three offices and forty-six affiliates around the globe.

Fleishman-Hillard

The roots of Fleishman-Hillard go back to pre-World War II St. Louis, Missouri, where Alfred Fleishman, then chief deputy circuit clerk for the city of St. Louis, met a reporter who was covering the courts for the *St. Louis Star-Times*. The reporter was Bob Hillard, and the two became good friends. After a wartime job at the Pentagon as chief information officer for the Air Force Rehabilitation Division, Fleishman decided to make public relations his post-war career. He invited Hillard to join him and, in 1946, the two rented three rooms above a Woolworth's Five and Dime store in midtown St. Louis. They sent out an announcement stating their aim 'to achieve better understanding and goodwill among employees, customers, stockholders, plant-city townspeople, and all other "publics".'

Al Fleishman and Bob Hillard tapped out the beginnings of a business on the keyboards of their manual typewriters. Over fifty-seven years later, Fleishman-Hillard has become a leader in global communications consulting. However, for twenty-some years, the firm served a mainly regional client base, until 1974 when John Graham was named president. Under his leadership, Fleishman-Hillard underwent the most dynamic period of domestic and international expansion. It grew from two offices in St. Louis and Kansas City, to over eighty offices located throughout North America, Europe, Asia, Latin America, Australia, and South Africa.

Hill & Knowlton

John W. Hill opened the doors of his first public relations office in 1927 in Cleveland, Ohio, following an eighteen-year career as a reporter, editor, and financial columnist. His early clients were banks, steel manufacturers, and other industrial companies. Hill, who was born on a farm in Shelbyville, Indiana, in 1890, managed the firm until 1962, and remained active in it until shortly before his death in New York City in 1977.

During the Depression when a client's bank went out of business, he took into partnership the bank's public relations director, Donald Knowlton. Hill moved the firm's headquarters to New York in 1934, to serve as public relations counsel to the American Iron and Steel Institute. Knowlton stayed in Ohio and operated Hill & Knowlton of Cleveland as a separate entity for several years.

Despite the Depression, Hill & Knowlton grew rapidly as Hill gained a reputation for effectiveness and as an advocate of enlightened corporate policies and straight-dealing with the press. The firm's business continued to expand through the 1940s and attracted corporate clients in growing numbers, including leaders in the steel, aircraft manufacturing, petroleum and shipbuilding industries.

In 1952, Hill & Knowlton became the first American public relations consultancy to recognize the business communication implications of formation of the European Economic Community. Hill & Knowlton established a network of affiliates across Europe and by the middle of the decade had become the first American public relations firm to have wholly-owned offices in Europe.

Additional expansion led to the firm's current network of offices. Hill & Knowlton became the first US public relations firm to open an office in Budapest, Hungary. Similarly, in 1984, Hill & Knowlton was the first to establish a presence in the People's Republic of China. In 1987, the firm became a member of the WPP Group plc family of communications companies. Currently, H&K's employees are spread worldwide throughout five regions: Asia Pacific; Canada; Europe; Middle East, Africa; Latin America; and the United States.

Indian PR Firms

Indian PR firms are much smaller and of relatively recent origin. Their global operations depend on their affiliation with global giants.

IPAN (India Public Affairs Network) is India's leading public affairs and public relations consulting firm. Founded in 1988, IPAN serves some of the finest organizations in the world including Commerce One, Hindustan Lever Ltd, Goldman Sachs, Glaxo SmithKline, Swatch Group, Special Olympics, Pramati Technologies and the HCL Group. An associate of Hill & Knowlton in India, in a non-exclusive relationship, IPAN has offices in New Delhi, Mumbai, Chennai and Bangalore, and representation in other major Indian cities.

IPAN has been in step with major business developments in the country consequent to the opening up of the Indian economy: among others, the entry of Pepsi in the face of a concerted campaign against it; the launch of Citibank's consumer banking business in what was then a highly regulated environment; the entry of foreign telecom majors like British Telecom, Hughes, Alcatel and Nokia; the clearance of the Enron power project in the face of orchestrated opposition; and the revolution in information technology spearheaded by companies such as Intel, Cisco Systems and the home-grown HCL Group.

IPAN has a significant portfolio of clients which includes many multinational and domestic corporations that are actively seeking to enter or develop the lucrative sectors of finance, information technology, telecommunications, infrastructure, health and consumer goods. IPAN has considerable expertise and experience in developing and implementing communication strategies for its clients that have helped to smooth their path in implementing successful business plans.

Perfect Relations is a major Indian public relations company that is an affiliate of Brodeur Worldwide which is a unit of the Omnicom Group. Perfect Relations was founded in 1992 and boasts a 'network of 14 wholly-owned offices across India and the SAARC countries of Sri Lanka, Bangladesh and Nepal' employing a staff of 200 and advising 100 long-term clients. In September 2003, Brodeur Worldwide announced that Perfect Relations had joined their Asia-Pacific network of affiliate companies. In March 2004 Perfect Relations was hired by the Indian National Congress political party for the May 2004 general election to oversee the strategy to counter the up-beat 'India Shining' advertising developed by Grey Global Group for the rival Bharatiya Janata Party (BJP).

Genesis Public Relations established in 1992 by Prema Sagar, claims its reach extends to all the leading state capitals in India and fifty countries around the world. This is through its network of offices, national affiliates and exclusive international affiliate — Burson-Marsteller, which agreed to acquire its entire share capital in December 2005.

PRCAI (Public Relations Consultants Association of India) mooted by a group of seven like-minded public relation firms that form the core founding members, has been established with a mission, 'To consistently establish benchmarks in Standards, Knowledge, Ethics and Expertise and to encourage and promote the progression of the Public Relations Industry in India, while endorsing the effectiveness of professional and ethical services.' Members: 20:20 MEDIA, Adfactors PR, CMCG India Private Limited, Concept Public Relations (India) Private Limited, Corporate Voice / Waber Shandwick, Dipayan Mazumdar and Associates, Genesis Public Relations, Good Relations (India), Hanmer & Partners, Integral PR, Madison Public Relations. Melcole Public Relations, Ogilvy Public Relations, Perfect Relations, Pressman Advertising and Marketing Limited, Text 100 (India) and The Practice.

Public Relations Society of India (PRSI) was established as a National Association of Public Relations practitioners in

1958 to promote the profession as a strategic management function. Over the years, the PRSI has grown into a big professional body with thirty-two Regional Chapters and over 10,000 members.

Government Public Relations

Governments were among the first to recognize the need to practice public relations, as we observe when we study history, though the term public relations was not used until the beginning of the twentieth century. By definition, democratic governments should reflect public opinion and work best when the citizens are well informed. Communicating with the public is one of any government's essential tasks. The government has a duty to explain its policies, decisions and actions; to inform the public about their rights and liabilities; and to provide the public with advice and warnings.

Governments have also felt the need for public relations outside their geographical boundaries to project their image. During the Cold War, there was a spread of libraries and cultural centres along with cultural exchanges all over the globe. The global dominance of Western media gave them an advantage over their rivals. The soft power of cultural diplomacy has emerged as a force to reckon with as it goes a long way in fulfilling strategic objectives. Most embassies have press and cultural attachés for the purpose, but some have separate organizations like the British Council and Indian Council of Cultural Relations.

United States

As public relations emerged in the United States, many of what we now call public relations exercises were undertaken by various federal departments, cities and states. California, for instance, conducted extensive and expensive campaigns to attract new residents. These government efforts paralleled what many businesses were doing at that time, and the government employees who performed these tasks had the same titles as their business counterparts. They were known by such terms as publicity agent, promoter, press agent, press secretary, and public relations specialist.

By 1913 there were enough concerns being expressed about the appropriateness and the directions being taken by government public relations practitioners that Congress sought to put limits on government spending for public relations. This came about in part because some big business interests resented the public relations successes of the United States Forest Service, that had led to the closing of some federal land to loggers, in part because of partisan political rivalries, and in part because of vague fears that a government propaganda machine could begin manipulating public opinion.

As a result, the Gillett Amendment was added to the Interstate Commerce Commission statute. It turned out to be one of those acts of Congress that ended up having much more power and influence than its actual language would suggest. It is often described as a ban on government public relations, but that's not what it started out to be. It doesn't prohibit government public relations; it simply said, *'Appropriated funds may not be used to pay a publicity expert unless specifically appropriated for that purpose.'*

Then came World War I and the extensive use of propaganda by all the warring nations. Ironically, when the war was over and the success of those propaganda efforts led people like Edward Bernays and countless businesses to increase their public relations efforts, there was a backlash against government propaganda and a rising fear of government manipulation. Any public relations activity by government became suspect, and the federal government, which had already seemingly taken a first step with the Gillett Amendment, backed away even further from public relations.

More accurately, the federal government backed away from the term 'public relations'. It didn't stop doing public relations. It simply gave the activity new, less offensive, and more public-spirited labels. The most widespread euphemism was 'public information', and a look at the job titles for almost any federal government agency will reveal multitudes of *public information officers*, *public information specialists*, *public affairs managers*, *public affairs officers*, *publication specialists*, *communication specialists*, *community facilitators*, *community relations coordinators*, and many other communicators. One mid-1980s study by the federal Office of Management and Budget found over 5,000 people who were designated as federal information specialists. It also estimated that the total number of people in public information or 'public affairs' positions in the federal government might be five to seven times higher.

And, as is true of so many other aspects of government in the United States, the public relations patterns set by the federal government were interpreted as virtual mandates by state and local governments. A variety of state and local laws and regulations were enacted to limit or prohibit public relations efforts by government, and many of them are 'strictly enforced' today. Consequently, there are very few people or agencies at any level of government who have the words 'public relations' in their titles or their job responsibilities, but there are thousands of public information officers and public information specialists throughout state and local governments.

In addition to government PR personnel, PR firms are also employed by US Government agencies and departments, for doing public relations for them. According to the US House Committee on Government Reform Minority Office, Hill & Knowlton received the following amounts for federal PR contracts: $286,000 in 1997, $1,250,000 in 1998, $1,980,000 in 1999 and $15,702,000 in 2000. Ketchum received the following amounts for federal PR contracts: $1,692,000 in 1999, $2,552,000 in 2000, $3,657,000 in 2001, $2,563,000 in 2002 $31,163,457 in 2003 and $58,895,846 in 2004. Fleishman-Hillard received the following · amounts: $33,589,000 in 1999, $2,344,000 in 2000, $5,011,996 in 2001, $23,903,419 in 2002, $3,433,690 in 2003 and $8,686,529 in 2004.

USIA

The United States Information Agency (USIA) was established by President Eisenhower in August 1953 as an arm of the White House responsible directly to the president. It operated under that name until April 1978, when its functions were consolidated with those of the Bureau of Educational and Cultural Affairs of the Department of State and the agency was called the United States International Communication

Agency (USICA). The agency's name was restored as USIA in August 1982. The agency promoted mutual understanding between the United States and other nations by conducting educational and cultural activities. USIA maintained 190 posts in 142 countries. Overseas, USIA was known as USIS, the United States Information Service. Pursuant to the Foreign Affairs Reform and Restructuring Act of 1998, USIA was integrated into the Department of State on 1 October 1999.

Some former directors of USIA[1] have described its functioning thus: Throughout those years the USIA assigned a public affairs officer experienced in journalism or public relations to nearly every American embassy. He — occasionally she — was always a full member of the country team yet sufficiently independent to advise the ambassador as an outside counsel might advise, rather than simply report to a corporate chief executive. A major duty of the public affairs officer was to recruit, train and supervise foreign service nationals, natives of the host country with backgrounds in journalism or academia and pro-American views who would represent the United States to their country's opinion leaders and media representatives — professionally, authoritatively and (most important) in their own language. In many countries the USIA also opened libraries[2] in high-traffic locations where ordinary citizens could have access to American newspapers, books and magazines.

The Department of State and the United States Information Agency were consolidated with the promise to facilitate the

1. Leonard H. Marks, Charles Z. Wick, Bruce Gelb and Henry E. Catto wrote in the *Washington Post*, 'America Needs a Voice Abroad' on Saturday, 26 February 2005, page A19.

2. American Libraries are still functioning in India but they are directly controlled by the US Embassy or Consulates.

merger of policy-making and public diplomacy.[3] After the recommendations of numerous organizations and task forces, and presidential directives of two administrations, the development of foreign policy is now beginning to include public diplomacy analysis and input in national security organizations.

But there is another version,[4] 'The USIA was a creation of the Cold War, born of the conviction that success in the struggle with the Soviet Union would require not only effective armaments and strong alliances but also steady progress in winning and retaining worldwide support for the aims and ideals of American-style liberal democracy. In this the USIA achieved remarkable success, as was demonstrated when the Cold War ended with the break-up of the Soviet Union and the freeing of its satellite states — an immense transformation that was welcomed almost everywhere. In the euphoria that followed, it was widely believed that the collapse of communism would lead to the embrace of liberal democracy almost everywhere. One influential book of the time even argued through its title that this trend could in time result in a world permanently at peace and thus in 'The End of History.' As a consequence, official Washington soon came to believe that the USIA was no longer needed. That view, combined with the ever-present pressure to trim the budgets of out-of-favour government departments, led to its being absorbed by the State Department — which had argued for years that the USIA really belonged there — and, in 1999, to its formal shutdown.

3. USIA which was in the business of public diplomacy for more than forty years, defined *'Public Diplomacy'* as follows: Public diplomacy seeks to promote the national interest and the national security of the United States through understanding, informing, and influencing foreign publics and broadening dialogue between American citizens and institutions and their counterparts abroad.

4. Leonard H. Marks, *et al*, 'America Needs a Voice Abroad'.

These days the Under Secretary for Public Diplomacy and Public Affairs, helps ensure that public diplomacy (engaging, informing, and influencing key international audiences) is practised in harmony with public affairs (outreach to Americans) and traditional diplomacy to advance American interests and security and to provide the moral basis for America's leadership in the world. On 23 September 2004, Congress approved the creation of the Office of Policy, Planning and Resources for Public Diplomacy and Public Affairs. This new office provides long-term strategic planning and performance measurement capability for public diplomacy and public affairs programmes. It also enables the Under Secretary to better advise on the allocation of public diplomacy and public affairs resources, to focus those resources on the most urgent national security objectives, and provide realistic measurement of public diplomacy's and public affairs' effectiveness. The office coordinates the Department's public diplomacy presence in close consultation with relevant bureaus.

The US Secretary of State Condoleezza Rice said in her confirmation hearing before the Senate Foreign Relations Committee on 18 January 2005, 'And if I am confirmed, public diplomacy will be a top priority for me and for the professionals I lead.'[5] Such is the importance of PR in international relations.

United Kingdom

In the United Kingdom as the communication role of the government grew, particularly during the First and Second World Wars (1914–1918 and 1939–1945) when propaganda

5. Website of the U.S. State Department.

was in high gear, a small number of professionally oriented public relations practitioners like Maurice Buckmaster[6] began to emerge. Besides there was the Empire Marketing Board, which was designed to implement imperial preference through market research, supply chain management and publicity. Its secretary, Sir Stephen Tallents, had an enthusiasm for national propaganda that was best encapsulated in his pamphlet, 'The Projection of England,' published in 1932. He offered patronage to the leader of the British Documentary Film Movement, John Grierson, whose interests encompassed democratic education and public relations, and about which he wrote extensively between the wars. Tallents' own ideas achieved realization in the formation of the British Council, which for all intents and purposes, is still the UK's largest public relations agency.

Many key figures of UK public relations scene also had a government background. J.H. Brebner had a distinguished career in the 1920s and 1930s at the Post Office and at the Ministry of Information where he was successively Director of the News Division, Special Overseas Operative, and at Supreme Allied Headquarters, Director of Press Communications. In1949, he wrote the first book that had 'public relations' in its title in Britain, *Public Relations and Publicity*.

Basil Clarke, a former *Daily Mail* journalist, worked for the central government at the Ministry of Reconstruction, the Ministry of Health and, finally as Director of Public Information in Dublin Castle at the time of the Irish conflict. He then set up his own agency, Editorial Services, which became a large and influential consultancy.

6. He was president of the Institute of Public Relations in 1955–56. It was local government officials who were most responsible for founding the Institute of Public Relations (IPR) in the UK in 1948, the first organization of professional practitioners.

The post-World War II era left new challenges for the UK, most notably its relationships with other countries, and during the process of de-colonization, which stimulated the growth of public relations. In terms of domestic politics, the major policy shift was nationalization, whereby government took ownership of core industries from the private sector. The threat of nationalization led to the formation of organizations that could lobby on behalf of private enterprises. Subsequent British governments have engaged in both nationalization and privatization, necessitating substantial communication.

However, the British history of government public relations should begin in the 1850s when the first dedicated publicity unit was set up by the Post Office (then a government department). The Postmaster-General deplored the public's 'imperfect knowledge' of his organization. He heralded 'this new way of bringing the activities of the Post Office to public and Parliamentary notice'. The publicity unit's first wide-scale publicity campaign was carried out in 1876. A million handbills were issued to alert the public to the virtues of government savings schemes, life insurance and annuities. The *Board of Trade Journal* was launched in 1886, providing facts for the business community. In 1912, Lloyd George realized that the success of the new National Insurance scheme depended on public understanding. He ordered a corps of lecturers to tour the country explaining its details to employers and workers.

During the The Great War of 1914–18 telegraph made it possible for news from the Front to travel at an unprecedented speed. The British Government invited Fleet Street editors to join its Information Advisory Committee, exploring ways to provide the public with war-related information. The Home Office opened an Information Bureau. In 1918 Whitehall's various units were consolidated into the first, short-lived,

Ministry of Information. Its apparatus was dispersed around Whitehall departments soon after the war ended.

In 1919, the Air Ministry was the first department of state in the UK to be set up with its own press officer from the outset. The General Strike of 1926 provided the government with a real communication challenge. The BBC resisted pressure to become a government mouthpiece in the absence of strike-bound newspapers. In response, Churchill produced a government newspaper, the *British Gazette*. During the 1930s and 1940s, departmental press offices moved from the simple role of answering enquiries to a more deliberate and proactive information policy. In 1932, the first Chief Press Secretary was appointed by 10 Downing Street, which built a special extension to house him.

During the Second World War the second Ministry of Information was set up in 1939 to mobilize opinion and information to help the war effort. Volunteers were needed for a host of tasks. People had to understand air-raid precautions. The public had to know about the rationing system, and how to make the best use of food and fuel. By 1944, the Ministry had a staff of 7,600, and a further 1,700 with similar duties were employed by other departments elsewhere. Many were working overseas, and a regional organization had been set up in the UK. After the war, the government decided that there was no further need for the Ministry.

In 1946, the Central Office of Information (COI) was established after the demise of the wartime Ministry of Information, when responsibility for information policy was resumed by departmental ministers. It was set up as a non-ministerial department, the status it still has in 2006, though there have been other changes. It was established as an Executive Agency on 5 April 1990 and then as a Trading Fund on

1 April 1991, in accordance with the Government Trading Funds Act 1973, as amended. COI is based in London, and employs around 350 people who are civil servants on permanent, fixed term or casual appointments.

COI's Chief Executive reports to the Minister for the Cabinet Office. The Minister is accountable to Parliament and its Select Committees for all COI's activities. The Minister also sets COI's annual objectives for efficiency, quality and financial performance. The aim of COI is to enable central government and public sector bodies to secure policy objectives through achieving maximum communication effectiveness and best value for money. COI's objectives are to improve the effectiveness of and add value to its clients' publicity programmes. COI achieves this through consultancy, procurement and project management services across all communication channels. COI works with government departments and public sector bodies on communication campaigns that cover a wide range of topics including health, safety, welfare, benefits and recruitment.

COI is basically a government procurement agency, not an end supplier. It is therefore uniquely placed to offer departments impartial advice on the best and most cost-effective ways of achieving PR objectives.

COI benefits to its clients:

- Aggregated buying power — client departments of all sizes benefit from the terms of business COI Communications negotiates using the leverage of its aggregated buying power.
- Specialist expertise — client departments gain from breadth of COI expertise during development of a campaign's strategy. Specialists in each medium then ensure expert contracting (for example, video production contracts that minimize repeat fee payments).

- Speed — in most areas framework agreements set strictly within EC rules — allow COI to place contracts with a speed that would be impossible if they had to be advertised individually.
- Allowing clients to ride peaks and troughs in spending — for most government organizations, publicity spending varies considerably from year-to-year in line with ministerial initiatives. Client departments are able to gain by piggybacking on continuing major market presence and involvement of COI.
- Effectiveness — departments can improve campaign effectiveness using COI developed techniques for measuring effectiveness of publicity spend. Departments also gain because accumulated COI knowledge provides expert strategic advice on planned campaigns.
- Getting it right first time — using COI minimizes the risk of failed campaigns.
- Propriety — COI has a comprehensive understanding of the role and constraints of government publicity, including political sensitivity, the need for absolute integrity and the observance of propriety.
- Innovation — COI is highly innovative in its approach, and exploits market developments to provide the best service to its clients.
- Specialization — client departments obtain economic access to specializations that they may require only rarely.
- Mix of values and skills — COI offers a unique combination of public sector values and private sector skills.

In the late 1940s, the government decided to review the way departments conducted their information work. The

Crombie Report proposed the setting up of the Information Officer class, which was duly done in August 1949, thus came up the Government Information Service (GIS). The Director-General of the COI took on the role of Head of Profession as part of his duties.

Another review of the GIS highlighted the lack of any formal qualifications that could be used to assess recruits. The Information Officer Management Unit was set up in 1984, and developed the assessment centre system that now underpins all recruitment and assessment. The Head of Profession role also moved away from the COI in 1990s to a full time post appointed by the Cabinet Secretary with the approval of the Prime Minister.

The Mountfield Report published in November 1997 reinforced the importance of political impartiality for government communication and made proposals to improve the coordination and consistency of communication across government and to enhance its capacity to operate in a 24-hour media world. It recommended that the Government Information Service, created in 1949, should be renamed the Government Information and Communication Service (GICS) to 'imply the proactive exposition and justification of policy rather than the reactive answering of questions'. Its main proposals were:

- to bring the standard of all government press offices up to that of the best;
- improved coordination across government;
- improved coordination within departments;
- closer and better working relations between policy civil servants and press officers;
- better leadership, training, development and personnel management; and

- retention of a politically impartial information service.

The mission of the GICS was to deliver a high quality professional communication service across government, which is respected as a partner in the development and delivery of policy, and recognized for creative, robust, effective and timely advice.

GICS objectives included:

- to work with departments to ensure a close knowledge of their needs; and to provide central support for recruitment and promotion, including a competency framework for each level of work, and appropriate assessment processes;
- to engage with the training of the Civil Service, particularly senior staff, to reinforce the importance of effective communication in the making and delivery of policy;
- to provide central services that support the work of departments collectively, including media monitoring and a regional news network;
- to support the handling of cross-government issues and emergencies, and reinforcement of departments under pressure, including a crisis communication coordination centre;
- to develop and support a process for the professional peer review of departmental communication directorates;
- to engage with relevant professional organizations with the aim of ensuring that GICS training is consistent with recognized best practice, and to gain recognition for its contribution to professional qualifications;

- to engage with professional organizations and other bodies, including foreign governments, to ensure knowledge and development of best practice; and
- to maintain a strong public service ethos and to support the highest ethical and professional standards, including compliance with all Civil Service guidance.

The GICS was a virtual organization. A member's departmental employer provided his / her current professional residence. The GICS was his / her common bond across government. The essential ingredient was the assessment centre process through which all GICS people are recruited and promoted.

Most GICS staff worked in the communication directorates of their departments. These units have various titles but they share a common purpose. They have a key role in achieving departmental aims and objectives:

- to create and maintain informed opinion about the department's subjects and work;
- to use all suitable methods of publicity to help the department achieve its aims and objectives; and
- to advise the department of the public's and the news media's reactions to its policies and actions, and to do this in partnership with minister's, officials, the centre and other departments.

The Director General of the GICS was responsible for setting GICS standards and for coordinating the presentation of major cross-government issues and emergencies. In August 2001 a new senior management team was created to support the Head of the GICS and to increase its corporate strength.

The role of the GICS Centre team was to:

- deliver services to departmental customers — be it media monitoring, training courses, recruitment campaigns, or regional media advice. The purpose was to help departments achieve their objectives within propriety boundaries and the Civil Service Code;
- act as change agents — inspiring, persuading and supporting communication directorates in departments to meet the constantly evolving challenges of the communication environment, be it through structural reviews, exchange of best practice or adopting different ways of working and managing their staff;
- be guardians of propriety and GICS professional standards. The GICS's credibility relied on its ability to offer impartial and honest advice. Operating at the 'hard edge' of delivery, the charge of politicisation is all too easy to make and their role was to protect core Civil Service values and uphold professional standards through their well-established assessment centres; and
- finally, to act as spokespeople and ambassadors for the GICS to other professional groups, the Civil Service as a whole and colleagues in other countries.

There were four central units: the *GICS Development Centre*, the central *Media Monitoring Unit*, the *GICS Operations Unit* and the *Government News Network*.

The *GICS Development Centre* helped departments and agencies to achieve the highest information and communication standards. It did this by managing staff recruitment and career development at all levels and by driving best practice. The Centre also published the *GICS Handbook*, which contains the central rules on propriety and professional advice.

The central *Media Monitoring Unit* keeps government departments and agencies informed of news developments 24 hours a day. The Unit provides coordinated round-the-clock news and current affairs monitoring, identifying and detailing media issues, and the way government policy is reported in print, on radio and on television. It keeps its subscribers aware of the bigger picture beyond their own departments and how their stories fit into the daily media agenda. The Unit is entirely funded out of subscriptions from government departments. Wherever appropriate it uses contractors or home workers to free up the Unit to monitor breaking news. The Unit has also established a sophisticated instant briefing service on major announcements, for example, keeping Government informed on coverage of Budget and Pre-Budget statements. In 2001 it expanded its service to respond to the vast media coverage generated by the foot-and-mouth disease crisis and the aftermath of 11 September, prompted the development of international media monitoring services.

The Unit provides:

- a coordinated watch for breaking stories;
- thorough early morning, lunchtime and evening thematic news summaries;
- tip-offs and intelligent read-outs of running stories;
- transcripts of selected items; and
- a media monitoring/cutting service to ministers on overseas visits.

The *GICS Operations Unit* was a central facility for handling major cross-cutting issues and emergencies. It provided contingency communications advice and services for the Civil Contingencies Secretariat. This included the delivery of cross-government responses to contingencies and providing support to individual departments facing crisis. When necessary it activated the *News Coordination Centre*, bringing in GICS volunteers drawn from around government. It collated briefings for ministers and departments, coordinated ministerial interviews and visits, and provided a central press office, websites and a call centre as required.

The *Government News Network* (GNN) moved to the GICS on 1 April 2002 from the Central Office of Information (COI), where it had been known as the COI Regional Network. This followed a recommendation in the COI Quinquennial Review. It concluded that transferring the network to the GICS in the Cabinet Office would ensure more effective presentation of cross-departmental and regional issues while maintaining links with government publicity and communications generally. Closer ties with the GICS Centre would speed information flow and help strengthen relationships with ministers and departments. The aim was to re-position the GNN as the respected adviser to all government departments and agencies on regional communication issues.

The other arm of the GNN operation was the News Distribution Service (NDS). NDS is the chosen delivery mechanism for nearly all Whitehall press notices, as well as departments' regional releases. It is therefore vital for NDS to develop its services in line with the ever-changing demands of a voracious media. NDS continues to pioneer new services which are both innovative, and cost-effective for all its departmental users.

By the time the Phillis Review[7] was commissioned in 2003

7. This Independent Review of Government Communications was launched in February 2003 when the Government accepted a proposal by the House of Commons Public Administration Select Committee that there should be a radical and external review of government communications. The Review Group was chaired by Bob Phillis (Chief Executive of the Guardian Media Group plc), so is known informally as the 'Phillis Review'.

the media environment had changed again with ever increasing competition for news stories and much wider use of digital media. Its report called for a redefinition of government communication into a more customer-focused two-way dialogue with the public, based on a strategic pan-media approach. 'The central recommendation is that communications should be redefined across government to mean a continuous dialogue with all interested parties, encompassing a broader range of skills and techniques than those associated with media relations. The focus of attention should be the general public.'

Among its recommendations were the recruitment of a Permanent Secretary for Government Communication and a new network for all government communicators, which became the GCN. The Head of Profession is now the Permanent Secretary, Government Communication (PSGC). He works closely with the Prime Minister's Press Office, and the Chief Executive of COI on cross-government issues. Working with the PSGC are the Director, Government Communication, and Director GCN. The group is made up of: Strategic Communications and Marketing; Professional Development and Business Management; GCN, Standards, Propriety, and the Media Monitoring Unit.

The Final Report of the Independent Review of Government Communications, chaired by Bob Phillis (Chief Executive of the Guardian Media Group plc), informally known as the Phillis Review and published in January 2004, *found a three-way breakdown of trust between politicians, the media and the general public* and recommended that new propriety guidelines and induction training should be developed by the Permanent Secretary, Government Communications to cover all those involved in communication, including special advisers. The principle of Civil Service impartiality must underpin these guidelines.

It recommended that all major government media briefings should be on record, live on television and radio and with full transcripts available promptly online. Ministers should deliver announcements and briefings relevant to their department at the daily lobby briefings, which should also be televised, and respond to questions of the day on behalf of the government.

The Phillis Review recommended that the central government website should be redesigned to meet the needs and perceptions of users, with individual departments only becoming 'visible' when this makes sense to the users. Information on local public services should be prominent and easily found. There should be increased investment in websites to reflect the increasing importance of this method of communication.

British Council

In the 1920s and early 1930s, the Foreign Office of the United Kingdom realized the need for an organization responsible for the promotion of British culture, education, science and technology in other countries, along the lines of existing French, German and Italian cultural organizations. This led to the setting up of the 'British Committee for Relations with Other Countries' in 1934. The name was later changed to the 'British Council for Relations with Other Countries, and then finally shortened to the 'British Council' in 1936. Working at first through British Embassies and High Commissions, the British Council appointed its first overseas representative to Egypt in 1938, followed by Portugal, Poland and Romania later that year.

Although set up and partly funded by the Foreign Office,

and working closely with it, the British Council had its own Chairman and Committee, and was responsible for its own policy and activities. The work of the early British Council included support to British institutes and societies, and English schools in other countries, recruitment of university lecturers, support to students and English teachers, books and periodicals for libraries, lecture tours, music performances and art exhibitions. Priority was given to the countries of the Middle East and Mediterranean region, Europe and Latin America.

During the Second World War in 1939 the Government considered amalgamating the British Council with the newly formed Ministry of Information, which was responsible for propaganda. However, the British Council Chairman, Lord George Lloyd, successfully argued for the value of the British Council as an independent organization, responsible for building long-term relationships. Although its information work was transferred to the new Ministry, the Government encouraged an expansion of its cultural and educational work.

As the War progressed, its activity had to be withdrawn and staff evacuated from all European countries except Portugal, Spain and Sweden. However, at the request of the Government, centres were set up in many cities in the UK to provide educational and cultural support to refugees and Allied service personnel. Centres for Allied servicemen in the Middle East were later set up in Egypt and Palestine. After the war, the UK centres continued to provide support to students and visitors from other countries. After 1945, the British Council restarted and expanded its work in the rest of Europe. However, in other parts of the world, reductions in Government funding meant that activity and staff had to be withdrawn from many countries.

There were regular Government reviews looking at such

questions as whether the Government should continue to support the British Council and what its priorities should be in terms of activities and geographical focus. These reviews were known as the Drogheda, Hill, Vosper and Duncan Reports, named after the chairmen of the review committees. By the end of the 1950s, the Drogheda Report had led to an expansion of activity in the developing countries of Africa and Asia, and the Hill Report had led to a move away from the teaching of English by British teachers towards more support and training for local English teachers. The setting up of the Government's new Department for Technical Cooperation in 1961, responsible for British aid to developing countries, led to important changes for the British Council. Throughout the rest of the 1960s and until the 1990s, the British Council took on an increasing share of responsibility for education programmes and student training schemes in the developing countries of Africa and Asia, and received a substantial proportion of its Government funding from the new Department.

The fall of the Communist regimes of Eastern Europe at the end of the 1980s and the beginning of the 1990s led to a huge demand for English language teaching and for training in areas such as management and law. The British Council responded by expanding its activity across the region, and by helping the British Government to develop its Know How Fund for Eastern Europe. The end of the Soviet Union saw a similar pattern further east, with new offices, projects and English teaching centres being set up in most countries of the former Soviet Union by 1995, and a big expansion in Russia itself.

From the mid-1990s onwards, internet-based and other electronic forms of communication became increasingly important, both as information resources and in developing new types of teaching and learning materials. By the early 2000s, this had led to an increasing number of British Council services being available on-line, but also to new 'Knowledge and Learning Centres' in British Libraries, designed to combine the best of virtual, distance and personal interaction. The first such centre was launched in Delhi in January 2002.

11 September 2001 brought renewed attention of the world to the importance of building understanding across countries and cultures, and the disastrous effects when this does not happen. In the US and elsewhere, people recognized the importance of the work of organizations such as the British Council in building the necessary bridges of understanding and trust. The British Council itself gave priority to its new project Connecting Futures, which brings together young people from the UK with those from countries in the Middle East, Asia, Africa and Eastern Europe.

There can be little doubt that the British Council facilitated the post-war emergence of English as an international language, or that its activities have aided the wider objectives of British foreign policy. The Council helped to ensure a cultural place for Britain in the modern world beyond that justified by its economic or political power: it has been a central organ of what the American scholar Joseph Nye Jr. has called 'soft power'.

During 2003 and 2004 British Council worked in 220 towns and cities in 110 countries, taught English to over 500,000 people, with an average of 120,000 students enrolled at any time in 126 teaching centres that employed 1,700 teachers who taught over 1.07 million class hours around the world, collaborated in 1,950 arts events globally, a quarter of which went on to reach a wider public on radio and television, administered 1.15 million professional and academic exams, issued 7.5 million books and videos to 300,000 British Council library members, dealt with 2.3 million enquiries in libraries and information centres and welcomed 8.5 million visitors, celebrated the fiftieth anniversary of the discovery of the double-helix structure of the DNA molecule with a touring exhibition, educational activities and talks by leading British scientists in more than 120 venues in 50 countries, attracting audiences of over four million, helped over 15,000 young British people aged 15 to 25 to meet and work with overseas partners in more than 600 projects, and placed over 1,000 young long-term volunteers in 30 countries, arranged nearly 2,500 work placements and more than 200 study visits in 31 countries across Europe and earned revenue of £ 198 million from clients and customers worldwide.

The Indian Scene

Pre-Independence Indian leaders understood the significance of public relations as they used newspapers and non-violent means to further their cause for independence. In many ways the Gandhian struggle had major PR components in it as he always used a high moral ground for its PR value. His interviews to eminent journalists were state of the art of PR. It is also interesting to note that one of the first national image cultivation activities after World War II was carried out by India in the US. The Indian Embassy hired none other than Edward L. Bernays for the job. He worked for India from October 1951 to May 1952.[8]

India has an elaborate government public relations set up which began with the appointment of a Chief Press Advisor

8. Edward L. Bernays, *Biography of an Idea: Memoirs of a Public Relations Counsel*, New York: Simon and Schuster, 1965.

immediately after the start of the Second World War by the British imperial administration. The Union Government has its PR outfits under the Ministry of Information and Broadcasting and the Ministry of External Affairs. State Governments in India have their own PR set ups, and many are happy to be called PR departments though some add information or publicity to their titles. The Indian Prime Minister's Office also has a separate Media Advisor like 10 Downing Street.

The main functions of the Ministry of Information and Broadcasting are:

- to create an environment and set up a policy framework for healthy development of various mass media in the country;
- to keep the people informed about government policies and programmes through the mass media;
- to educate and motivate the people for greater participative involvement in the various developmental activities and programmes of the Government;
- to liaise with State Governments and their organizations in the field of information and publicity; and
- to serve as a constant link between the Government and the Press and act as a clearing house of official information and authentic data pertaining to the Union Government's plans and programmes.

Significant from the Public Relations point of view are the following:

Press Information Bureau (PIB)

The Press Information Bureau is the nodal agency of the Government of India to disseminate information to the print and electronic media on government policies, programmes, initiatives and achievements. Functioning as an interface between the government and the media, the PIB also provides feedback to the government with people's reaction as reflected in the media. With its eight Regional Offices and thirty-two Branch Offices and Information Centres, the PIB disseminates information through different modes of communications, such as press releases, press notes, feature articles, backgrounders, and organizing press briefings, interviews, press conferences and press tours. The information material released in Hindi, Urdu and thirteen other regional languages reaches over 7,000 newspapers and media organizations.

The Bureau headquarters has a team of officers who are exclusively attached to various ministries and departments for the purpose of assisting them in disseminating information to the media. They also provide feedback to their respective ministries and departments. As part of the Special Services, the Feedback Cell in the PIB prepares a daily digest and special digests based on news stories and editorials from national as well as regional dailies and periodicals. The Feature Unit of the Special Services of the Bureau provides backgrounders, updates, features and graphics. These are circulated in the national network and also sent to the Regional and Branch Offices for translation and circulation to the local Press. PIB arranges photo coverage of government activities and the photographs are supplied to dailies and periodicals published in English and other Indian languages all over the country.

The PIB is linked with its Regional and Branch Offices over computer networks to facilitate speedy feeding of information. The Bureau has a Home Page on the Internet, which makes available publicity material such as press releases, features, photos and graphics. The PIB internet home page is accessible at its website http://pib.nic.in.

The press releases from the Bureau are sent by fax and through computers to local newspapers as well as all resident correspondents of important outstation newspapers. PIB has started photo transmission by computer to its offices, and is connected to its twenty-two regional-centres by video conferencing systems. This enables media persons at regional centres to participate in press conferences in New Delhi and also in other parts of the country.

PIB provides an accreditation facility to media persons so as to make easy access to information from the government sources. A National Press Centre set up in the Press Information Bureau, New Delhi serves as a nerve centre for both the national and international Press. The Centre has facilities like a telecommunication centre, a press conference hall and a cafeteria. The PIB acts as an interface between the government and the media.

Research, Reference and Training Division (RR&TD)

Set up in 1945, The Research, Reference and Training Division[9] functions as an information servicing agency for the Ministry of Information and Broadcasting, its media units and their field offices. It serves as an information bank as well as an information feeder service to the media units to help in their programming and publicity campaigns. It also studies trends in Mass Communication Media and maintains a reference and documentation service on Mass Communication. The Division provides background reference and research materials and other facilities for the use of the ministry, its media units and others engaged in mass communication. The Division also

9. Training was added to it in early 1990s.

looks after the training aspect of the Indian Information Service (IIS) officers in collaboration with the Indian Institute of Mass Communication (IIMC).

The Division compiles two annual reference works entitled *India — A Reference Annual*, an authentic work of reference on India, and *Mass Media in India*, a comprehensive publication on mass communication in the country.

Publications Division (PD)

The Publications Division is one of the leading publishing organizations of the country and the largest in the public sector. It is engaged in dissemination of information about the nation on various spheres of activity, to facilitate the task of national integration by promoting greater awareness and understanding of the different regions and of people adhering to various faiths and beliefs. It publishes and sells books and journals at affordable prices. Some of the important journals published by the Division include *Yojana*, *Kurukshetra*, *Employment News*, *Aajkal*, etc.

The Division carries out sales of publications through its own sales outlets located at important cities as well as through agents. It also takes part in exhibitions and book fairs to promote the sale of books and journals. It has so far published more than 7,000 titles, out of which more than 1,500 titles are live today. The Division has published *The Collected Works of Mahatma Gandhi* in 100 volumes. Besides books, the Publications Division brings out twenty-one journals on issues of national importance and social issues.

Photo Division

The Photo Division is the biggest production unit of its kind in the country in the field of photography. It provides photographs to the media units of the Ministry of Information and Broadcasting and other central government organizations and state governments. The Division also supplies on payment, photographs and transparencies to the general public. It has its headquarters in New Delhi, with well-equipped laboratories and equipment for handling and processing different kinds of photographic jobs and assignments both in black-and-white and in colour. A system exists for easy retrieval of different kinds of photographs stored in the photo-library.

A News Photo Network has also been installed at its Head Office in New Delhi with links to all regional offices. It has now switched over to a digital mode of photo transmission. The process of digitally storing photographs on current events in the News Photo Network is currently on. It also feeds photographs to the Press Information Bureau, which makes these photographs available on their web site. The Division has four regional offices at Mumbai, Chennai, Kolkata and Guwahati.

Directorate of Field Publicity

This Media Unit of the Ministry of Information and Broadcasting is engaged in the task of publicizing various programmes and policies of the government through its network of 268 Field Publicity Units spread over the country, mostly located at District headquarters. They are under the control and supervision of twenty-two Regional Offices, usually located at State capitals, each controlling ten to seventeen Field Publicity Units.

The Directorate of Field Publicity came into existence in 1953 with thirty-two Field Publicity Units under the control of four Regional Offices. The set-up was created under the integrated publicity programme named 'Five Year Plan Publicity

Organization'. The ministry directly exercised administrative control over the units and regional offices. A full-fledged Directorate was constituted in 1959 to supervise and control the activities of the Regional Offices and the Field Publicity Units and it came to be called the 'Directorate of Field Publicity'.

After the Sino-India war in 1962 and the Indo-Pak War in 1965, some radical changes in the approach and working of DFP became necessary in view of the urgent need for boosting the nation's morale and for mentally preparing the people to meet any external threat. Accordingly, thirty-four more new units were created in 1963 and another thirty-three in 1965 for publicity exclusively in the border areas. Realizing the urgency of family welfare in the wake of the 1965–66 famines, Health and Family Welfare units were set up for the first time in the country in 1966. Presently, out of the present strength of 268 Field Units, seventy-two are Border Units and thirty, Family Welfare Units

Broadly, the aims and objectives of the Directorate are:

1. To project the policies and programmes of the government to the people and to inform them about the plans and schemes formulated for their benefit.
2. To educate the people about fundamental national values like democracy, socialism and secularism and to reinforce their faith in them through constant personal contacts.
3. To establish a rapport with the people at the grassroots level for their active participation in the developmental activities, as also to mobilize public opinion in favour of implementation of welfare and developmental programmes.
4. To gather people's reactions to the programmes and

policies of the government and their implementation and to report them back for appropriate and corrective action by the government. The Directorate thus acts as two-way channel of communication between the government and the people.

One of the main formats of publicity used by the field units are audio-visual programmes in the form of film shows. Messages are put across to the audience in the form of entertaining documentary films. Sometimes feature films are also screened as crowd pullers.

Apart from film shows, the Field Units also organize Song and Drama programmes, which comprise the following popular categories:

(a) Dramas, and
(b) Composite Programmes which include music concerts, ballets, folk dances, *qawalis*, etc.

Traditional cultural media like folk songs and plays, *Harikatha* (narration of stories from the epics and Puranas, interspersed with musical compositions), Puppet shows, *Raslila* (plays centred around Sri Krishna), *Aalha* (Aalha and Udal were two warrior brothers whose tales of valour are sung all over northern India in a very dramatic manner), poetic symposia, and other modes are also utilized by the field units

The most important mode of communication used by the Field Publicity Unit, is oral communication or inter-personal communication. Seminars, symposia, group discussions, etc., are the various methods of oral communication. Since the field officers come face-to-face with the people, they have the advantage of using this medium for communicating various messages. The Field Officer through these programmes has the advantage of watching the reactions of the people. While he removes the doubts raised to the extent possible on the spot, he reports back to the headquarters the reactions where action at a higher level is called for.

Field Publicity Officers organize special programmes in the form of competitions with the objective of having wide public participation and involvement. Some of them are — essay competitions, debates, elocution contests, patriotic song competitions, healthy baby shows, local talent competitions, painting and drawing competitions, rural sports, and Rangoli. Attractive prizes like books and other utility items are awarded to the winners.

Field Publicity units are equipped with portable exhibition kits. Apart from the exhibition sets supplied by the Directorate of Advertising and Visual Publicity (DAVP), DFP has also produced three 16-panel exhibition sets on AIDS Awareness, Pulse Polio Immunization and Child Labour.

Song and Drama Division

Set up in 1954 as a unit of All India Radio it was given the status of an independent media unit in 1960 as a subordinate office of the Ministry of Information and Broadcasting. It was established for tapping the resource rich live media, particularly the traditional and the folk forms, for plan publicity. It has the advantage of instant rapport with the people and flexibility in its forms to incorporate new ideas effectively. It utilizes a wide range of stage forms such as drama, folk and traditional plays, dance-drama, folk recitals and puppet shows besides the sound and light medium to focus the attention of the audience on important aspects of the country's life and development in different fields. On an average, the Division puts up about 36,000 programmes all over the country every year.

The Division has ten Regional Centres at Bhopal, Chandigarh, New Delhi, Guwahati, Lucknow, Chennai, Pune, Kolkata, Bangalore and Ranchi. It has nine Sub-Centres located at Bhubaneshwar, Hyderabad, Patna, Imphal, Jodhpur, Darbhanga, Nainital, Shimla and Srinagar.

A Border Publicity Scheme was introduced in the Song and Drama Division in 1966 with the objective of boosting up the morale of the people along the sensitive international borders. The Border Publicity Centres are situated at Jodhpur, Jammu, Shimla, Nainital, Darbhanga, Imphal and Guwahati. In 1967 an Armed Forces Entertainment Wing was set up with the view of entertaining armed forces personnel posted in the forward areas. Of the nine troupes one is located in Chennai and the rest at Delhi. The Song and Drama Division adopted a new medium, an amalgam of sound, light and live action in 1967 after seven years of trials. There are three Sound and Light units one each at Delhi, Bangalore and Allahabad. In 1981, the Division set up a tribal centre at Ranchi for the participation of tribes in the programme activities for the welfare of the tribal people. The scheme covers Jharkhand, Orissa and Madhya Pradesh.

The Song and Drama Division puts up field programmes in coordination with the sister media units of the Ministry of Information and Broadcasting, Central/State Government Departments and voluntary organizations.

Directorate of Advertising and Visual Publicity (DAVP)

The origin of the Directorate of Advertising and Visual Publicity (DAVP) can be traced to the start of World War II, when the erstwhile Government of India appointed a Chief Press Advisor. Among other things, advertising was also one of his responsibilities. A post of Advertising Consultant was created in June 1941 under the Chief Press Advisor. This is where DAVP has its roots. On 1 March 1942, the Advertising Consultant's office became the Advertising Branch of the Department of Information and Broadcasting. Following the expansion in its scope, functions and activities, this advertising unit was declared an Attached Office of the Ministry of Information and Broadcasting on 1 October 1955 and was designated as the Directorate of Advertising and Visual Publicity (DAVP).

DAVP acts as a service agency for undertaking multi-media advertising and publicity for various ministries and departments of the Government of India, including production of media inputs as well as dissemination of messages and information. Some public sector undertakings and autonomous bodies also route their advertisements through DAVP. It helps central government departments in formulating communication strategies and media plans, and helps in implementing them at the grass-root level by providing multi-media support.

Films Division of India

The Division was established in 1948. For over fifty years, the organization has maintained a record of Indian history on celluloid. It is the main film-medium organization of the Government of India and is equipped with trained personnel, cameras, recording and editing facilities. This infrastructure is put to use to assist in-house as well as free-lance film makers and producers. The Films Division holds about 8,000 titles of documentaries, short films and animation films in its archives.

The Division produces documentaries and news magazines from its headquarters at Mumbai, and films on defence and family welfare from New Delhi, and short feature films with a rural bias from its regional centres at Kolkata and

Bangalore. It caters to over 12,600 cinema theatres all over the country and to non-theatrical circuits like units of the Directorate of Field Publicity, mobile units of the State Governments, Doordarshan, field units of the Department of Family Welfare, educational institutions and voluntary organizations. The documentaries and newsreels of State Governments are also featured in the Division's releases on the theatrical circuit. It sells prints, stock shots, video cassettes and distribution rights of documentaries and short feature films in India and abroad.

Directorate of Film Festivals

Set up by the Government of India in 1973, to organize International and National Film Festivals within the country, it facilitates India's participation in festivals abroad, arranges programmes of foreign films in India, Indian films abroad and holds the National Film Awards function. As a vehicle of cultural change, DFF promotes international friendship, provides access to new trends in world cinema, generates healthy competition and in the process, helps to improve the standards of Indian Cinema.

National Centre of Films for Children & Young People

Earlier known as Children's Film Society, India, it was formed in 1955 with the aim of harnessing the medium of films to provide healthy entertainment to children and young people, thereby providing an alternate to commercial cinema which is said to cause an adverse impact on children.

The aim and hope has been to contribute to the process of better upbringing of the younger generation, utilizing this highly effective medium — Cinema and TV.

The present activities include:

a) Production and procurement of films and TV serials and their dubbing in Indian languages.
b) Exhibition of these through Theatres, Schools and TV.
c) Conduct of International Festival of Films for Children and Young People and participation in such festivals abroad.
d) Production of animation films.

Films produced by the Centre are entered in various National and International Film Festivals. The Centre also organizes its own International Film Festival, which is held every alternate year. The 10th Film Festival was held in Hyderabad in November 1997. A decision has been taken to the effect that Hyderabad would be the permanent venue for the International Film Festival for Children and Young People.

External Publicity Division

The External Publicity Division of the Ministry of External Affairs is responsible for international image building. A Joint Secretary who also serves as the spokesperson of the Ministry of External Affairs heads it. The Division commissions films and publications for the use of Indian missions worldwide. It facilitates travel and working of foreign journalists in India and of Indian journalists who go abroad with Indian dignitaries. It coordinates with PIB the coverage of international events in India.

ICCR

The Indian Council for Cultural Relations (ICCR), an autonomous organization of the Government of India, was established in 1950. The objectives of the Council, as defined in its Memorandum of Association, are:

- to participate in the formulation and implementation of policies and programmes relating to India's external cultural relations;
- to promote cultural exchange with other countries and peoples;
- to promote and strengthen cultural relations and mutual understanding between India and other countries;
- to establish and develop relations with national and international organizations in the field of culture.

The Council, located at Azad Bhavan, New Delhi, carries out this mandate of cultural diplomacy through a wide spectrum of activities, which include: exchanges of visits by scholars, academicians, opinion-makers, artists and writers; facilitation of the organization of and participation in seminars and symposia abroad; exchanges of visits by performing arts groups; exchanges of exhibitions; commissioning of busts and statues of Indian leaders for installation abroad; presentation abroad of informatics, audio-visual material, books on India and Indian musical instruments; active collaboration in the operations of some Foreign Cultural Centres in India (e.g. nine of the thirteen British Libraries in India — the ones outside the four metropolitan cities — are run jointly by the ICCR and the British Council); administering of scholarship schemes for foreign students for studies in India; assisting organization of and participation in seminars and symposia in India; maintaining the Council's Regional Offices in India and its Cultural Centres abroad; establishing and maintaining Chairs and Professorships for Indian Studies in Universities abroad and Centres abroad; administering the Jawaharlal

Nehru Award for International Understanding; organizing the Maulana Azad Memorial Lecture; conducting the Maulana Azad Essay Competition and bringing out publications.

The Council has Cultural Centres abroad in: Georgetown, Paramaribo, Port Louis, Jakarta, Moscow, Berlin, Cairo, London, Tashkent, Almaty, Johannesburg, Durban, Port of Spain and Colombo, and regional offices in Bangalore, Chandigarh, Chennai, Hyderabad, Kolkata, Lucknow, Mumbai and Thiruvananthapuram.

Indian Technical and Economic Cooperation 'ITEC' was launched by a decision of the Indian Cabinet on 15 September 1964, as a bilateral programme of assistance of the Government of India. Under it and its corollary SCAAP 156 countries in Asia, Africa, East Europe, Central and Latin America, Pacific and Small Island countries are invited to share the Indian development experience. India spends about Rs 500 million annually on ITEC activities.

South Africa

While the above examples of Government PR from the US, the UK and India show historical development, South Africa presents the latest thinking as its Government Communication and Information System (GCIS) was launched only in 1998. GCIS was established in terms of Section 7 (Subsections 2 and 3) of the Public Service Act of 1994.

GCIS's vision is helping to meet the communication and information needs of government and the people, to ensure a better life for all.

GCIS's mission is to provide leadership in government communication and to ensure that the public is informed of government's implementation of its mandate.

GCIS's strategic objectives are to:

- ensure that the voice of the government is heard;
- foster a more positive communication environment;
- have a clear understanding of the public information needs and government's communication needs;
- promote interactive communications between government and the public;
- set high standards for government communication.

GCIS is located in The Presidency and is responsible for setting up the new Government Communication System and transforming the communication functions in government. The CEO of GCIS is the official spokesperson for the government and attends and services Cabinet.

GCIS is primarily responsible for communication between government and the people. A high premium is placed on development communication that emphasizes direct dialogue, especially with people in disadvantaged areas. GCIS is involved in drafting communication strategies and programmes for the whole of government at national level, and integrating the communication operations of all government departments. To reach its objectives, GCIS aims to:

- provide excellent media and communication services to government departments;
- make Government Information Centres (GICs) and Multi-purpose Community Centres (MPCCs) critical elements of government communication;
- assist in developing government media, communication and information policy;
- ensure efficient services to the media;
- produce information products for dissemination to citizens;

- integrate the international marketing of South Africa;
- continually transform GCIS and to develop its management and employees to meet the demands of its mandate.

There is no mention of 'PR' in the above description of GCIS only 'communication' and 'information'.

Corporate Public Relations

Though the principles and practices of Government and Corporate PR are similar, there is at least one significant difference. Corporate PR has government as one of its major publics and therefore PR agencies offer 'Government Relations' as a major service to corporate clients. In the mid-1980s, there were plenty of academics and think tanks providing analysis of business and public policy issues, and more than enough law firms, bankers, public relations firms and lobbyists to implement specific strategies. However, no existing firm had the expertise in a sufficiently broad range of advisory disciplines to capably counsel corporate and institutional leaders on how to transform analysis into smart, purposeful strategy.

Clark & Weinstock (Omnicom Group), based in New York, decided to meet this need and proceeded to recruit experienced consultants from diverse fields. In 1994, Clark & Weinstock established an office in Washington, D.C. headed by former six-term congressman Vin Weber (R – Minnesota). Over the years Clark & Weinstock has become one of the most influential firms in Washington, D.C. as well as New York. In 2003, Clark & Weinstock added Weber Merritt Strategies to its Washington, D.C. office. Weber Merritt Strategies brings a team of professionals who collectively have over thirty years of successful grassroots campaign experience.

Consultants with Clark & Weinstock have worked in the Executive branch, in Congress, at major law firms, think tanks, leading investment and commercial banks, major universities, leading public relations firms, national political campaigns, and in the media. Clark & Weinstock consultants also contribute to opinion-leading journals and provide public policy commentary on television and radio.

Depending on the organization, corporate PR can include: investor relations, employee relations, community relations, media relations, labour relations, government relations, technical communications, training and employee development, marketing communications, management communications. Many organizations also include philanthropic activity, crisis and emergency communications, and advertising as part of corporate PR functions. Corporate PR makes the public image of an organization vigorous and understandable for the audience. It is the basic instrument for brand strategic positioning and management of the brand and contributes most for building substantial brand equity. In a competitive marketplace, every company's and organization's objective is to establish long-term relationship with the consumer and to enlarge its customer share. Customer satisfaction with the quality of products or services, as well as their support is obligatory, but not sufficient conditions for their loyalty. Long-term relationships between companies and their customers, current and future, are built upon satisfactory communication for both parties.

Though both Ivy Lee and Edward Bernays worked for corporate clients, Lee loved to call himself 'physician to corporate bodies', Arthur W. Page (1883–1960) is credited as being the founder of corporate public relations. Arthur W. Page was Vice President of Doubleday Page, the publishing company founded by his father. He was in charge of the company's magazine group. His special passion was a magazine titled *The World's Work*, a periodical devoted to commerce, manufacturing, agriculture and business in general. In *The World's Work*, which he edited, Page wrote many powerful editorials describing and explaining the special obligations of corporations in a democratic society. In 1927 Walter Gifford, the Chief Executive of the AT&T asked Page if he would be interested in writing a book about AT&T. Page declined. Gifford referred to the editorials Page had been publishing in *The World's Work*, and asked if he would be interested in going to work for AT&T and putting his ideas into practice. Page said 'yes,' but only if the position would be a policy-making job. He said he was not the least interested in being a publicity man. Gifford affirmed the responsibilities of the position — and corporate America got its first-ever vice president in charge of what we call public relations. Arthur Page remained a vice president of AT&T[1] until his retirement at the age of 64 in 1946.

1. Page's PR work was not limited to AT&T. He was a member of the boards of directors of the Chase Bank, Westinghouse, Kennecott Copper, and Continental Oil. He was a trustee of Bennington College, Teachers College at Columbia University, the Carnegie Corporation, Metropolitan Museum of Art, the Morgan Library, the Southern Educational Foundation and Farmers Federal of Asheville, North Carolina. He was also a member of the Board of Overseers of Harvard University. He was Chairman of the Joint Army Navy Committee on Welfare and Recreation. Following World War II, he was a founder of the Free Europe Committee, which, among other things, created Radio Free Europe. Throughout his life, he remained an unpaid consultant to US Presidents from Theodore Roosevelt to Dwight Eisenhower, as well as to countless cabinet secretaries and to the State Department and the War Department. He was summoned to Washington in 1945 by his friend, Henry Stimson, the Secretary of War. His task was to prepare President Truman's announcement of the atomic bomb.

Page wrote to one of his contemporaries. 'For a long time, business men figured that if they produced goods at a price that the public would buy, that was ample evidence that they deserved and had public approval. But it turned out not to be as simple as that. Business found it could lose public approval by having trouble with labour, by being unpopular in its hometown, by using selling methods that didn't suit the government, and by an infinite number of other things, some of them seemingly quite harmless.

'So it has become generally accepted that a corporation must be a good citizen in all kinds of ways besides a good producer and distributor. Failing to meet an ever changing and sometimes whimsical definition by the public of what is a good corporate citizen may be the biggest hazard a company runs.

'So it is worthwhile to put some first-class effort on the somewhat nebulous job of being a good citizen. And having done this, it is just common sense to let your light shine where it can be seen. Publicity is the art of telling a good story well. If the story isn't good fundamentally, there is no one who can tell it well, and it is a waste of money to try.

'So our public relations are mostly what we do, but if what we do isn't exposed to view, we may not get the benefit of it.'

The Arthur W. Page Society founded in 1983 is a select membership organization for senior public relations and corporate communications executives who seek to enrich and strengthen their profession. According to this society, Arthur W. Page viewed public relations as the art of developing understanding and communicating character — both corporate and individual.

The successful corporation, Page believed, must shape its character in concert with the nation's. It must operate in the public interest, manage for the long run and make customer satisfaction its primary goal. He described the dynamic this way: '*Real success, both for big business and the public, lies in large enterprise conducting itself in the public interest and in such a way that the public will give it sufficient freedom to serve effectively.*' He also said, 'all business in a democratic country begins with public permission and exists by public approval' and, therefore, public relations as a function of executive management is central to the success of the business organization.

The Page Principles

Page practiced six principles[2] of public relations management as a means of implementing his philosophy.

- *Tell the truth*. Let the public know what's happening and provide an accurate picture of the company's character, ideals and practices.
- *Prove it with action*. Ninety per cent of the public perception of an organization is determined by what it does and ten per cent by what it says.
- *Listen to the customer*. To serve the company well, understand what the public wants and needs. Keep top decision makers and other employees informed about public reaction to company products, policies and practices.
- *Manage for tomorrow*. Anticipate public reaction and eliminate practices that create difficulties. Generate goodwill.
- *Realize a company's true character is expressed by its*

2. These principles were not put together by Arthur W. Page but by the society created in his name from his work, writings and speeches.

people. The strongest opinions — good or bad — about a company are shaped by the words and deeds of its employees. As a result, every employee — active or retired — is involved with public relations. It is the responsibility of corporate communications to support each employee's capability and desire to be an honest, knowledgeable ambassador to customers, friends, shareowners and public officials.

- *Conduct public relations as if the whole company depends on it*. Corporate relations is a management function. No corporate strategy should be implemented without considering its impact on the public. The public relations professional is a policy maker capable of handling a wide range of corporate communications activities.
- *Remain calm, patient and good-humoured*. Lay the groundwork for public relations miracles with consistent, calm and reasoned attention to information and contacts. When a crisis arises, remember that cool heads communicate best.

John Graham of Fleishman-Hillard in his Hall of Fame Lecture to the Arthur W. Page Society[3] said, 'Many of us in this room have worked through periods where public relations people were buried in the corporate hierarchy . . . reporting to the legal department, human resources, the marketing group, or the executive support organization. Those days are rapidly receding as more and more CEOs come to understand what Arthur Page knew all along: Companies operate with the blessing of the public.'

3. 'Public Relations: Coming Of Age In The New Economy' at 17th Annual Conference September 2000.

Like Governments more and more corporations are giving up the term public relations and are switching over to Corporate Communications.

Corporate Communications or Corporate PR can be defined as a management function encompassing all intentional forms of internal and external communications in a way the organization creates and keeps a positive image among its major target groups or publics. Technologies, such as the Internet, underscore the global character of communication. In practice, corporate communication is a strategic tool for the corporation to gain a competitive advantage. Corporations use it to lead, motivate, persuade, and inform employees — and the public as well. Understanding corporate communication provides the vision a company requires in an information driven economy for strategic planning. Corporate communication is more of an art than a science. Its body of knowledge is interdisciplinary, drawing on the methods and findings of — anthropology; communications; language and linguistics; management and marketing; semiotics; sociology; and psychology.

Corporate communication promotes: strong corporate culture, a coherent corporate identity, a reasonable corporate philosophy, a genuine sense of corporate citizenship, an appropriate and professional relationship with the press, quick, responsible ways of communicating in a crisis, understanding of communication tools and technologies, and sophisticated approaches to global communications. In good corporations, PR professionals ensure that external interests concerning the needs of society are considered within the corporate decision-making process. They also update the employer on political and social issues affecting corporate operations.

Corporate PR also involves coordinating sponsorships —

activities ranging from Olympic games, to a bike race, to a charity activity. Corporate-sponsored events enhance a corporation's reputation, give product brands high visibility, provide a focal point for marketing efforts and sales campaigns and generate publicity and media coverage.

Media provide the basic source of public information about a company and its products and events. Very often, there is misunderstanding between the media and a corporation because of a lack of communication. PR professionals ensure that information released by media is accurate by distributing news releases and holding press conferences, so that the media can verify their facts.

Businesses also use PR tools and tactics to support their marketing and sales objectives. This is called marketing communication or marketing public relations — planning, executing and evaluating programmes that encourage consumer satisfaction through communication that identifies companies and their products with consumer interests. PR professionals are responsible for drafting and distributing printed materials, including press releases, feature stories and newsletters. In a corporate PR campaign, activities are geared towards generating awareness and credibility for a product through publicity: news stories, hosting sales promotions, corporate sponsorships and advertising.

When corporate crises arise, it is the role of PR professionals to take responsibility and be accessible. They set up information centres and provide a constant flow of information to the media and public. PR professionals must know media needs and deadlines, as well as monitor news coverage and telephone inquiries.

It is important for businesses to become involved in the well-being of society, or corporate citizenship. Such concern improves the quality of life, creates public support for business and enhances a company's image. Recently, environmental concern has been a way of expressing corporate citizenship. Applying the tools of PR, corporations have addressed the need to follow good environmental practices and have implemented environmental clean up campaigns. Corporate citizens also contribute at the time of national or international crises such as tsunami's or earthquakes.

Though initially corporate PR involved producing publicity material, issuing press releases, organizing press conferences, bringing out newsletters, house journals, editing annual reports and writing speeches for top executives, it now involves all this and much more.

Corporate Positioning

An articulate, well-defined and properly communicated corporate positioning programme can directly support a company's business mission, improve its standing with its constituencies, and create a base of allies who can be useful in advocacy of specific issues of importance to the company. Proper positioning results in company messages, regardless of subject or issue, being clearly communicated to match perception with reality. Companies develop programmes that enhance and improve perceptions among the full range of key stakeholders: investors, consumers, employees and analysts, to name a few.

Optimal corporate positioning involves crucial areas, including corporate reputation, CEO reputation and corporate citizenship. Corporations must pay close attention to these areas to safeguard their bottom line.

Corporate Reputation

Warren Buffett wrote to the employees of Salomon Brothers on August 26, 1991, when he was called in to take over after the removal of John Gutfreund, '*If you lose money for the firm by bad decisions, like I've done plenty of times for Berkshire, I will be very understanding. If you lose reputation for the firm, I will be ruthless.*'

In today's global marketplace, companies are judged more and more on Intellectual Capital; intangible assets such as reputation, knowledge and potential. Corporate reputation is an essential component of a company's Intellectual Capital. A good reputation sets a company apart from its peers and ensures a healthy bottom line. Corporate reputation has many facets and must be strategically managed and tailored to individual stakeholder audiences or publics. Corporate Reputation Management begins with a reputation audit and identification of stakeholders and their expectations, setting of communication objectives, messaging, and training for effective message delivery, focussed outreach programmes and finally measurement of impact. It includes branding and corporate identity development by identifying consumer needs to synergize communication — corporate literature, copywriting and design, also website creation, design and management, brand launch, extension and repositioning communication strategies at each stage of the brand life cycle to ensure preference.

CEO Reputation

In today's increasingly competitive marketplace, the importance of a CEO's reputation is on the rise more than ever before.

Whether it's regarding a crisis, earnings report or succession plan, a CEO's reputation plays a critical role in determining how internal and external audiences evaluate — and respond to — a company.

In a Burson-Marsteller research,[4] when asked about the most important leadership characteristic, it was found that chief executives, influentials[5] and opinion leaders around the world put 'belief in the CEO' at the top of the list, identifying credibility as the single most critical leadership ingredient. Burson-Marsteller research data shows that CEO reputation accounts for a staggering 48 per cent of a company's reputation — this percentage continues to climb. The overall visibility of Chief Executive Officers is increasing exponentially. These days, when companies make the news, so do their CEOs. Consequently, companies must carefully convey the proper information about their CEOs. If the person at the top is perceived to be credible, then financial capital, human capital and 'trust' capital will follow. These intangible assets are priceless and must be invested in and sustained.

Investor Relations

Investors are the most significant public for a corporation. Effective investor relations enable a company to unlock shareholder value. It begins with a thorough analysis to identify perception gaps, and to develop a communication strategy based on professionally carved communication tools for building a long-term relationship between the company and

4. The most recent US study titled, 'Building CEO Capital' was released in October 2001.

5. CEOs and other senior executives, financial analysts, institutional investors, members of the business media and government officials are called business influentials.

the financial world. Corporate reputation and the CEO's reputation play a critical role in investor relations.

Issues Management

It involves identifying emerging situations and indicators that could impact the corporation, and dealing with them in a non-crisis scenario. Issues management prevents issues from flaring into crises. It proactively addresses public policy and activism issues, helping the company monitor, mitigate and manage these concerns effectively. It involves competition watch, media tracking, competition message analysis, opinion tracking and analysis, and periodic perception audits. Some PR consultancies have specialized in Change Communication services to help maintain credibility in situations of change — like Mergers and Acquisitions, Joint Ventures, Takeovers or Re-engineering and Rationalization.

Crisis Communication

It involves communicating proactively with confidence and transparency in times of crises to minimize damage to corporate reputation. It needs a crisis preparedness plan with clearly defined communication and response strategies; detailed training to ensure smooth execution in times of need; controlled media outreach in times of crisis by providing a rapid reaction press office; and finally post-crisis management to ensure open channels of communication. Undertaking crisis audits and risk analysis helps creation of crisis systems and control. Rehearsing crisis scenarios and role-plays helps in developing experienced spokespeople. Senior executives should undergo media training to be effective spokespersons during periods of crisis.

Media Relations

An organization's media relation strategy is often the most critical element of its communications programme. Everyone regularly accesses one branch or another of the news media — television, radio, print or the Internet. Credible, influential, and universal, the news media is an indispensable channel for the delivery of key public relations messages. A media relation strategy is at the core of every integrated communications programme.

Far stronger than a mere vehicle for publicity, the media presents an audience to build trust through transparency, and an influencer through endorsement. Designing and implementation of media campaigns, positioning strategy, day to day press office functioning — writing press releases, articles, statements, on-line and electronic news distribution, providing trained spokespeople, managing press conferences, media training for executives, photo library maintenance, media measurement and evaluation are covered in media relations. Media relations involves keeping updated on in-house media databases, editorial calendars, events, reviewing past print, broadcast and online coverage. By reviewing past news coverage PR professionals determine different editorial slants and approaches for the media.

Product Launch

Depending on the relevance of the product a full strategy is planned to launch a product. Ideally a product is given for review to key publications before the actual roll-out of the product to the press. The product is introduced to the press via press releases and product demonstrations at major events and trade shows. Appointments are set with the press based on well-rehearsed mini-presentations. Promotional collateral's for the product, produced in accordance with the research and creative designs, are distributed at the product launch, which can be instrumental in stimulating interest amongst the press and industry contacts at major trade shows.

Special Events

Special events are ideal opportunities to attract media coverage. Thorough planning and follow-through are keys to the success of these events. Speaker sessions and interviews are the major ingredients of special events. Special events like Seminars, Conferences, Road Shows, Exhibition and Fairs allow Corporations opportunities where corporate executives can interact formally with media.

Press Release Creation

A press release is an information disbursement tool. Well-written press releases have contributed in increasing client product sales thereby exposing a company to the masses, and greatly enhancing their image. This important tool of PR will be dealt with in a separate chapter.

Press Conferences

This formal and structured interaction with the media is a very important tool of media relations. It is used to provide significant input to media and deserves a separate chapter.

Editorial Offensive

Creation of a series of articles tailored for specific media for communicating key messages in line with the desired positioning of the company. These articles help in high recall value. There is a related PR service where information on editorial opportunities is available when a journalist is planning a story and corporate PR may chip in with relevant information to help him or her do the job.

Journalist Adoption Programme

With or without this name, it is another tool used most effectively to build evangelists in the media for a company. Some ten to fifteen journalists are selected and informal meetings are set up with the company's spokespersons. They may be taken around plants and establishments and information is continuously fed to them some time resulting in exclusive stories.

CEO Visits

A CEO visit is the most sensitive of activities to be handled by PR. Any CEO's visit needs the highest level of strategic planning coupled with impeccable coordination of multiple activities including media exposure.

Speaker Opportunity

Speaker opportunities allow clients to present their views on a personal basis to a large receptive audience. They create the credibility aura around the company and the person and can really boost the PR effects. Round Table is a forum for discussion on a newsworthy topic. This is a platform to facilitate a discussion in a non-news environment. This tool is most effectively used to build a relationship with the media.

User Stories

User stories also called success stories help in getting a favourable story in print about how a customer or organization is reaping benefits by using a company product. This coverage can then be used by the company for sales collateral.

Advertising

Companies spend significant amounts on advertising. The advertising budget is normally placed under PR or the Corporate Communication department. Advertising campaigns provide the power of integrated communications and help PR departments in placement of stories in media.

News Monitoring and Tracking

News and media tracking is a significant activity as part of media relations and helps to understand the media. This helps in planning future courses of action and gives an immediate response when needed. Today, one can choose from dozens of networks, 24-hour news channels, 24-hour business channels, 24-hour sports channels and there are 24-hour food and cooking channels. We're now making pop culture celebrities of chefs. Shopping channels, history channels, old movies . . . the list goes on and on. And then there is the Internet. The public square has grown geometrically. In such an environment where the deadline of media is now, media tracking is a very important activity of PR.

Online Communication or e-PR

For PR professionals the use of online communications has emerged as the latest technology-aided tool. The increasing spread of the use of the Internet has made on-line communication an important PR activity. It not only means communicating with on-line media but also corporate website design and content management, e-mail campaigns, multi-media presentations, CD-ROMs and use of interactive software for PR purposes.

The Internet is here to stay and will play an even more important role in reaching out to target groups (publics) in the future. The focus should not be limited at targeting online media and content sites but extend to include electronic delivery to members of the press within regional, and national media organizations. The Web can be put to work by targeting electronic press sites, Internet coverage tracking, targeted online events, promotions and contests, Web research and competition analysis. Websites can supplement or supplant other PR activities including internal communication. Corporate PR need to better embrace the more pervasive communications channel of the Internet, especially during a crisis or when the reputation of the company or the industry reputation is under attack. Research has shown us that there are some very new elements to be taken care of and the most critical one is speed and it is here that the Internet plays a very powerful role. Mark Twain said 'A lie can travel halfway around the world while the truth is putting on its shoes.' That was when information travelled as fast as the telegraph. There is just no corollary to that today. Mark Twain would have no concept of what speed means to us. For us, it means we have to think in terms of real time responses to bad information. Not in terms of the next news cycle, but right now, because, there is no news cycle anymore.

Internal Communications

Internal communications helps communicate with existing employees and creates an environment that fosters motivation, belongingness, and attracts better talent which is critical for any knowledge based organization. Besides newsletters or house journals are now e-mailed and intranets are used for internal communication. There is need for integration of internal and external messaging regarding major news so that the internal publics do not feel left out. Media relations around company best practices and unique employee achievements/ stories are very helpful. Analyses of external communications affecting employees help assist internal communications and HR.

Integrity is a quality that leaders need to own and communicate tirelessly throughout the organization, through both words and deeds. And, as we are reminded time and again, integrity is precious. *It is earned*, only if it is genuine and consistent. *It is earned*, only if it is communicated through behaviour. Words alone do not suffice. *Integrity is the way companies behave when no one is looking*. When asked what keeps him up at night, Jeff Immelt, Chief Executive Officer of the General Electric Company, remarked, 'It's always an integrity issue of some kind. With 300,000 people, you always worry that someone doesn't get it. We can survive bad markets. What you can't live through is anybody who takes from the company or does something wrong in the community.'[6]

Government Relations

Government relations are a very important component of PR these days involving strategic advice based on political analysis and intelligence, policy evaluation and interpretation. It

6. Quoted by Christopher P.A. Komisarjevsky, President and Chief Executive Officer, Burson-Marsteller Worldwide in his address before The Conference Board's Corporate Communications Conference, New York City on 1 May 2003.

requires contact building and liaising with policy makers, regulatory bodies and influential NGOs, trade associations and industry group campaigns. It also requires research and monitoring, community relations and corporate citizenship. Burson-Marsteller describes its GR practice thus:

Burson-Marsteller undertakes government relations programmes through its wholly owned specialist company, BKSH.[7] The combined resources of Burson-Marsteller and BKSH offer an unparalleled breadth and depth of experience in public affairs and government relations. The company has strong working relationships with decision makers and opinion leaders at the centres of power. In Washington, these range from Congress to the White House, from the State Department to the Pentagon, from national associations to the National Press Club. We understand the Washington D.C. community's own unique rhythm and set of unspoken rules, and we are skilled at negotiating for our clients to maximum effect. BKSH also works with decision makers in all 50 US states.

In Europe BKSH is based in Brussels, the political centre of Europe, with a network of offices spanning all the major national capitals of the European Union. Each centre is staffed by consultants with expertise in their own political systems which meshes seamlessly when working with their counterparts in other countries on cross-border issues.

Access to the political systems of Asia and South America is secured through the local Burson-Marsteller public affairs practice in each country.

We assist clients at all levels, from 'front-page' issues to those that need quiet work behind the scenes. Wherever in the world clients seek help influencing governments — national,

7. Black, Kelly, Scruggs & Healey (BKSH).

transatlantic, pan-European or global — they can rely on BKSH for the same level of professionalism and commitment and the promise of efficiency, effectiveness and excellence.

John D. Graham, Chairman and Chief Executive Officer of Fleishman-Hillard International Communications, announced on 13 February 2004 the formation of Fleishman-Hillard Government Relations. This rebranding of the agency's Washington, D.C., lobbying subsidiary (formerly FH/GPC), underscores Fleishman-Hillard's continued focus on growing its global public affairs business. Fleishman-Hillard Government Relations would be led by former US Representative Larry LaRocco, who has been a senior lobbyist with Fleishman-Hillard since January 2002. Fleishman-Hillard Government Relations provides strategic counsel and government relations services to clients with issues pending before the US Congress and executive branch agencies. The firm's specialties include: international trade; banking and finance; energy and natural resources; homeland security; strategic marketing to the federal government; healthcare; technology; transportation; and state and federal appropriations.

Globalization

For PR practitioners in the corporate world, the key client is the Chief Executive Officer. It is the CEO who has primary responsibility for defining the corporation's expectations of its chief public relations officer. The PR chief needs to have an open, vibrant and effective continuous relationship with the CEO, which demands that the PR chief meets the CEO's expectations. Those expectations are a combination of the CEO's personal aspirations, his vision for the corporation, and evolving developments within and without the corporation that are determining business success. More CEOs than ever know that they must look at the world differently if they are to succeed in the early years of the twenty-first century. The PR chief needs to be on the same wavelength as the CEO. And keeping up will become harder as the pace of corporate change accelerates. And the changes in corporate structure, product base and geographical span, force changes in the image of the corporation.

The combination of shareholders, and competitive and organizational pressures, results in an ever greater premium being placed on top management's skills to be flexible, adaptable and efficient in decision-taking. Key functions become still tighter and team relationships between the leadership group become ever more vital. To be a player, the PR chief must be sensitive to each of these factors providing swift and expert information to the leadership team on a continuous basis, and demonstrating the skills to secure a place at the top management table.

If a company is going global, its PR should be at the forefront of its effort to position itself in the worldwide marketplace. Organizations with a global business strategy also need a global communications strategy — with an agreement on objectives, priority messages, target publics and product promotion plans from New York to New Zealand, so each country's public relations activities not only support local operations but also reinforce the corporation's global plan.

The tempo of globalization will continue to accelerate. The global paradigm will increasingly dominate the planning, the definition of corporate vision and the cutting-edge strategic issues preoccupying top management. Globalization will impact every aspect of the PR chief's work. Analysis of competitive factors demonstrates that going global is not a question of choice. It is a necessity. Leading corporations, in most business sectors that do not become increasingly global will fail. The choice is globalize, or be wiped out. In 1994, the Conference Board of New York surveyed 1,250 publicly traded US manufacturers to understand more about globalization trends. Of the firms surveyed, 92.5 per cent reported direct foreign investment, foreign sales or other forms of international activity. The Conference Board's conclusion was that the internationalization of marketing and manufacturing activity has become irreversible even for relatively small companies. The survey suggested that profitability rises for firms with broad global scope.

The typical path of corporate development is to undertake international roll-outs in stages, moving from development of exports and sales infrastructure abroad to eventual production overseas, noted the Conference Board. But, its study of smaller multinationals indicated that there may be an alternative approach. By advancing to multinational engagement well before the milestone of $ 1 billion in annual sales, a firm may compress or even leapfrog the intervening stages. And, not only is size no obstacle to international expansion, but early entry into the global market may be a clear sign of success.

While multi-lingual fluency may not be a set criteria for hiring tomorrow's corporate PR chief, it is probable that CEOs will increasingly seek PR advisers with a broad and firm grasp of the global environment. They will want to feel assured that their PR advisors are presenting them with speeches for foreign audiences, and tips on foreign cultures, that avoid embarrassment because of cultural insensitivity. More importantly, CEOs will want PR chiefs at the top management table who have something of real value to add to strategic discussions on international challenges — especially in crisis situations.

In an increasingly integrated world economy full of opportunity, where 'doing business' means having a vision about where the world is going, and restructuring companies to make them genuinely multinational. It means being right on top of the latest global developments that can influence business decisions, knowing the strategies of foreign competitors, and having the right contacts.

Going global also means establishing a reputation of excellence on a global level, a reputation that secures respect, and, in turn, an advantage among the corporation's employees, customers, suppliers, sources of finance, public sector regulators, and other stakeholders.

The degree to which a corporation enjoys a high reputation has a direct impact on its ability to gain entry to new foreign markets, to find the best joint venture partners, to win the confidence of governmental authorities, sources of finance, suppliers and customers. Reputation management in the global arena is a bottom line competitive issue. It has to be a top priority for the CEO.

Positive global reputations are won with difficulty and lost with ease. The slightest hint that a corporation, or one of its foreign affiliates, is willing to pay a bribe to gain new market access, or a governmental contract in a remote region of the globe, can damage the corporation's reputation for integrity on a worldwide basis.

Communications systems and the establishment of global civil society organizations, be they concerned with the environment or animal rights, are posing increasing challenges to global corporate reputation management. They will do so even more in coming years as communications technologies improve and civil society organizations become more experienced.

Global networking by interest groups is forcing corporations to an increasing degree to accept the reality that they dare not seek to apply one set of environmental (or employment, or public policy) standards in one country and a much different and lower set of standards in another. Inevitably the corporate PR chief will need to be insistently attentive to these issues, and increasingly effective in encouraging regional and national senior corporate managers to adhere to business ethics and standards that do not put the corporate global reputation at risk.

Globalization requires that the PR chief will: need to acquire an increasingly broad range of skills for herself, or himself, and for the PR department; obtain greater knowledge of corporate global operations, international affairs in general, and international economic and business issues in particular; secure enhanced efficiency of global corporate resources deployed for communications; find increasingly sophisticated ways to communicate effectively with growing numbers of audiences; need to have substantial management skills to tackle, for example, the mounting potential turf battles with national and regional corporate managers; and, need to redefine the corporate image, its vision, its culture and confront the many ethical issues that such challenges pose.

Centralization versus Decentralization

Globalization accelerates the trends towards increasing delegated responsibilities to unit, regional and national managers, and this creates a dilemma for corporate public relations. PR decentralization of responsibility is difficult. Globalization may enhance needs for stronger central managerial and executive capacities and resources in the public relations area. Globalization means that an unprecedented range of audiences have to be handled, yet each must have a sense that they are being addressed by one corporation, with one image and one set of messages. Decentralization risks conflicting messages reaching external audiences, it risks the establishment of a less than crystal clear corporate identity; indeed, it risks an image over time of a corporation that appears to external audiences as out of its depth in the competitive global business ocean.

Then, the growth of the Internet, the evolution of global media entities (CNN, *News Corporation*, *The Financial Times*, *Dow Jones*, etc.), and the rapidly increasing integration of financial markets and institutional investor communications across national borders, means that PR chiefs can swiftly talk to many audiences in many countries in a uniform way from a single base. It sounds efficient. Yet, can PR continue to be centralized, or seek a new form of centralization, in a corporation where almost all business areas are enjoying unprecedented decentralization? Does PR centralization make sense where the CEO is creating his office as a type of holding company relative to growing numbers of semi-independent business units, and where unit, regional and national corporate senior executives are urged by the CEO to be increasingly sovereign? There are no simple answers. Some functions may need to be centralized, or, at a minimum, there will be a need for a head office capability to act globally on urgent PR issues. At the same time, it may be the case that the overall corporate forces of decentralization leave the PR chief with few organizational choices.

Instead of a large central department, the PR chief may be better served with a tiny high-powered team. That team could in turn have direct lines of communication to corporate PR professionals based in the key offices of senior corporate regional and national managers, and who have a direct reporting accountability to such managers. In addition, it could be that the overall structure is complemented by the engagement of PR agencies to provide services direct to the PR chief and his team, as well as to the senior corporate regional and national managers.

The PR chief has to develop effective relationships not only with the CEO and the top management team, but with the increasingly important unit, regional and national managers who drive the corporation's dynamic global operations. It will be a direct function of the mounting independence of action devolved to these managers in increasingly globalizing corporations by corporate headquarters.

While Finance can demand worldwide reporting standards and procedures from managers across the globe and monitor their operations with intensity, PR does not lend itself to similar approaches. While corporate Legal departments can seek to enforce compliance to distinct norms upon corporate managers around the world and wave the threat of severe sanctions in the event of non-compliance, PR can attain cooperation and partnership only by more subtle approaches.

In fact, the impact of the corporate PR chief on unit, regional and national managers, comes first and foremost from the PR chief's ability to win respect and be viewed as credible by these managers. Winning on this front by the PR chief demands a combination of being seen to enjoy the esteem of the CEO, occasional demonstrations of wisdom (but not arrogance), tact and diplomacy, sensitivity to diverse regional and cultural situations, and a willingness to move with skill and speed to assist unit, regional and national managers resolve real PR problems that they face.

And, arguably in no single area is the requirement of forging these relationships more important than in employee communications. Few CEOs would deny that employee motivation and productivity is significantly influenced by effective communications to all employees of a clear global corporate identity, by a set of admirable global core values, by a sense of success throughout the corporation, and by an array of factors particular to the immediate national and regional location of the employee.

While the latter local area may be the sole province of managers in the field, the other components are best designed and implemented in a partnership between the head office, where the PR chief should have lead responsibility for the CEO, and the unit, regional and national senior corporate managers.

There are no simplistic solutions. Creating an employee magazine at head office for 100,000 employees in 20 countries is both probably expensive, probably of marginal value, and full of risks of inadvertently touching some sensitivities in distant places. Producing reports — print, audio or video — in numerous languages may at best serve to supplement proactive programmes of employee communications in the global corporation, but they cannot be the heart of such communications.

The most effective communications is provided by immediate supervisors to their staff groups. The most effective communications to the supervisors is by their managers and so on up the chain of command. The PR chief can at most strive to see that head office communicates well with a relatively limited number of middle level and senior corporate managers around the world, and assists them to be the chief communications officers to the employees directly under their umbrellas.

To make this work the PR chief must enjoy the respect of the managers with whom he communicates; the chief must be seen as a source of support for their communications efforts;

and, the chief must demonstrate sensitivity to their problems. Perhaps nowhere in the PR domain is the PR chief more tested than in this area on an ongoing basis. And, the more global and the more decentralized the corporation becomes, so the tougher this challenge will be.

Corporate Social Responsibility

There is no question that we are in a demanding era. Corporations must have built-in sensing devices that can detect changes in the social winds. The job of detecting those changes and charting a new course belongs to the public relations professional. The real measure of PR efficiency of a corporation is not whether it has organized itself to lead, but whether it has organized itself to respond to social change.

One of the prime functions of the professional public relations practitioner is to act as mediator between the corporation and society. The public relations executives provide qualitative evaluation of social trends to help formulate policies that enable the corporation to.adapt to these trends and communicate — both internally and externally — the reasons for those policies. Understanding the concerns of stakeholders and the views of the public are important to corporate leaders. Carefully listening to others and doing the right thing are key qualities to leadership and long-term success in the corporate world.

The Harvard Business Review published an excellent article by Roger Martin, dean of the Joseph L. Rotman School of Management at the University of Toronto. He wrote: 'But corporations don't operate in a universe composed solely of shareholders. They exist within larger political and social entities and are subject to pressures from other members of those networks, be they citizens concerned about environmental protection, employees seeking to strike a balance between work and family, or political authorities protective of their tax bases. . . . Clearly, then, shareholder value and social responsibility are not necessarily incompatible.'[8] Christopher P.A. Komisarjevsky, President and Chief Executive Officer, Burson-Marsteller Worldwide called his address before The Conference Board's Corporate Communications Conference, New York City on 1 May 2003, 'A New Era of Responsible Communications'.

He said, 'what the future holds for this new era of "*responsible communications*" — communications that are candid, transparent, timely, clear, ethical . . . messages that reach well beyond the usual portfolio of stakeholders . . . and messages that get there with lightning speed.' There is no substitute for complete disclosure, integrity and speed. The mandate is: *be honest, leave nothing out, genuinely care for others and get there first with the news*. And this is the responsibility of corporate PR professionals.

8. Roger L. Martin, 'The Virtue Matrix: Calculating the Return on Corporate Responsibility', *Harvard Business Review*, vol. 80, no. 3, March 2002.

Theories and Models

Public relations is like many other professions where practice leads theory. In fact theory emerges out of practice of leading professionals, as the Page Principles of Corporate PR have emerged out of the work done by Arthur W. Page. Lasswell's Model of Communication emerged during the period of the Second World War and should be applicable to PR as it is basically a communication activity, and theories and models of communication should apply to public relations as well. As this model was associated with propaganda and propaganda being a bad word now, it is ignored by PR theorists these days.

Kenneth Plowman of Brigham Young University[1] pointed out that the convergence and mutual understanding of diffusion of innovations leads to pre-eminent models and situational theories in public relations. The ideal model is the two-way symmetrical that leads away from the context/distribution of rhetorical theory to collaboration and mutual problem solving of the two-way symmetrical model. In the past, rhetorical

1. 'Theory in Public Relations Brings Sense to Teaching Communications Theory', *Journalism and Mass Communication Quarterly*, no. 60, Summer 2003, (Public Relations Division of the Association for Education in Journalism and Mass Communication).

theory has emphasized one-way persuasion but recently Heath[2] has described a mutual persuasion model of communication. Like rhetorical public relations theory, the two-way symmetrical model emphasized the receiver or audience view of an issue in strong alignment with the post-modern view, the listening and caring view of feminist theory and the deconstructionist stance of culture and chaos theory. In public relations terms, these audiences are called publics. Publics arise in response to the consequence, pro or con, that an organization has on people as it pursues it mission. Publics organize around problems and make issues of problems that actively affect them.[3] Mass communication researchers have done little to define and explain the behaviour of publics, the most extensive research being Rogers (1983)[4] diffusion of innovations. The situational theory (J. Grunig and Hunt, 1984[5]; J. Grunig and Childers, 1988[6]) is the most researched of the segmentation of publics theories and could contribute greatly in this era of mass media publics being delineated through technology. Indeed, audiences of media are no longer mass in the classic sense.

2. Robert L. Heath, 'A Rhetorical Approach to Zones of Meaning and Organizational Prerogatives', *Public Relations Review*, 19 (2), 1993, pp. 112–55.

3. James E. Grunig, 'Implications of Public Relations for Other Domains of Communication', *Journal of Communication*, 43 (3), 1993, pp. 164–73.

4. Everett M. Rogers, *Diffusion of Innovations*, New York: Free Press; London: Collier Macmillan, 1983.

5. James E. Grunig and Todd Hunt, *Managing Public Relations*, New York; London: Holt, Rinehart and Winston, 1984.

6. James E. Grunig and Linda Childers, 'Reconstruction of a Situational Theory of Communication: Internal and External Concepts as Identifiers of Publics for AIDS'. Paper presented at the meeting of the Communication Theory and Methodology Division, Association for Education in Journalism and Mass Communication, Portland, OR, July 1988.

Publics

The publics in public relations are groups whose common interests are affected by the organization, or whose acts and opinions affect the institution. There are basically two types of publics: one active and the other latent. Organizations need to identify and list all publics and identify primary publics. The focus of a PR effort should be the primary public. Identifying and prioritizing publics need research.

It is important to correctly identify and characterize the relevant publics. A public, is 'a group whose members face a similar problem, recognize that the problem exists, and organize to do something about it.' Grunig and Hunt (1984)[7] assert that there are three stages in the evolution of publics. In the first, the latent stage, the public does not recognize the problem. A public moves to the awareness stage when it recognizes a problem. The final stage is the active stage in which the public organizes to do something about the problem. According to James E. Grunig and Todd Hunt the idea is to communicate with an aware public before it actively opposes an organization, thus becoming an activist public.

Four PR Models

Public relations scholars like James E. Grunig,[8] have identified four models of public relations through the history:

1. *Press agentry / publicity model* is a one-way communication model that uses persuasion and manipulation to influence audiences to behave as the organization

7. James E. Grunig and Todd Hunt, *Managing Public Relations.*
8. James E. Grunig (ed.), *Excellence in Public Relations and Communication Management*, Hillsdale, NJ: Lawrence Erlbaum Associates, 1992.

desires. This model was practiced from 1850 to1900. The great showman Phineas Taylor Barnum (1810–1891) is mentioned as a great practitioner of this model. Current use: entertainment, sports, and as a component of marketing (under 'Promotion').

2. *Public Information model* is also a one-way communication model that uses press releases and other one-way communication techniques to distribute organizational information to general public. A public relations practitioner is often referred to as the 'journalist in residence'. This is also called Government model or Journalistic model and aims at dissemination of accurate information. It was evolved between 1900 and 1920. Ivy Ledbetter Lee (1877–1934) was a great practitioner of this model. Current use: still prevalent in businesses, non-profits, government entities.
3. *Two-way asymmetrical model* is again a communication model that uses persuasion to influence audience to behave as the organization desires by communicating only acceptable characteristics of the organization. Uses feedback to evaluate whether objective met. This model is in use since 1920s. Edward L. Bernays (1891–1995) is recognized as pioneering practitioner of this model and is credited for bringing social science into public communication-using social science theory and research about attitudes and behaviours to persuade publics. It is also called the advocacy model. Current use: prevalent in businesses and in public causes.
4. *Two-way symmetrical model* is a two-way communication model that uses communication to negotiate with publics, resolve conflict, and promote mutual understanding and respect between the organization

and its public(s). In this model, also called relationship management model, the focus is on mutual understanding, conflict resolution between organization and its publics. It was evolved during 1960s. Research is used to explore perceptions and values and feedback is used in adjusting communication strategies. Uses social science theory and methods, theories of communication, rather than persuasion, for planning and evaluation. Here research is for understanding, rather than just changing attitudes, for counselling management on public reaction to policies; how policies can serve public interest and help create specific communication objectives. Current use: responsible businesses, non-profits, government entities, and movements. Professional leaders James Grunig, Scott Cutlip, Arthur Page.

Modernity (Best and Kellner, 1991)[9] began after feudalism and the Middle Ages. It opposed traditional societies and is characterized by innovation, novelty and dynamism. Modernity denotes the processes of industrialization, individualization, commodification, bureaucratization, and rationalization. Best and Kellner averred that modernity's promises of liberalization masked forms of oppression and domination. Post-modernism was said to begin with the advent of computers and modern media technologies — leading to the global village. It celebrates relativism and interpretivism, theories that at best provide partial perspectives on the world. Post-modern theory rejects modern assumptions of social coherence and notions of causality in favour of multiplicity, plurality, fragmentation and indeterminacy. Modernist theories relevant to the discussion here include:

9. Steven Best and Douglas Kellner, *Postmodern Theory: Critical Interrogations*, New York: Guilford Press, 1991.

Logical Positivism. Logical positivism (Tan, 1985)[10] is the traditional scientific method of explain, predict and control. It assumes there is a real world outside the scientist. The theorist set up hypotheses to test and see how close those theories come to objective reality. Objectivism and empiricism are other labels for this perspective on theory.

Structural-functionalism. It suggests that social phenomena occur from the interactions of social structures and the functions those structures serve (Prior-Miller, 1989).[11] This theory traces its roots directly to logical positivism and is an outgrowth of the writings of Durkheim (1947)[12] and Weber (1968).[13] Of paramount importance to structural-functionalism is the whole, assuming that organizations and relationships exist as part of a larger system, much as any single part of the human body exists to serve the whole. The processes that occur in organizations, such as cooperation, conflict, or communication, adjust to each other to maintain the whole. Organization structures then, are a result of the functions they serve; the functions served determine the structures. In the early '70s, communication scholars noted the lack of consideration of structural-functionalism in mass communication research. Systems theory extends from structural-functionalism.

10. Alexis S. Tan, *Mass Communication Theories and Research*, (2d ed.), New York; London: Macmillan, 1985.

11. M. Prior-Miller, 'Four major social scientific theories and their value to the public relations research', in Carl H. Botan and Vincent Hazleton, Jr. (eds), *Public Relations Theory*, Hillsdale, NJ: Lawrence Erlbaum Associates, 1989, pp. 67–81.

12. Emile Durkheim, *The Division of Labor in Society* (Tr. from the French *De la Division du Travail Social* by George Simpson), Glencoe, IL: The Free Press, 1947.

13. Max Weber, *The Theory of Social and Economic Organization*, (Parsons, Talcott and A.M. Henderson, Trans.), London: Collier-McMillan, 1968.

Congruence between modernism and post-modernism has led to several theories. Some of them are:

Scientific Reality. The first one, closest to modernism and related to American pragmatism, is scientific reality. Its premise is one of external reality, apart from social construction of reality by individuals (Fitzpatrick, 1993).[14] However, that reality may never be reached. It is informed by emergent and socially created realities. Subjectivity serves to prove objectivity (Greenwood, 1991).[15] Scientific reality moves beyond a positivist philosophy to consider social relationships in context. A realist view of human relationships examines not only how external events affect them but also how internal events, the purpose and reasons behind them, affect human interaction. The realist philosophy supports developing objective, causal explanations for relationship processes. All the while it considers also clear, subjective justifications for its claims.

Interpretive Empiricism. Putnam and Cheney (1983, 1985)[16] described social scientists who set up hypotheses to be tested from the ground up using naturalistic inquiry to find what the subjects of study describe as their own situation. The results, however, may be that the conclusion reached by the theorists may not match those of the subjects of study. Interpretive empiricism, despite this shortcoming, is an approach

14. M. Fitzpatrick, 'Communication and the new world of relationships', *Journal of Communication*, 43 (3), 1993, pp.119–26.

15. John D. Greenwood, *Relations and Representations: An Introduction to the Philosophy of Social Psychological Science*, London; New York: Routledge, 1991.

16. L.L. Putnam and G. Cheney, 'A critical review of research traditions in organizational communication', in Mary S. Mander (ed.) *Communications in Transition: Issues and Debates in Current Research*, New York: Praeger, 1983, pp. 206–24; L.L. Putnam and G. Cheney, 'Organizational Communication: Historical Development and Future Directions', in Thomas W. Benson (ed.), *Speech Communication in the 20th Century*, Carbondale: Southern Illinois University Press, 1985, pp. 130–56.

to merge the objective and subjective dichotomy. Social scientists construct theories and by doing so construct meaning for the reality they observe and measure.

Positive Relativism. L. Grunig (1992)[17] described a medium between the objective and the subjective or modernist and post-modernist as positive relativism, a position that neither asserts nor denies an objective reality. Its roots are psychological (Bigge, 1971)[18] and deals with a reality defined as that which people make of their experiences. It needs the results of the five senses to prove a theory or hypothesis worthwhile. Objects derive their qualities from the total situation rather than apart from their context. This notion of nothing existing apart from a larger scheme is consistent with systems theory.

Differencing. Dervin (1993)[19] weighed into the controversy between positivism and relativism or the empirical versus the rhetorical/hermeneutic when she used the tried and true metaphor of the blind men and the elephant. She described the problem as each blind man feeling a different part of the elephant and describing accurately their share of the whole. Her position is culture versus agency, culture being the whole, and agency being the plurality and free will of the parts. The structure or culture versus agency distinction is most often identified with Giddens (1984).[20]

Dependency Theory. DeFleur and Ball-Rokeach (1976,

17. Larissa A. Grunig, 'Toward the philosophy of public relations', in Elizabeth Lance Toth and Robert L. Heath (eds), *Rhetorical and Critical Approaches to Public Relations*, Hillsdale, NJ: Lawrence Erlbaum Associates, 1992, pp. 65–91.

18. Morris L. Bigge, *Positive Relativism: An Emergent Educational Philosophy*, New York: Harper & Row, 1971.

19. B. Dervin, 'Verbing communication: Mandate for disciplinary invention', *Journal of Communication*, 43 (3), 1993, pp. 45–54.

20. Anthony Giddens, *The Constitution of Society: Outline of the Theory of Structuration*, Berkeley: University of California Press, 1984.

1989)[21] interpreted Newcomb's symmetry model (1956)[22] of self and other, orienting to the object in a triangulation toward society. Their three points of the triangle are audience, society and mass media. They said that people have various levels of dependence on mass media based on the amount of disorder, conflict and change in society among these three poles. They essentially used Weaver's (1977)[23] concept of need for orientation, where the effect of mass communication depends on message relevancy and uncertainty of an individual about a particular subject. The key seems to be peoples' need to reduce ambiguity. Mass communication is very powerful if it reduces ambiguity through defining and structuring reality.

Conflict Theory. The conflict perspective assumes that conflict is the basis of social interchange and the product of social interchange (Conrad, 1990).[24] Organizations, rather than being the products of the consensus of individuals or organizations interacting with each other (subjective, critical/ rhetorical, and symbolic interactionism), are products among participants in conflict. Conflict theory assumes that conflict is an inevitable part of social interactions because of the incompatible, competing goals and values of individuals and organizations. Conflict theory looked predominately at how conflict can be resolved within and without the organization — that it is good to solve conflict for society to progress. Rush

21. Melvin L. DeFleur and Sandra J. Ball-Rokeach, *Theories of Mass Communication*, (5th ed.), New York: Longman, 1989.

22. T.M. Newcomb, 'An approach to the study of communicative acts', *Psychological Review*, 60, 1953, pp. 394–404.

23. D.H. Weaver, 'Political Issues and Voter Need for Orientation', in Donald L. Shaw and Maxwell E. McCombs (eds), *The Emergence of American Political Issues: The Agenda-Setting Function of the Press*, St. Paul, MN: West Publishing Co., 1977, pp. 107–19.

24. Charles Conrad, *Strategic Organizational Communication: An Integrated Perspective*, Ft. Worth, TX: Holt, Rinehart, and Winston, 1990.

investigated how the mass media can serve as a mediator in society to resolve problems among competing groups.

Post-modern theories include:

Critical Theory. It stems from Marxist and authoritarian viewpoints in that the media is manipulated by those in power. The theory's mission is to expose oppression, alienation, and injustice in organizations (Putnam and Cheney, 1983).[25] The mass media flows in a one-way direction, to sway audiences and it is incumbent on audiences to critique the powerful — to change the system so communication is more audience-centred. Critical studies are significant breaks with the old, established order, and the new is regrouped around a different set of premises or themes. Rather than looking at how communication assists societal structures, the critical scholar would ask whose interests are served in society and what role do they play in creating and maintaining power and domination.

Culture Theory. It views society as hermeneutic, the 'parts and whole' cannot be considered separately. L. Grunig (1992) saw culture as symbols and meanings in communication (back to symbolic interaction) and cited its fit with systems. Systems theory, however, views society as a whole. Culture views the two as inseparable and together, and symbolic interaction views the process as communication from part to whole. Wagner (1981)[26] and Agar (1993)[27] viewed culture as the co-construction of meaning. Hall (1959)[28] and later Carey (1989)[29]

25. L.L. Putnam and G. Cheney, 'Organizational Communication'.

26. Roy Wagner, *The Invention of Culture*, Chicago: University of Chicago Press, 1981.

27. Michael H. Agar, *Language Shock: Understanding the Culture of Conversation*, New York: William Morrow, 1994.

28. Edward T. Hall, *The Silent Language*, Garden City, NY: Doubleday, 1959.

29. James W. Carey, *Communication as Culture: Essays on Media and Society*, Boston, MA: Unwin Hyman, 1989.

saw communication as culture and culture as communication. He said communication does not create laws to explain events but seeks to understand events and diagnose meanings.

Feminist Theory. Feminist theory is audience and receiver-oriented. Logical positivism has been extensively criticized in feminist research for its division between theory and practice, between researcher and the object or the audience of the research. Liberal feminists work with the male-dominated system and radical feminists work to overturn and transform it (Van Zoonen, 1991).[30] Creedon (1993)[31] criticized system theory because it supports existing, patriarchy systems. Reinharz (1985)[32] discussed the making explicit of implicit values and norms; those values being feminist, more person-oriented. Toth (1992) said research must not be separated from its subject. There is a mutual process of creation occurring between researcher and subject. Fine (1993)[33] called for an infrasystem rather than a supra or subsystem in systems theory that would transform patriarchy to the implicit values and norms that L. Grunig (1992) also mentioned.

Chaos Theory. Chaos theory (Cottone, 1993)[34] makes

30. L. Van Zoonen, 'Feminist perspectives on the media', in James Curran and Michael Gurevitch (eds), *Mass Media and Society*, London; New York: Edward Arnold, 1991, pp. 235–66.

31. P.J. Creedon, 'Acknowledging the Infrasystem: A Critical Feminist Analysis of Systems of Theory', *Public Relations Review*, 19 (2), 1993, pp. 157–66.

32. S. Reinharz, 'Feminist Distrust: Problems of Context and Content in Sociological Work', in David N. Berg and Kenwyn K. Smith (eds), *Exploring Clinical Methods for Social Research*, Beverly Hills, CA: Sage, 1985, pp. 63–84.

33. M.G. Fine, 'New Voices in Organizational Communication: A Feminist Commentary and Critique', in Sheryl Perlmutter Bowen and Nancy Wyatt (eds.), *Transforming Visions: Feminist Critiques in Communication Studies*, Cresskill, NJ: Hampton Press, 1993.

34. L.P. Cottone, 'The Perturbing Worldview of Chaos: Implications for Public Relations', *Public Relations Review*, 19 (2), 1993, pp. 167–76.

sense at the global level. It is the extreme allowance of relativism, intepretism and agency. Its pluralism is chaos or disorder. It sees order in disorder, and it sees sudden and profound changes, fluctuations and transformations. If positivist science dismisses data that is not relevant, chaos states there is nothing that is insignificant. To be fruitful in mass communication studies, Cottone (1993) said chaos theory must look at three themes: a multidisciplinary effort, an investigation of extreme cases, and work that is tranformative in nature.

Modernity and post-modernity, can be brought together in convergence and mutual understanding of diffusion of innovations and leads to the pre-eminent models and situational theories in public relations (J. Grunig and Hunt, 1984).[35] The ideal model is the two-way symmetrical that leads away from the context/distribution of rhetorical theory (Heath, 1992;[36] 1993)[37] to collaboration and mutual problem-solving of the two-way symmetrical model.

Diffusion of Innovations. One way the poles could come together is through the diffusion of innovations concept of Rogers (1983).[38] This theory is a process and the interacting of systems theory that begins with: (1) innovation; (2) channels; (3) time; and (4) with society — that Rogers used to describe how knowledge (the mass media) interrelates on an interpersonal level (persuasion/rhetorical) to reach what Rogers and earlier Kincaid (1979)[39] called convergence to mutual under-

35. James E. Grunig and Todd Hunt, *Managing Public Relations*.

36. Robert L. Heath, 'The Wrangle in the Marketplace: A Rhetorical Perspective of Public Relations', in Elizabeth Lance Toth and Robert L. Heath (eds), *Rhetorical and Critical Approaches to Public Relations*, Hillsdale, NJ: Lawrence Erlbaum Associates, 1992, pp. 3–15.

37. Robert L. Heath, 'A Rhetorical Approach to Zones of Meaning and Organizational Prerogatives'.

38. Everett M. Rogers, *Diffusion of Innovations*.

39. D. Lawrence Kincaid, *The Convergence Model of Communication*, Honolulu, HI: East-West Center, 1979.

standing. Rogers and Kincaid (1981)[40] claimed the combination of the mass media and the interpersonal is the most effective for attitude change. Mass media channels reach large audiences, spread information and change weakly held attitudes. Interpersonal channels provide a two-way exchange of information and are more effective than mass media in dealing with resistance or apathy from the audience. Rogers' (1987)[41] view of the diffusion process is based on the convergence model of communication that he and Kincaid developed. Communication is a process where participants create and share information with one another to reach mutual understanding. In most communication models, the individual is the unit of analysis. In the network model of Rogers (1986),[42] the dyad linked by communication and the groups within the group are studied. Mass media effects, in this context, arise from joint activity and affect all participants. Rogers characterized a communication network as consisting of interconnected individuals linked by patterned communication flows.

Rhetorical research in public relations comes into play when symbolic behaviour influences issues (Heath, 1992).[43] People or publics use words and visual symbols to 'share and evaluate information, shape beliefs, and establish norms for coordinated collective action.' Rhetoric also helps explain how people and organizations manage their relationships in a situation that requires a response to a problem that arises from that situation.

40. Everett M. Rogers and D. Lawrence Kincaid, *Communication Networks: Toward a New Paradigm for Research*, New York: Free Press; London: Collier Macmillan, 1981.

41. Everett M. Rogers, 'The diffusion of innovation perspective' in Neil D. Weinstein (ed.), *Taking Care: Understanding and Encouraging Self-protective Behavior*, Cambridge: Cambridge University Press, 1987.

42. Everett M. Rogers, *Communication Technology: The New Media in Society*, New York: Free Press; London: Collier Macmillan, 1986.

43. Robert L. Heath, 'The Wrangle in the Marketplace'.

One or more publics channel messages in the situation surrounding each message. This situation influences which facts and arguments in the message are relevant. It constrains what can be said and how it can be phrased on an interpersonal level. Issues management studies such as those by Crable and Vibbert (1983, 1985)[44] and Heath and Nelson (1986),[45] asserted that an issue can be created by the organization and that through the use of symbolic strategies, communication can influence the public policy debate. Although typically thought of as one-way persuasion, Heath (1992, 1993)[46] argued against one-way rhetoric intended to dominate and persuade the opposition, and instead recommended mutual persuasion.

Systems Theory of PR

A system is a set of interdependent units, which endure within an established boundary by responding and adjusting to change pressures from the environment. Systems can be of the following types:

A *closed system* has an impermeable boundary: and therefore cannot exchange matter, energy or information with its environment. It is static and does not adapt to external change and eventually disintegrates.

An *open system* has a permeable boundary: and therefore

44. Richard E. Crable and Steven L. Vibbert, 'Mobil's epideictic advocacy: "Observations" of Prometheus Bound', *Communication Monographs*, 50 (4), 1983, pp. 380–94; Richard E. Crable and Steven L. Vibbert, 'Managing issues and influencing public policy', *Public Relations Review*, 11 (2), 1985, pp. 3–16.

45. Robert L. Heath and Richard Alan Nelson, *Issues Management: Corporate Public Policymaking in an Information Society*, Beverly Hills, CA: Sage Publications, 1986.

46. Robert L. Heath, 'The Wrangle in the Marketplace'; 'A Rhetorical Approach to Zones of Meaning and Organizational Prerogatives'.

exchanges inputs and outputs through its boundary. It is responsive — adjusts and adapts to environmental change. The survival and growth depend on interchange with the environment. Inputs from the environment can be reactions to the system's outputs, can be result of change independent of outputs, can have impact on the system's goals. Adjustments are directed internally/externally. The internal outputs can change/maintain goals. Similarly, external outputs change/ maintain environmental conditions. The interchange with environment is cyclical and therefore continually adjusts in order to maintain equilibrium.

In *relatively open/closed systems*, no social system is totally open or totally closed. Systems are relatively open or relatively closed. Relatively closed systems use reactive programme planning and management. Activated only when disturbed-reacting to crises, problems. Relatively open systems rely on feedback — positive or negative. Negative feedback is most important for equilibrium. When negative feedback gives error-messages the system adjusts. Positive feedback results in amplifying or maintaining course; anticipating change; influencing the environment. Proactive action is possible by actively probing and monitoring environment. Early warnings can be used to make adjustments to prevent or avoid disturbances or problems later.

PR is part of an adaptive subsystem, distinct from production, maintenance and managerial subsystems. PR is a boundary-spanner. Proactive PR keeps organizations sensitive to environmental changes. In an open system PR actively monitors social environments and makes adjustments. The most-open systems use a two-way symmetrical model: PR practitioners are managers of change. Public relations establish and maintain mutually dependent relationships between an organization and its publics.

PR efforts are part of an organization's managed behaviour to achieve goals. Goals can be achieved by maintaining existing relationships in the face of changing conditions; continually adjusting relationships with publics in response to changing social environments and adapting goals to accommodate change pressures. PR employs communication as a tool to help an organization and its publics solve problems: sharing information; solving problems. Proactive corrective actions may be most useful aspect of the open systems model as it reduces amount of effort required and trauma associated with crisis-oriented reactive PR.

Systems theory considers the whole paramount over the parts (von Bertalanffy, 1969)[47] but emphasizes the integration of the parts — like the human body (Toth and Heath, 1992)[48] where the parts are vital to keep the system functioning. Systems theory is known, too, as hermeneutics, the concept where the whole cannot be known without the parts and the parts cannot be known without the whole. Windahl and Signitizer (1992)[49] cited Katz and Kahn (1978)[50] and Goldhaber (1986)[51] in creating a systems model. In systems terms then, the unit of analysis is not any one thing, person or event in isolation but a relationship between people and environments. These relationships can be approached partly through communication.

47. Ludwig von Bertalanffy, *General System Theory: Foundations, Development, Applications*, (2d ed.), New York: G. Braziller, 1969.

48. Elizabeth Lance Toth and Robert L. Heath (eds), *Rhetorical and Critical Approaches to Public Relations*, Hillsdale, NJ: Lawrence Erlbaum Associates, 1992.

49. Sven Windahl and Benno H. Signitzer, with Jean T. Olson, *Using Communication Theory: An Introduction to Planned Communication*, London; Newbury Park, CA: Sage Publications, 1992.

50. Daniel Katz and Robert L. Kahn, *The Social Psychology of Organizations*, (2d ed.), New York: Wiley, 1978.

51. Gerald M. Goldhaber, *Organizational Communication*, (4th ed.), Dubuque, IA: W.C. Brown, 1986.

The assumption being that social structures stay together through meaning shared by people who belong to the system (Windahl and Signitzer, 1992).[52]

Situational Theory of PR

Grunig's (1977)[53] situational theory consists of two dependent variables and three independent variables. The two dependent variables, active and passive communication behaviour, can also be called information seeking and information processing. *Information seeking*, as described by Clark and Kline (1974), is 'the planned scanning of the environment for messages about a specific topic.' *Information processing* is 'the unplanned discovery of a message followed by continued processing of it,' Clark and Kline (1974). The independent variables are situational because they describe the perceptions that people have about specific situations, especially problematic ones causing conflict. Grunig defines these three variables: *Problem Recognition*. People detect that something should be done about a situation and stop to think about what to do. *Constraint Recognition*. People perceive that there are obstacles in a situation that limit their ability to do anything about the situation. *Level of Involvement*. The extent to which people connect themselves with a situation.

According to the theory, research has confirmed that high problem recognition and low constraint recognition increase

52. Sven Windahl and Benno H. Signitzer, with Jean T. Olson, *Using Communication Theory*.

53. James E. Grunig, 'A Situational Theory of Environmental Issues, Publics, and Activists', in Larissa A. Grunig (ed.), *Environmental Activism Revisited: The Changing Nature of Communication through Organizational Public Relations, Special Interest Groups and the Mass Media*, Monographs in Environmental Education and Environmental Studies, vol. 5, Troy, OH: North American Association for Environmental Education, 1989.

active information seeking and passive information processing. The level of involvement also increases, however it has little effect on information processing. People seldom seek information about situations that do not involve them. They will however randomly process information.

Game Theory

The basic premise of game theory holds that conflicts of interest can be modelled as games of strategy. Game theorists model these conflicts by considering the participants as 'players' in the game. One player is the organization and the other is the activist group in which each player has certain preferences and dislikes. Each one has to select 'plays' or strategies for reaching the preferred outcome while simultaneously considering the opponent's strategies. Game theory examines various approaches to conflict by applying specific models. These models can be divided into two types of game: *zero sum* and *non-zero sum*.

On the pure conflict extreme is the *zero-sum* game which can be defined as: 'one in which the payoffs to the players in any outcome add up to zero; what one player gains, the other must necessarily lose,' Colman (1982). These types of games are based on pure opposition, as there is no possibility of profitable collaboration.

The *non-zero sum* game is dominated by mixed motives. In this game, each side retains 'a strong sense of self-interest but is motivated to cooperate, to a limited extent, in order to maximize very different benefits for each,' Colman (1982).

As public relations is a communication activity and uses mass media as well, certain theories and concepts emphasizing media effects need mention here. The *Magic Bullet theory* is one of the earliest and has enormous belief in the power of media. It suggests the effect of messages through mass media is like a magic bullet and is predictable, immediate, direct and uniform on everyone who receives it. Two major studies of 1933 on effects of movies on children gave empirical data to support it. Herbert Blumer's Payne Fund study on movies and children found films as a source of imitation, unintentional learning and emotional possession. The Peterson-Thurston Study found uniform and cumulative effect on children's attitudes toward issues and found an attitude change leading to change of behaviour. Several scholars in later studies found that media effects were not uniform but depended on individual differences, social categories, critical ability and education.

In 1948 Paul F. Lazarsfeld found media as part of the *Web of Influence* which include family, friends, associates, etc. In fact, The Rockefeller Foundation funded the Radio Research Project on the effects of radio through Princeton University, with Paul F. Lazarsfeld as director of the project from his base at the University of Newark. In 1939, Lazarsfeld moved with the Radio Research Project to Columbia University, where he became a faculty member in the Department of Sociology. The Rockefeller Foundation project on radio effects became the Bureau of Applied Social Research in 1944. Among the most noted of the studies conducted by the bureau was the Erie County (Ohio) investigation of the role of the mass media and of opinion leaders in the two-step flow of communication. The 1944 book that resulted from this study, *The People's Choice* (written by Lazarsfeld, Bernard Berelson, and Hazel Gaudet), helped establish the specialty of political communication and ushered in a scholarly era of the minimal effects of mass communication. Lazarsfeld and his colleagues found that the mass media of radio and print had relatively minor direct effects on how people voted in the 1940 presidential election in the United States. People mainly decided for whom to vote on the basis of interpersonal communication with peers. Another famed bureau study followed, the Decatur (Illinois) research in which Lazarsfeld sought further understanding of the two-step flow of communication — in which ideas move from the media to opinion leaders and then to their followers through interpersonal networks. The results of the Decatur study appeared as a book, *Personal Influence* (written by Lazarsfeld with Elihu Katz, 1955), and illustrated the importance of media-stimulated interpersonal communication between opinion leaders and their followers as they made consumer decisions about movies, fashions, and so on.

The *two-step flow theory* recognized opinion leaders who attend to media and have personal influence on others and have a intermediary role in diffusion of innovations, cultural and technical change.

The *uses and gratification theory* found that based on uses and gratification specific messages from specific media are selectively attended to. Audiences actively and freely select content and are not passive as in the Magic Bullet. Personal interests, desires, values and habits of seeking gratification influence decisions.

The *accumulation of minimal effects theory* postulates significant changes in beliefs, attitudes and behaviour over time, if media focus repeatedly on an issue and are consistent in presenting uniform interpretation, especially when the audience knows little or nothing about the issue from other sources. Watergate, Vietnam and Saddam Hussein are good examples.

Media helps society adopt new technologies, ideas, standards, fads and fashions in the *adoption of innovation theory*. The adoption curve begins with awareness, and media-spread information, ads play a major part. Early adopters become opinion leaders but the flow may not be confined to two-step but may be a multi-step flow. If the innovation is useful it will lead to diffusion and widespread adoption.

Persuasion

There are six steps to persuasion: presentation, attention, comprehension, yielding, retention and finally overt behaviour. There are seven barriers to it namely, selective perception, selective exposure, selective retention, group norms, multi-step flow, ego-involved attitudes and nature of media in a free society.

Source credibility is determined by seven factors: trustworthiness, expertise, dynamics, similarity, power, idealistic (intentions) and goodwill (intentions). If a low credibility source is used hard specific facts and first-hand experience are needed.

The *sleeper effect* has been noticed after month or so — the source is often forgotten or disassociated from the message. The impact of a persuasive message will generally tend to decrease over time. However, under the right circumstances the sleeper effect predicts that a message from a low-credibility source can actually increase in persuasiveness. Low credibility may be caused by a discounting cue, such as when a prediction of improving economic conditions is given by a government spokesperson (who is presumed to be biased). However, when the message eventually gets separated from its source (by *dissociation*), the message may gain more credibility.

Attitudes and Behaviour

Attitudes and behaviour have been seen shifting towards consistency according to several theories:

In the *congruity theory*, incongruent attitudes move together attitudes regarding objects more than attitudes regarding people. More polarized attitudes are harder to change. Magic Johnson — AIDS; Michael Jordan — Nike, Hanes.

Cognitive dissonance (L. Festinger)[54] is defined as tension over two inconsistent cognitions (acting contrary to one's attitudes). According to the cognitive dissonance theory, there is a tendency for individuals to seek consistency among their cognitions (i.e., beliefs, opinions). When there is an inconsistency between attitudes or behaviours (dissonance), something must change to eliminate the dissonance. In the case of a discrepancy between attitudes and behaviour, it is most likely that the attitude will change to accommodate the behaviour. Conflict in beliefs/actions; after incongruent choice, leads to a feeling of discomfort: Consistency overcomes discomfort by (1) upgrade choice made; (2) downgrade or ignore choice not made; (3) revoke decisions (rare).[55] If you can get someone to act differently than their attitudes, attitudes will change: No dissonance if they realize they are being forced, duped or compensated. Rewarding people for what they enjoy leads to attribution to reward. When a choice made is inconsistent with beliefs, it will generally change attitudes. However, commitment is difficult to overcome. Dissonance theory applies to

54. Leon Festinger, *A Theory of Cognitive Dissonance*, Stanford, CA: Stanford University Press, 1957.

55. Consider someone who buys an expensive car but discovers that it is not comfortable on long drives. Dissonance exists between their beliefs that they have bought a good car and that a good car should be comfortable. Dissonance could be eliminated by deciding that it does not matter since the car is mainly used for short trips (reducing the importance of the dissonant belief) or focusing on the cars strengths such as safety, appearance, handling (thereby adding more consonant beliefs). The dissonance could also be eliminated by getting rid of the car, but this behaviour is a lot harder to achieve than changing beliefs.

all situations involving attitude formation and change. It is especially relevant to decision-making and problem-solving.

The *self-perception theory* states that: 'Individuals come to know their own attitudes, emotions and internal states by inferring them from observations of their own behavior and circumstances in which they occur. When internal cues are weak, ambiguous, or uninterpretable, the individual is in the same position as the outside observer'.[56] Self-perception theory further states that if external contingencies seem sufficient to account for the behaviour, then the individual will not be led into using the behaviour as a source of evidence for his self-attributions. If any source implies irrelevance or low credibility, then self-attributions will not occur. It thus has two basic postulates: (1) attitudes are inferred from behaviour and (2) reward undermines attitude. Impression management is necessary and there is need to appear consistent.

The *assimilation-contrast theory* says we accept messages close to our own viewpoint; they may appear closer than they are. This is called latitude of acceptance. We reject messages that are too far from our own viewpoint; they may appear further away than they are. This is called latitude of rejection. There is also latitude of neutrality. When the ego is involved there is a narrower latitude of acceptance and a wider latitude of rejection.

Attitudes predict behaviour, (1) if specific to the behaviour, as specific attitudes toward specific health-related practices; (2) self-awareness, from experience or inner-direction, think about attitudes (reminded), or acquired in a way that make them strong (from experience, self-interest); and (3) if other influences are minimized.

56. D. J. Bem, 'Self Perception Theory', in L. Berkowitz (ed.), *Advances in Experimental Social Psychology*, vol. 6, New York: Academic Press, 1972, pp. 1–62.

Behaviour determines attitudes, where choice plays a major role, as behaviour is not internalized if there is no choice. There is a foot-in-the-door phenomenon where (escalating commitments) spiralling action and attitude lead to momentum of compliance. Commitment, obligation to requester, is a significant factor. Voluntary initial act affects attitude. Cognitive dissonance leads to change in attitude and self-perception to change in self-image.

The *attribution theory* was developed over time from the theories of Fritz Heider, Edward Jones, Keith Davis, and Harold Kelley, all social psychologists. Heider first wrote about attribution theory in his book *The Psychology of Interpersonal Relationships* (1958) which played a central role in the origination and definition of the attribution theory. Jones and Davis' systematic hypotheses about the perception of intention was published in 1965 in the essay 'From Acts to Dispositions'. Kelley published 'Attribution in Social Psychology' in 1967.

Attribution theory is about how people make causal explanations; about how they answer questions beginning with 'why?' The theory deals with the information they use in making causal inferences, and with what they do with this information to answer causal questions. The theory developed within social psychology as a means of dealing with questions of social perception. For instance, if a person is aggressively competitive in his/her behaviour, is s/he this kind of person, or is s/he reacting to situational pressures. If a person fails a test, does s/he have low ability, or is the test difficult? In both examples, the questions concern the causes of observed behaviour and the answers of interest are those given by the man on the street. This is why Heider refers to attribution theory as 'naïve' psychology. Attribution theory describes the processes of explaining events and the behavioural and emotional consequences of those explanations. When we offer explanations about why things happened, we can give one of two types. One, we can make an external attribution, or two, we can make an internal attribution. An external attribution (get ready for this) assigns causality to an outside agent or force. Or as kids would say, 'The devil made me do it.' An external attribution claims that some outside thing motivated the event. By contrast, an internal attribution assigns causality to factors within the person. Or as the sinner would say, 'I'm guilty, grant me forgiveness.' An internal attribution claims that the person was directly responsible for the event. We attribute behaviour to either attitudes or situations. Our own good behaviour to attitudes; others' to situations and vice versa.

The *social learning theory* was put forth by a psychology professor Albert Bandura.[57] It emphasizes the importance of observing and modelling the behaviours, attitudes, and emotional reactions of others. Bandura (1977) states: 'Learning would be exceedingly laborious, not to mention hazardous, if people had to rely solely on the effects of their own actions to inform them what to do. Fortunately, most human behaviour is learned observationally through modelling: from observing others one forms an idea of how new behaviours are performed, and on later occasions this coded information serves as a guide for action.' Social learning theory explains human behaviour in terms of continuous reciprocal interaction between cognitive, behavioural, and environmental influences. The component processes underlying observational learning are: (1) Attention, including modelled events (distinctiveness, affective valence, complexity, prevalence, functional value)

57. Albert Bandura, *Social Learning Theory*, Englewood Cliffs, NJ: Prentice Hall, 1977.

and observer characteristics (sensory capacities, arousal level, perceptual set, past reinforcement); (2) Retention, including symbolic coding, cognitive organization, symbolic rehearsal, motor rehearsal; (3) Motor Reproduction, including physical capabilities, self-observation of reproduction, accuracy of feedback; and (4) Motivation, including external, vicarious and self-reinforcement. Because it encompasses attention, memory and motivation, social learning theory spans both cognitive and behavioural frameworks.

Key components are modelling (observational learning), and social reinforcement (feedback). It involves interaction between environment and thought. Fundamental assumptions are: majority of behaviours are learned; observing behaviour is an effective way to initiate behaviour change. Learning occurs when a person knows what to do and produces the desired outcome. Behaviour is facilitated through reinforcement. People expect (expectancy learning) events to occur in given situations.

Media has a great effect in high threshold issues, as agenda setting is done through the media and issues are defined; saturation leads to salience (pronounced, highlighted), concordance — agreeing on and repeating idea and then there is a cumulative effect. Here media monopoly is a significant factor.

Asymmetrical *versus* Symmetrical Communication in Activism

Public relations theory suggests that conflicts are most efficiently resolved when 'participants evolve compatible ground rules for play.'[58] This concept is the underlying principle in

58. Priscilla Murphy and Juliet Dee, 'Du Pont and Greenpeace: The Dynamics of Conflict between Corporations and Activists Groups', *Public Relations Research*, 4 (1), 1992, pp. 3–20.

Grunig and Hunt's (1984) definition of symmetric two-way public relations. This communication, according to J.E. Grunig and Hunt (1984), 'resolves conflict through negotiation, communication, and compromise.'

L.A. Grunig[59] was able to conclude that because organizations fail to effectively deal with activist publics using the other three models of public relations, there was an implied need for the two-way symmetrical model. Her five assertions about two-way symmetrical communication between organizations and activists are:

1. Organizations need two-way communication to learn the consequences of what they are doing on all of their relevant publics.
2. Organizations need two-way communication to tell the publics what they are doing about the negative consequences.
3. The two-way symmetrical approach to public relations is an on-going process.
4. An on-going, balanced, and proactive programme of constituency relations must acknowledge the legitimacy of all constituent groups regardless of size.
5. Research is an important variable in the two-way symmetrical model of public relations. Organizations must learn to measure their effectiveness in terms of more than simplistic short-term gains or losses.

59. Larissa Grunig, 'Activism: How it limits the effectiveness of organizations and how excellent public relations departments respond', in James E. Grunig with David M. Dozier (eds), *Excellence in Public Relations and Communication Management*, Hillsdale, NJ: Lawrence Erlbaum Associates, 1992.

Public Relations Planning

Edward L. Bernays in his famous book, *The Engineering of Consent*, says 'Like Columbus, you can sail west and reach new land by accident. But if you have charts, you can do better; you can arrive at a destination decided upon in advance. . . . It is careful planning more than anything else that distinguishes modern public relations from old-time hit or miss publicity and propaganda.'

Most public relations practitioners have probably heard at a conference or workshop: 'You should do more planning. It's good for you; it will make you more successful.' Most practitioners believe it and follow it. There are others who don't do as much planning as they could have, lamenting at not having more time to devote to it. Planning is good for public relations people, and it can contribute to the success of public relations activities. But, it takes time and effort. It can be tedious, and it's neither glamorous nor exciting. It lacks the appeal and the challenge of media relations or crisis communication and, for most practitioners, falls short of providing the satisfaction and sense of accomplishment that completing a publication or a special event does. It's generally viewed as one of those things that should be done rather than something people want to do.

Sometimes 'quick and dirty' planning is all that is needed. However, the most effective planning is slower and more methodical.

In simplest terms planning is figuring out the best way to accomplish whatever you want to do or to get wherever you want to be. The basic concept is clear, simple, and straightforward. But, over time planning has become a specialty field in its own right and has developed its own special jargon. Traditional planners set goals, identify objectives, and define action steps to reach their goals and objectives. Contemporary planners have added buzz words like strategic, visioning, and organizational advancement to the planning lexicon. They shift into an 'organizational advancement mode' to draft 'strategic planning documents that enunciate organizational visions.'

Public relations planning is simply identifying with whom you want to have a relationship, what you want from that relationship, and what you can do to achieve it. It seems rudimentary, but it's surprising how often such basic forethought is overlooked.

A public relations plan helps maintain self-discipline as well as being an excellent informational tool. This is especially true for public relations practitioners who have recently changed jobs or taken on new clients. Planning forces them to ask questions and review their underlying assumptions. Each successive step in the planning process sharpens their focus on how the organization operates and where it's going, as well as clarifying public relations' role in that operation.

Planning has two different types:

Strategic planning defines an overall framework, focus, and goals for a long-term or indefinitely on-going process or operation.

Tactical planning is an outgrowth of strategic planning that often focuses on a specific time period, e.g. a five-year plan, an annual plan, or a monthly plan, rather than the entire life of the organization.

Although some people try to do tactical or project planning without first having a strategic plan, it's rarely successful. It's far more common to view tactical planning as an extension of strategic planning.

The best public relations practitioners are equally comfortable doing both types of planning. They work together. Think of an organization's strategic plan as its global view of the world and its tactical plan as its local street map. The tactical plan converts the broad brush strokes and goals of the strategic plan into a series of objectives which are practical, do-able tasks involving specific campaigns, audiences, programmes, or activities. Each of these tactical objectives — or projects — can be completed independently of the others, but they are ultimately intended to move the organization toward its long-range goals. A written plan is a guide for future action. Public relations plans range from single-sentence, common sense aphorisms to hundred-page, hard-bound documents, and the time practitioners devote to planning ranges from nil to nearly full-time. In a similar way, the importance they attach to planning ranges from insignificant to life-saving. There are almost as many approaches to PR planning as there are practitioners.

At its most basic level public relations planning can be compared to the rudimentary technique Professor Harold Lasswell developed for analysing and modeling mass communication. His oft-quoted approach to studying communication boiled down to four simple questions: Who says what? In which channel? To whom? With what effect? For public relations, the critical questions become: *What is to be communicated? In what way? To which audience? For what purpose?*

Public relations people who can answer these questions can be said to have done at least rudimentary planning. All planning does not require the same amount of work, nor does it produce the same tangible evidence. The brevity, or even the complete absence, of a planning document does not necessarily indicate a lack of planning.

The best starting point for public relations planning is to review the organization's mission statement and goals. These documents summarize what the organization is and what it's trying to accomplish, and they should provide the focus for every decision the organization — or any sub-unit within it — makes and every action it takes. This should be especially true of public relations efforts. Consequently, many public relations plans start with a copy of the organization's mission and goals. The next element these plans include is a mission statement for the public relations unit which spells out what that unit does and how it assists and supports the organization in carrying out its mission.

Target audiences, or publics can be the next focal point for planning. Beyond this point, different planners structure their plans in different ways that reflect their views of what public relations is and what it does. Some put primary emphasis on policy research and issues management, others on activities like publications, special events, speech writing, and media relations. And, those who see relationship-building as the essence of public relations often build their strategic plans around their organization's most important publics and target audiences.

Identification of Publics

Depending upon the nature of the audiences or publics, these listings may be as short and simple as the names of key people, organizations, and communities or as long and complex as psycho-demographic profiles of prospective buyers of a particular product. For most organizations the list will include a mix of short and long identifications. Consistency isn't the goal; useful information is. Long audience identifications, if they include unique characteristics, appeals that are particularly effective with this audience, or the best ways of reaching the audience, can be very useful.

With whom does the organization need to have relationships? What does it want these people to think about the organization? These questions can be answered after a little introspection and discussion with top management. Keep in mind that these are ultimately top management's decisions, not the public relations practitioners'. The public relations people should speak out and try to influence who is included and who is excluded from this list, but they rarely make the final decision. Probably the most effective way of dealing with these questions is for the public relations staff to develop a preliminary list of publics and relationships and then meet with key managers to review and discuss them.

No matter how obvious it seems, each public should be evaluated in terms of its relevance and importance to the organization. Data about the abstract or general importance of a public, how big it is, how politically influential it is, or how rich its members are — is not enough and can, in fact, be very misleading. The critical information needed is how and why this public affects the organization. What does it, or could it do, to help, or to hinder, the organization in reaching its goals? Padding an audience list with people or organizations who have little or no direct bearing on the organization is a waste of time. It serves little purpose, no matter how prestigious these audiences may be. It might even interfere with or delay meaningful planning. There is a tendency among some public relations people to become enchanted by various élite media and to make them a regular part of their media relations audience simply because of their prestige. It may be waste of effort.

What view does the organization want this public to have of it? Or, what kind of relationship does the organization want to have with this public? It is a reflection of what the organization hopes to accomplish by interacting with this public. It may be having them to purchase products or services, or supporting new legislation, or any other issue depending upon the organization and public. The more clearly and concretely this view is expressed, the more helpful it will be for future planning and relationship building.

Research

Once the publics and desired relationships have been nailed down, the next step is to explore the existing relationship the organization has with each of those publics and to decide whether it needs any adjustment. This calls for more than internal discussion. Simply letting the public relations staff and/or organizational managers speculate will never yield reliable information. Carefully conducted research, whether it's done by the public relations staff or by hired research consultants, is the only way to get vital and meaningful information about the publics you need to reach. It's critical to successful planning that such research be done, and that its findings then be incorporated into the plan as it is being developed.

What is this public's current view of the organization? Or, what is the organization's current relationship with this public? This is to ascertain where the relationship is now compared to where the organization wants it to be. This is not something to be guessed at. This question, more than any other part of the strategic planning process, requires accurate, non-ambiguous answers. Virtually all the rest of the planning process, including the setting of specific objectives and the measurement of success, is based on the information gathered at this step.

What issues and appeals are important to this public? Which media does this public use and trust the most? Some planners consider these to be extraneous questions as they are not absolutely essential for properly assessing the organization's current relationships or for determining what can be done to improve them, but the information they provide can be extremely helpful later, during tactical planning and while carrying out a public relations campaign. Answering these two questions helps ensure that only the most effective and efficient media for reaching the target publics are used and that the messages the organization sends via these channels will include the best possible themes and concepts for a response from the publics. If these questions are included in the planning process, they should be asked in the broadest possible ways. Responses about preferred media or channels of communication should not be limited to the major mass media, but should also take narrower and more selective communication techniques — everything from interpersonal conversations to public speeches to telephone calls to direct mail to the Internet — into account. And the list of important or appealing issues should not be restricted only to issues which are directly related to the organization and its mission.

Plan Development

At this stage the planning process integrates the first two stages with a series of questions that build upon and further explore the responses to the earlier questions. How does this public's current view of the organization differ from the desired one? Or, how does the organization's current relationship with this public compare with what the organization wants it to be? This comparison lets the organization know which of its relationships are moving along on track and which are most in need of adjustment. A frequent outcome of this planning step is a prioritized list of relationships which need immediate attention.

What message themes will have the greatest impact on this public? Something that has become increasingly common in recent years as organizations seek more and more ways to establish additional linkages to their constituents is that the perceived strength of an audience's feeling about a particular topic will 'inspire' the organization to take a similar public stance on that issue even though it has no direct bearing on the organization and would otherwise have gone unnoticed by its management.

What are the best ways of reaching this public? There are some instances in which responses to this item are nearly identical to the media preferences identified for the publics. At other times, the public's stated preferences may not be suitable or affordable for the organization to use. The means of reaching the audience which are identified here need to be appropriate, available, and affordable. In many instances, it may be most effective to list several different means of communicating with each audience, specifying which means and medium is most appropriate for various types of situations.

Who will serve as the organization's primary contact for working with this public? Even though public relations is concerned with all of an organization's relationships, the public relations practitioners themselves are not always the most appropriate 'point persons' for working with every public. Some high-profile publics — political figures, major business executives, etc. — may not be satisfied dealing with public relations staff members. They may expect the personal attention of the CEO or the chairman of the board. Other publics may be so engrossed with technical issues that they need to be dealt with by subject matter specialists and technical experts. Still others may not care who they deal with, just so long as someone from the organization pays attention to them. Therefore, primary audience contacts can include a mix of public relations people, management executives, technical specialists, and others, all of whom are chosen for their rapport with a particular public rather than their job titles.

Tactical public relations objectives are developed by analysing the organization's strategic plan, after ascertaining how each public's current view of the organization differs from what the organization would like it to be. In addition to identifying which relationships are most in need of attention, this analysis allows the organization to identify common threads among its various relationships and its publics' perceptions of it: What do people think it does well? What do they think it does poorly? What do they like about it? What do they dislike about it? What would they like to have changed? These findings then become the basis for developing a prioritized list of objectives — specific, short-term goals — which often include or are linked to a project, publication, special event, or other task whose achievement can be readily measured. The assumption and intent is that successfully completing these objectives will, over time, ultimately lead to the realization of the organization's long-term goals.

What short-term objectives will lead to the goals of the strategic plan? There are any number of potentially useful ways public relations objectives can be identified, organized, and prioritized. A useful classification can be:

Project-oriented objectives focus on specific work products (e.g. news releases, publications, etc.) or tasks (e.g. holding an open house, press conference, testifying before a legislative sub-committee, etc.) that end up on a giant 'to do list' of projects that will enhance the organization's public relations. These can be either new initiatives or a continuation of current activities. Usually the first consideration in trying to prioritize such a list is predicting how many people will be affected. The more people it will impact, the higher its priority is likely to be, although some consideration is also given to cost, ease of completion, and precedent. If it's relatively cheap, easy to do, and is something the organization has been doing for a long time — e.g. publishing a monthly employee newsletter — continuing to do it may rise to the top of priority list regardless of how many people are actually affected by it.

Relationship-oriented objectives focus on the organization's various publics and the quality of its relationships with each of them. Recognizing that the ideal of having a perfect relationship with each and every public is rarely attained and that it is almost impossible to devote equal time and attention to every separate audience, this approach tries to list the organization's relationships in the order in which they should be given attention. The priority given to any particular relationship is based on a combination of that public's importance to the organization and an assessment of how far from ideal its current relationship with the organization is. The more important the public is and the further from ideal its relationship is, the higher its priority becomes.

Performance or production oriented planners, especially

public relations practitioners who are using a first or second phase approach to public relations, are likely to prefer the first approach and to emphasize task-oriented planning. Third-phase public relations practitioners and relationship-builders are more likely to use the second approach. Regardless of which approach is used, the end result of this step in tactical planning is a list of objectives the organization will attempt to achieve.

What specific actions or messages will lead to achieving this objective? This question really requires multiple answers and may involve far more members of the organization than the public relations staff if the actions that appear to be needed involve more than communication activities, require large expenditures of time and/or money, or if they will require any changes in established policies and procedures. Planning the communication aspects alone can be an enormous task requiring that media choices and formats be specified down to the level of identifying a spokesperson, selecting styles, tones, themes, and linked appeals, as well as message content. Each of these decisions needs to take into account all available information about the public's media preferences special interests, and issues or appeals that are of particular concern to them.

What resources will be needed for these tasks? This may take a lot of time and effort to fully answer. Honest and realistic estimates of the personnel, time, equipment, and money required to achieve each objective let planners compare the expected effort and expense of completing the project with the likely outcome — a rudimentary cost-benefit analysis. It also helps with scheduling and work assignments when/if the project is actually undertaken. For both reasons it is important to estimate the necessary resources as accurately as possible. Resource estimates need to include routine staff time and effort plus everyday office expenses such as postage and copying in addition to obvious and extraordinary expenses such as hiring freelancers, purchasing materials or outside services, or renting special equipment. When appropriate, estimates should be reported on both a per instance basis and as a total cost over the life of the plan.

When should it be done? In some instances, this answer is a specific day, date, or time or perhaps a recurring, periodic response, e.g. once a year, once a month, or each pay-day. In other cases, the answer may outline a contingency that may, or may not ever, occur.

How will success in achieving each objective be evaluated? In selecting or setting up evaluation mechanisms, public relations people need to keep a sharp eye on what it is they really need/want to measure so they don't inadvertently end up measuring something easy to measure but irrelevant. Not everything measurable is meaningful in all contexts. The number of people who attend an open house, for instance, is easy to count but, in and of itself, doesn't indicate how these people feel about the organization or if their tour of its facilities changed their opinions in any way. To find out the latter, you may have to ask them. That's much more difficult than doing a headcount, but it's also much more likely to provide meaningful information.

Similarly, some media relations people measure their success by the number or percentage of their news releases that are used by the media or by the number of inches or minutes of coverage their stories receive. Still others have a complex formula that assigns a monetary value to each story that is used based on audience size and amount of coverage. While these measures may gauge the amount of media coverage an organization receives, and perhaps its success in placing stories in the media, they do not necessarily measure the organization's success in building relationships with its key publics because they do not show how much or what kind of impact this media coverage has on the people who see it. They often do not even indicate whether the people who see the coverage are the people the organization really needs to reach. It should be kept in focus that the ultimate goal of public relations is helping an organization maximize the benefits of its relationships with all its various publics. Its goal is not necessarily getting news coverage or publishing employee publications or having a large turn out for an open house. Whatever evaluation methods are used must focus on how well the organization's relationships are being handled, not how quickly or how well the 'to do' list is completed.

Remember Women

Do women want to be considered in the context of minorities when they are actually the majority of the population? Of course, not. But are their needs — ranging from women as single parents to women working in sectors where they are clearly a small minority fully addressed? The issues are diverse and include some single parents having insufficient time or resources to access media and possible prejudice within male dominated sectors not being taken seriously enough by news and magazine media.

Women form an important part of the target audience both in their own right and also as a gateway to others. Campaigns have long since targeted women with messages about personal responsibility such as crime prevention and environmental protection, because it is clearly established that they are generally more sensible than men in taking advised actions. In other words, they are targeted both as members of the public in general and as drivers of action by others.

It is clear that for every campaign covering any subject, women should be considered as part of the audience. In each supplier brief specifically ask for needs of women to be addressed. This consideration should influence the creative design, content and medium (or media) used.

One aspect of planning in relation to targeting women is family decision-making. When the message has a particular relevance to the family as a group or the home environment women are often the key decision-maker and lead any discussion. Targeting the message and placing it in a media environment where the family are together as a unit can be effective in prompting a debate about the issue which the female Head of Household would lead or be particularly concerned about. However, we must be mindful that family behaviour is changing with more people living alone, one-parent families and fewer occasions when the family sit down together, etc.

Overtly targeting any sector of the population can be interpreted as demeaning and patronizing; at the very least heavy-handed. None of us like to be categorized. Clearly women are not a homogeneous group. Important differences exist, for example, between women of different ages and social class and between mothers and those without children. Because of the changing roles and attitudes in recent decades this is truer today than ever before. In some cases it may be useful to build a lifecycle framework into youı definition of the target audience.

Not only do we need to avoid patronizing our audience but we also have a wider responsibility to society to think carefully about how we represent women. The challenge for advertising and marketing materials is to embrace the diversity of possible roles rather than showing only limited stereotypical roles, even if the stereotype is now the working mother rather than the 50s stay at home housewife.

As for any audience, the best way to communicate with women is to create a marketing strategy that is built on understanding of the audience it is designed to reach. Many mistakes can be avoided by investing in qualitative research at an early stage in the planning process. This will help you to understand how the issue in question relates to women's lives and what their concerns are. Certainly any creative development research should explore the attitudes and views of women and explore any differences in reactions by gender.

Building the Right PR Team

PR as a management function has grown beyond day to day media relations, press releases, media alerts, and tradeshows. PR has assumed an overarching marketing role that often encompasses brand creation, channel marketing, marketing communications, direct marketing, and product marketing. Building the right PR team is crucial. The goal is to focus on capabilities and then hire to match a budget. In most cases the budget may need to be raised or lowered based on the ideal prospects. On the other hand, hiring primarily based on budget — in order to save money for example may dramatically prolong the delivery timeline for results or prevent them from being obtained altogether.

Internal versus Outsourcing

One of the clear advantages of building an internal PR group is the fact that the team (or person) is dedicated entirely to the company. Internal teams also have an opportunity to bond with other departments to extend internal PR. A potential disadvantage could be that internal communications persons may lose touch with industry perception because they are too close to the corporate story. As the company grows, the need for PR direction and management becomes pervasive, requiring the need for a virtual 'mini' agency inside the company which may be very costly and may be affordable to only big corporations or government departments.

Outsourcing PR carries its own set of pros and cons. PR agencies/consultants offer a tremendous potential for offloading the overwhelming task of building an internal PR department from all business administration angles including Information Technology and Human Resources. If the team is knowledgeable about the industry and they have maintained current relations with target reporters, influencers, and analysts, chances are an entire team could be commissioned for the price of one internal salary. A team can focus on an expanded set of opportunities which will increase the potential for enhanced brand equity. An external team may also provide a balance of internal visibility combined with an outsider's view to provide expert opinions and marketable vision.

Disadvantages surrounding the outsourcing of PR usually focus on the potential distraction from other clients. Depending on the budget size as well as other client events, the team may be pulled away or prevented from focusing on your account. Many times, the fact that most agencies are not 'next door' to their clients prevents strong relationship ties from forming. An external team can be perceived as expendable if it is not integrating itself within the dynamics of the internal team. Unless the outsourced team is incredibly communicative through an internal PR champion for the overall PR programme, executives and accounting departments have a hard time justifying the expense on a monthly basis.

The most common team structure these days usually combines a mixture of both internal and outsourced PR services. By hiring an internal PR manager to manage and direct an external team based on day to day company communications directives, the foundation for a scalable, cost-effective, results oriented team is set. It allows companies to enjoy the best of both worlds by maintaining someone on staff who is directly in touch with executive management, corporate culture and mission, and also in-step with the leaders of their outsourced team for real-time market feedback, strategy, and direction. PR in turn can work together to grow alongside the company to provide the day to day results necessary to increase sales and brand resonance as well as justifying its existence and expense.

There are an infinite series of combinations for internal and outsourced PR services and every executive and communications professional has their preferences based on past successes. What is common throughout every winning combination is that the right people were involved at the right level at the right price. Whether internal or outsourced, or a combination thereof, building a qualified, motivated, cost-effective, and scalable PR team is ultimately the key to success.

Hiring a PR Agency

Finding the right public relations firm will pay off in time, money and performance. The right firm is one that requires a minimum amount of education about your business. You need a firm that shares your financial prudence and will allow you to demonstrate a strong return on investment for your communications operations. You need an agency as a partner that will have good chemistry with your staff and is comfortable with your company's culture, while retaining a healthy independence of thought.

The process of PR agency selection should begin with selection of two or three members of your staff to assist you in the selection process. Assign them to handle administration, scheduling and communication with the candidate agencies. This review team should include those members of your staff who will be working most closely with the agency. It may also include one or two of your internal clients, such as a key brand manager, HR VP or finance officer.

Do determine the communications objectives the agency will be helping to achieve. The more actionable and measurable the objectives, the better they will be to guide and evaluate the agency. Having the objectives well articulated prior to beginning the search also allows you to determine how much you can accomplish with internal resources and to discuss those tasks with your own staff before beginning the agency search.

An objective should:

1. Specify a desired outcome (increase awareness, improve relationships, build preference, adopt an attitude, generate sales, etc.).
2. Directly specify one or several target audiences.
3. Be measurable, both conceptually and practically.
4. Refer to 'ends', not 'means'. If the statement outlines a means to do something, it is a strategy rather than an objective.
5. Indicate a time frame in which it is to be achieved.

In general, process goals, such as 'get publicity', 'launch a product' or 'create a brochure', make poor objectives. They do not relate to broader organizational goals and are not measurable in any specific, concrete or truly meaningful manner. A useful way to replace 'process' objectives is to ask yourself, 'What is the purpose of (insert objective)?' The answer to this question is likely to move you closer to a clear, actionable objective. Once you have your objectives defined and an understanding of where you need outside help in achieving those objectives, you can determine what you want the agency to do.

To communicate your needs, you will want to prepare a needs document that is clear and concise. Start by stating your 'actionable and measurable' objectives. Then identify the audiences and stakeholders that you want the agency to help you reach, and the local, national or international markets where you will be operating. Describe past and current efforts that might support or affect the proposed engagement. Estimate the anticipated duration of the assignment — whether a finite project or ongoing relationship — and the amount of funding you have budgeted for agency support during the first year of the assignment.

This description of the problem, the expected solution and the available funding should be thorough enough to permit candidate agencies to identify their capabilities for helping you. But it should not be so prescriptive that it dictates to the agencies which capabilities they must use. Avoid, for example, asking for a list of functional capabilities such as media relations, event management and crisis communications. You want to see which capabilities the agency thinks are necessary to solve your problem, and you don't want to miss out on innovative capabilities that you may not have asked to be listed.

While providing flexibility in how agencies may profile their capabilities (staff C.V.'s, functional listings, awards, etc.), you should specifically request examples where the agencies solved similar problems or addressed identical audiences for other clients. These case studies illustrate a lot about an agency — its strategic mindset, creativity, media relations and accountability for measurable results. They also are good sources of possible references by clients, partners and even journalists.

Since you will be the recipient of your agency's cumulative experience and acquired knowledge, the request for credentials should ask the agency to describe its experience and knowledge about your industry and its process for sharing knowledge with its clients. As public relations has become an increasingly strategic business tool, agencies have invested heavily in research, databases and measurement protocols. You want an agency with a solid knowledge base that it can draw on for your benefit. But you also should be budgeting for research by the agency that is tailored to guide your unique plans, to develop timely market intelligence and to measure the results of your programme. The letter should request an explanation of the firm's knowledge sharing process and a description of measurement protocols.

You want to know how easy an agency will be to work with administratively and how prudent they will be in managing your investment in their work. Ask them to describe their account management process and their procedures for ensuring quality and performance among the different individuals and offices that may work on your account. You'll also want to understand how they bill for their staff time and for other costs. Finally, you should provide the agencies a chance to demonstrate whether they will be a good cultural fit. To identify your priorities and success factors associated with the upcoming engagement, you might consider, for example, using the industry's annual client survey that rates the importance of various attributes.

This completes the development of a request for credentials

that gives prospective agencies enough insight to demonstrate their credentials for helping you achieve your objectives. You'll note that it does not ask the agencies to propose strategies and creative solutions addressing your objectives. While it may be tempting to ask for that information, it is counterproductive. It's presumptuous to think that an agency can provide strategic solutions and creative ideas based on the superficial background that can reasonably be provided to a group of bidding firms. You'll find out how good the agency is in pitching for new business, not necessarily how well it will serve your unique needs.

Those who want substantive strategic plans and full creative solutions from all candidates should be prepared to pay the agencies for their time in creating the plans and solutions. They also must be willing to spend considerably more time in developing a formal request for proposal (RFP), providing research and access to others in the company, sharing confidential information and offering to respond to questions from the agencies. Lacking that thoroughness, it's understandable that an agency may produce a proposal that appears attractive, but that is unlikely to offer innovative solutions tailored for your company.

An efficient agency search usually considers three to five firms. Any more will tax your staff resources and prolong the search. In identifying those candidates, clients can use a variety of directories published by the various newsletters serving the public relations industry. They should also investigate each firm's record in retaining long-term clients. One of the most efficient resources for creating a short list is an Internet-based interactive screening process that searches our firms based on size, location, industry experience and professional specialties.

In creating a short list, try to allow for some variety in sizes and types of firms. For example, a healthcare company may want to consider a mix of healthcare specialty firms and full-service agencies with healthcare divisions. For clients outside the cities where major national firms are based, it's also useful to consider a mix of local firms and regional offices of the national firms.

Send a letter to the CEO of each of your selected candidates with the request for credentials that you prepared. The letter should describe how you will conduct the search, provide a timetable for the pitches and identify any potential issues, such as specific client conflicts, that would make the firm ineligible to compete for your company's business. Provide the name and phone number of your staff member with responsibility for managing the search. Ask the agency to call to confirm its intention or inability to compete within 72 hours of receipt of the letter. If any agency drops out, you should have a list of alternates ready to invite.

You should request that the agencies provide a written credentials summary within three to four weeks and be prepared to make a presentation about two to three weeks later. The written response permits your staff to consider and discuss the candidates' credentials ahead of time, to prepare questions for the presentation and to see how well the agency organizes and presents written material — a good indicator of the quality of their work for clients.

As the agencies prepare their submissions, they will naturally want to know the competition. To avoid unnecessary, and sometimes disruptive, speculation, it's wise to let them know the names of all competitors. You should also require that they sign an agreement to keep confidential all information you provide them, and agree to similarly protect the information they give to you.

By the time that the written responses are received, the presentations should already have been scheduled. Assuming that all the written submissions are of high quality, all firms should make presentations. While some clients solicit a large number of bids and shorten the list based on the written submission, they overburden staff who must review the written proposals, unfairly impose work on multiple agencies and miss out on an important element of their decision making. Personal interaction is the key to learning whether a firm will fit in with your company.

With the recommended three to five candidates, the presentations can be accomplished in two days. Allow at least two hours for each, emphasizing to the firms that at least half of that time must be reserved for questions and discussion. It should be your choice whether to host the presentations or to visit the agencies, recognizing that agency visits offer an opportunity to add to your overall impressions of the firms. You should ask for a tour of the agency.

Although you would like to meet the people who will be working on your account, it is unrealistic to demand that an agency introduce its entire proposed account team. Such demands encourage 'bait and switch' tactics by agencies that are put in an impossible position. On the other hand, you do not want just to meet a new business team that will be unavailable to service your business. The ideal 'presentations' are informal discussions that illustrate the thinking and capabilities of an agency to meet your needs. The agency leaders who will be responsible for setting up and supervising your account team should be prepared to tell you what they would do to staff the account if it is awarded to their agency and how they will ensure that you get the best service from the different specialists within the agency. They will introduce individuals who will play a role on your account and some of the specialists who will be assisting your account team. Most important, you want to have a discussion with the group that illustrates their innate intelligence and personality, their knowledge of your industry and their experience and success in dealing with similar challenges that you face.

You will be looking for how well the agency group interacts, particularly in describing similar projects they have worked on together. You'll also be looking for how the proposed account manager proposes to take responsibility for every aspect of your service, from assembling your account team to delivering tangible, bottom line results. Finally, you and your team will be trying to get a feel for the more subjective elements of the agency — creativity and chemistry — which are best conveyed in person.

During the entire process, from the review of written submissions to the agency meeting, the members of the review team should complete evaluation forms that address their impression of the skills, capability and character of the agency. With those checklists in hand, the review team should meet within two days of the completion of the final presentation. Each member should state his or her first choice. If the decision is not unanimous, then the members should discuss their numerical scores as well as their qualitative impressions of the different teams.

As soon as a decision is made, the corporate public relations officer should call the senior executives at the competing firms to tell them of the decision and to provide a general critique of their proposals. Since the losing firms will want to learn from their investment of time and effort, a frank and specific critique is important. Highlighting for the winner the strengths and weaknesses of his or her firm will be invaluable guidance in assembling your account team.

The assigned administrative person on the selection team should immediately work with a designated person at the agency to prepare a contract, establish confidentiality procedures, arrange for the transfer of background documents and company data, and create smooth online communications. While those administrative responsibilities are being accomplished, the senior agency executive is beginning to set up the account team through transfer of agency employees or recruitment of talent from outside the firm. If activities are to start immediately, an interim team will usually be assembled. Within a month, the permanent agency team should be established, up-to-speed about the company's knowledge base and building relationships with the media and other opinion-influencers following the company. Once that is completed, it's wise to schedule a meeting with the new account team and the company's communications staff to collaborate in developing a plan for working together to accomplish the communications programme. This kick-off meeting should become the first of many successful team efforts on behalf of your company.

Briefing Contractors

Whatever work you may be contracting out, there are key elements you should always cover in your brief:

- background issues (e.g. if you're briefing on a newsletter which is to be part of a broader awareness raising initiative, make clear the role of the newsletter);
- your audience and its needs;
- communication objectives;
- exact details of what is expected (e.g. for a newsletter how much of the text and photography you expect your suppliers to create, and how much you will provide);

- timing — include delivery date and other key stages;
- budget; any mandatory constraints; and
- how the activity will be assessed. Any additional information, background research, documents, statistics, etc., should be included as attachments.

Part of Policy

Communication is integral to policy development. When a final policy plan is put forward, a presentational strategy and handling plan should be included. A typical media-handling plan should have the agreement of top management on at least the following points:

1. The strategy and objectives, including core message, core information, core audiences, targeted routes, budgets and evaluation proposals.
2. Preparatory briefing — using briefings and other opportunities to alert the media to the context of forthcoming announcements and its context.
3. Launch — detailed timings and proposed allocation of spokespersons to: main and localized press briefings, national broadcast interview arrangements, regional broadcast interviews and signed articles; embargo or lock-in arrangements, third-party endorsement, press pack content and distribution, regionalized material.
4. Follow-through monitoring arrangements, contingency plans for follow-up briefings, interviews, and articles; regional visits; opportunities to restate and reinforce the message and information. There is need to discuss how to handle the uncertainties and the effect on the plan.

PR people must think strategically and deliver tactically. A well-written annual report or brochure is of no strategic value if it does not contribute to meeting corporate goals and objectives. The development of communication strategies must take place alongside the development of policy. It is one of the dynamic roles of PR staff to work alongside policy colleagues and relevant outside bodies from the earliest stages of setting overall policy strategies. A core communication strategy, setting out desired outcomes, should be developed at an early stage. Now more than ever the key to the success of the PR is through integrated campaigns and teamwork. The only means through which a company / government department can convey precisely what they wish, to whom and how often is paid publicity. Much that government / corporate needs to convey in support of securing policy objectives involves persuasion, fostering of behavioural change, targeting hard to reach audiences. Publicity and campaigns work is sometimes the only way to meet all these needs. PR will work alongside this on presentational and media handling strategies to enable the government / company to speak with one voice, and take a strategic approach to communication and cross-departmental policy and messages to allow all concerned to share relevant information; to time announcements to the best advantage of the government / company as a whole.

Press Releases

A press release, now also called news release, is simply a statement prepared for distribution to news media. The purpose of a press release is to give journalists information that is useful, accurate and interesting, and therefore newsworthy.

Initially a press release was considered a form of advertising because of the self-serving content and charged for accordingly by some media during the early years of use. Soon it became accepted as a free source of news and information that can be used by newspapers and other media in their coverage as they see fit. This workhorse of public relations was perhaps invented in the late 1800s, but Ivy Lee got credit for inventing the press release for its successful use in 1906.

Written in the form of a conventional news story, a press release presents the point of view of the organization that disseminates it. Newspaper editors and reporters often use facts, quotes and other information from these releases. If a press release is printed 'as is', without changing even one word, then it has conformed to the journalistic standards of that particular medium. It is the ultimate success of a PR effort.

In fact, the UK Government Information and Communication Service (GICS) clearly mentioned this objective of a news release: *To produce written work of such a high standard that it is difficult for the media to improve on it.*

Press releases were first used in the US by big railroads, although they rapidly became the norm in all corporations and large organizations, both for-profit and non-profit. In the early years of the twentieth century, Ohio Bell Telephone discovered that if it handed out 'canned' news in this form, newspaper reporters would stop going to telephone rate hearings to get the information in person, thereby minimizing uncomfortable inquiries about the rates and related matters.

Basics

Depending upon the outfit and the purpose, press releases present a great variety of format and content. However, good press releases are normally printed on a letterhead or stationery with logo, clearly identifying on whose behalf the press release has been issued. Normally the issuing company, government agency or department or organization has its name, address and phone number as part of the letterhead, some also carry the web address. Press releases distributed by e-mail normally carry these details with the name of the contact person.

PRESS RELEASE is usually spelled out in all CAPS and centred in bold. It is also clearly mentioned if the press release is for IMMEDIATE RELEASE or is Embargoed. If a press release does not mention an embargo, that is, to be used on and after a specified date and time, then it means that it can be used immediately. Embargoed press release is issued for the convenience of journalists for a planned forthcoming event or speech or address to be delivered and scheduled date and time is mentioned as embargo. Where there is chance of change an embargoed speech circulated as a press release carries, 'Check against delivery'.

Another essential component of the press release is the *Headline* or *Title*. It is usually centred, and is in bold. The title of the press release or headline is usually short and snappy, indicating the content and hopefully grabbing the attention of the journalist. These days many important press releases have more than one headline or a multi-deck headline, highlighting several points in the press release. Such headlines are to help journalists know about the content and help decide a headline for the story written on the basis of the release.

After the headline the press release should clearly put the city and date of origin of the press release. This is called the *dateline*, normally carried or referred to by news media using the press release and answers two important elements of news — where and when. The rest of the body may differ according to the content of the release but should be as close to newspaper writing style as possible. It is then that the press release has more possibility of being used and the journalist may also use the same language as used in the press release. It should give the most important information in the first paragraph also called the *lead paragraph* or *intro* and then should give details. The decision of what is important is crucial and it should keep in mind the news values. The release should try to answer all the five Ws (who, what, when, where, why) and one H (how). Page numbers should be clearly marked if the press release exceeds one page and a clear indication of the end of the press release should also be indicated — ### or Ends etc.

The traditional format (one or two pages of double-spaced text with standardized spelling and punctuation) was developed to help journalists edit the text with editorial markings to help proper typesetting of the text. As more and more press releases are distributed via e-mail and with print media increasingly moving to digital printing, the format of a press release has become less important. Many public relations practitioners now also disseminate their press releases to many key publics such as employees and investors as well besides media. So now there is an immense variety of writing styles.

Here is a press release received by e-mail from International Press Institute, Vienna:

Press Release
Vienna, 9 November 2005

IPI Alarmed by Defamation Charges Against Zambian Editor

According to information provided to the International Press Institute (IPI), on 9 November, Fred M'membe, the editor and chief executive officer (CEO) of the privately owned daily newspaper, the Post, was arrested and detained in a police station in Zambia's capital Lusaka.

The arrest came after the editor voluntarily surrendered to the authorities at the Kabwata police station. Accompanying M'membe were his lawyer Sam Mujuda, and Post managing editor Amos Malupenga.

The editor was then warned and cautioned under the laws of Zambia, questioned for over an hour, charged with the defamation of President Levy Mwanawasa, and then detained in a police cell. M'membe's decision to attend the police station ended a 48 hour siege at the Post by the country's security forces. The editor was later released from detention and told to appear before a magistrate's court on 10 November.

According to the information contained in the statement warning and cautioning M'membe, "It was alleged that between November 6 and 7, 2005 in Lusaka, with intent to bring the President into hatred, ridicule and contempt, [you] did publish defamatory matter against President Mwanawasa."

The charge apparently relates to an editorial in the Post during that period criticising President Mwanawasa for his "foolishness, stupidity and lack of humility." The editorial was written in response to a speech given by the president attacking former President Kaunda for implying that the new constitution would have a smoother passage if members of civil society were consulted.

An award winning journalist, M'membe has had ongoing problems with the Zambian authorities. On 29 June, the editor was told to report to police headquarters for calling on President Mwanawasa to resign, and, on 12 July 2002, he was acquitted, along with three other defendants, of criminal defamation when he alleged that former President Chiluba was a thief.

Commenting on the decision to arrest and detain M'membe, IPI Director Johann P. Fritz said, "This is the second time in six months that M'membe has been forced to attend a police station and face charges of defaming the president."

"The use of criminal defamation to silence the work of journalists and to foster self-censorship is little more than a tool of repression in the hands of government.

"If an open society is to be encouraged in the country, the Zambian government must accept the principle that politicians can expect greater criticism than the average person and they should not be tempted to the use the criminal law as protection," said Fritz.

"I would urge the Zambian President to do everything possible to drop the charges against M'membe and to instigate a review of all the country's laws that infringe press freedom and remove them from the statute books. Journalists must be free to practice their profession without fear of harassment and intimidation."

International Press Institute (IPI)
Spiegelgasse 2/29
A-1010 Vienna
Austria
Tel: + 431-512 90 11
Fax: + 431-512 90 14
E-mail: ipi@freemedia.at
http://www.freemedia.at

IPI, the global network of editors, media executives and leading journalists, is dedicated to the furtherance and safeguarding of press freedom, the protection of freedom of opinion and expression, the promotion of the free flow of news and information, and the improvement of the practices of journalism.

In the above press release sent by e-mail one can mark the writing style is very close to news writing. The headline is not bold but can be understood. The dateline is just after 'Press Release'. At the end of the press release there is a complete address with phone, fax and website link. A click on that leads you to the IPI website. This is a new PR tool, which is now being used by good PR professionals who are up-to-date with new technology. It also gives a paragraph of information on IPI at the end of the press release. Good PR.

The UN Information Centre (UNIC), New Delhi, sends press releases issued from New York or other places to Indian journalists by e-mail. Here is an example:

9 October 2005

UNIC/PRESS RELEASE/155-2005

FROM THE UN SECRETARY-GENERAL

Statement Attributable to the Spokesman of the UN Secretary-General about the Earthquake in South Asia

8 October 2005

The Secretary-General is deeply saddened by the loss of life and destruction caused by the earthquake that hit Pakistan, with impact extending into India and Afghanistan on the morning of 8 October 2005, and extends his sincere condolences to all the victims and their families.

The UN Office for the Coordination of Humanitarian Affairs is in contact with the governments of Afghanistan, India and Pakistan to explore ways in which the United Nations can assist in all efforts required to support relief and rescue operations and in subsequent recovery and reconstruction. END

This press release was used by large number of media organizations being timely, brief and to-the-point. "Statement Attributable to the Spokesman of the UN Secretary-General" is basically unnecessary and smacks of officialese. The place of issue of this release is not specified so the journalists would presume that it should be New York, but the UN Secretary-General may be travelling.

At least one recent example of contemporary corporate press release is essential here to give an idea how top technology companies are using this important PR tool:

FOR IMMEDIATE RELEASE

MICROSOFT AND YAHOO! ANNOUNCE LANDMARK INTEROPERABILITY AGREEMENT TO CONNECT CONSUMER INSTANT MESSAGING COMMUNITIES GLOBALLY

Consumers will be able to exchange instant messages, see presence, share emoticons and add friends from Yahoo! Messenger or MSN Messenger

Sunnyvale, CA, and Redmond, WA — October 12, 2005 — Yahoo! Inc. (NASDAQ:YHOO – News) and Microsoft Corp. (NASDAQ: MSFT – News) today announced a landmark agreement to connect users of their consumer instant messaging (IM) services on a global basis. The industry's first interoperability agreement between two distinct leading global consumer IM providers will give MSN(r) Messenger and Yahoo!(r) Messenger users the ability to interact with each other, forming what is expected to be the largest consumer IM community in the world, estimated to be more than 275 million strong.

Being able to instant message between IM communities is one of the features most requested by MSN Messenger and Yahoo! Messenger users, and Microsoft and Yahoo! share a commitment to provide IM interoperability while keeping consumer security and privacy first and foremost. In addition to exchanging instant messages, consumers from both communities will be able to see their friends' online presence, share select emoticons, and easily add new contacts from either service to their friends' list, all as part of their free IM service. Yahoo! and Microsoft plan to introduce these interconnectivity capabilities between MSN Messenger and

Yahoo! Messenger to customers around the world in the second quarter of 2006, and in doing so expect to help make IM an even more useful part of consumers' online communications and communities.

"Yahoo! and Microsoft share a commitment to providing the highest-quality experience possible for consumers, and today's groundbreaking announcement underscores our desire to provide consumer interoperability between our thriving IM communities," said Terry Semel, chief executive officer, Yahoo! Inc. "This is truly a turning point for the IM industry, and we believe our agreement with Microsoft will help usher in a new era of IP communications." "Microsoft and Yahoo! look forward to bridging the divide between our global communities, creating richer and easier ways for our customers to connect," said Steve Ballmer, chief executive officer of Microsoft. "IM interoperability is the right thing for our customers, our businesses and the industry as a whole, and Microsoft is delighted to help lead these efforts with Yahoo!"

About Yahoo! Messenger

As one of the most popular instant messaging services on the Internet, Yahoo! Messenger with Voice (http://messenger.yahoo.com) makes it easier than ever for people to express themselves, interact and manage relationships with friends and family. Yahoo! Messenger with Voice has a unique and proven history of innovation in instant messaging as the first to offer Webcam functionality, the first to introduce an interactive and shared experience with IMVironments(r), and the first to introduce animated emoticons. Yahoo! Messenger with Voice continues to the lead the marketplace by integrating with leading Yahoo! services including games, music, photos and search, and providing the greatest choice for consumers to stay connected to one another through text IM, voice calling, e-mail, video or mobile messaging.

About MSN Messenger

MSN Messenger (http://messenger.msn.com) is a world-leading free instant messaging service that allows people to connect with others in real time, expressing themselves in a rich, convenient and fun way. MSN Messenger is available in 26 languages and is used in nearly every country in the world by more than 180 million active accounts each month. MSN Messenger provides customers with a window into their contacts – enabling them to chat with friends, family and colleagues online via text, voice, mobile phone or video conversation; express themselves with winks and dynamic display pictures; and share photos, files, searches and more instantly. MSN Messenger works well with other MSN services including MSN Hotmail(r), MSN Spaces, MSN Search and MSN Music to give customers a more flexible way to connect to the people and information that matter most to them.

About MSN

MSN attracts more than 420 million unique users worldwide per month. With localized versions available globally in 41 markets and 21 languages, MSN is a world leader in delivering Web services to consumers and online advertising opportunities to businesses worldwide. The most useful and innovative online service today, MSN brings consumers everything they need from the Web to make the most of their time online. MSN is located on the Web at http://www.msn.com. MSN worldwide sites are located at http://www.msn.com/worldwide.ashx.

About Microsoft

Founded in 1975, Microsoft (Nasdaq "MSFT") is the worldwide leader in software, services and solutions that help people and businesses realize their full potential.

About Yahoo!

Yahoo! Inc. is a leading provider of comprehensive online products and services to consumers and businesses worldwide. Yahoo! is the No. 1 Internet brand globally and the most trafficked Internet destination worldwide. Headquartered in Sunnyvale, Calif., Yahoo!'s global network includes 25 world properties and is available in 13 languages.

Press Contact:

Jessie Anderson,
Hill & Knowlton for Yahoo!,
(212) 885-0662, Jessie.anderson@hillandknowlton.com

Rhian Rotz,
Waggener Edstrom for Microsoft,
(503) 443-7000, rhianr@wagged.com

Rapid Response Team,
Waggener Edstrom for Microsoft,
(503) 443-7070, rrt@wagged.com

###

Take note of the double deck headline briefly stating the most important points to attract the attention of journalists. Also take note of dateline where two cities are mentioned with one date. This means that this press release has been issued simultaneously from two different cities where the headquarters of the two companies are located. There are quotes in the text. These serve two purposes. It enhances credibility and quotes are also a journalistic requirement. A press release in itself is a complete news story, just three paragraphs, and 344 words, which can be used as is by a news organization with minor changes of style.

Then there is one paragraph each about Yahoo! Messenger, MSN Messenger, MSN, Microsoft and Yahoo! This is a great way of communicating about each brand. Note the links to websites in the 'about' paragraphs and NASDAQ symbols of the two companies along with links to news about the companies. The click of a mouse on these can lead to more information if the journalist gets interested.

Also take note of press contacts 'Jessie Anderson, Hill & Knowlton for Yahoo' and 'Rhian Rotz, Waggener Edstrom for Microsoft.' The press contacts are from PR agencies hired by the companies.

Writing Tips

When an organization issues a news release it is putting its own story in words and delivering it to the media in a format the media can make use of. The most common form of release remains words on a page, although many of these pages are now electronically transmitted rather than being delivered as hard copy.

A news release which is perceived as newsworthy by the media is edited and/or rewritten in ways that turn it into the media's version of the story rather than the public relations person's view of the story. What happens to releases once they're issued is beyond the control of the public relations person who releases them. These decisions are strictly the prerogative of the gatekeepers of the media. Large or small, local or national, the media control their own content, and public relations practitioners cannot demand anything be included or excluded as editorial content. Usually the journalist will cut out self-serving, old news, or unsupported commentary. Sometimes, releases are simply trimmed to fit the space available or to make them more consistent in terms of style. The media may add additional information to make the story more complete or more relevant to their perceived audiences.

From a public relations point of view the best is if the media use a release exactly as issued without changing anything. In that case, the organization is telling its own story in its own words instead of having a third party tell it from his or her perspective. But, that won't happen unless the public relations person who writes the release is thoroughly knowledgeable about media style and values and reflects that in what and how they write. This has to be understood by the highest in management, to make it easy for PR professionals to do their job professionally.

Styled and structured as a news story, the news release is meant for the most cynical, influential and impatient clients. The writing objective is to creatively produce copy that is so clear, accurate and reader-friendly that the editorial process finds it impossible to improve. It is essential that the first few lines stand alone — informing, intriguing and selling the story. News releases are queued in newsroom computers with large number of other stories. Copy-tasters make their initial, critical selection only on the basis of those vital, few lines. A news story is usually written in inverted pyramid order. The most important point is at the top, and details follow in descending order of importance. Good news copy can be pruned from the bottom up without any problem of comprehension. If the top of a news release is boring, any journalist will reasonably assume the rest is worthless. Journalists expect copy to be written as a news story, not an essay.

Here is a good British example from an internal official guide for writing a news release: **Do not start** by saying:

> 'The Rt. Hon. Freda Smythe, Secretary of State for Administrative Affairs, today announced that from 31 July 2001 the preferred fuel for official vehicles will be liquefied petroleum gas owing to its environmentally preferable exhaust characteristics.'

Do start by saying:

> 'A cleaner, greener government car fleet will be in use by the summer of 2001.Today's announcement by Administrative Affairs Secretary Freda Smythe means Ministers' cars will be powered by liquefied petroleum gas (LPG) from August 2001.'

Some US practitioners advise: NEVER WRITE A PRESS RELEASE OVER ONE PAGE. If an editor wants more information, they will contact you. Say it economically, the shorter the better. Never waste a word. The point is to get the editor's attention. If they need more information, they WILL call. However, in modern PR practice one cannot limit or prescribe the length of a press release. It should depend on the content or the story, which the press release tells. You may just miss the mark because the journalist handling the story may not have enough time to call and fill in the details that were left in the hope of that call. In many cases the press release is all what may be seen and therefore it should give as complete a story as possible. There is no problem about economy of words, but it should not be at the cost of the story. Paragraphs should be kept as short as practicable — two or three sentences.

Do not issue a news release without a headline. The headline is simply a label to attract the reader. It should be as short as practicable, contain an active verb and be no longer than a line. Good punning headlines attract the reader, but they must be appropriate and not misleading. Multi-deck or multiple headlines are preferred when the purpose is to give options to journalists or to highlight different points.

This advice from a US practitioner is worth noting if you want to say how great you are, quote someone who thinks so. (And hopefully, not your mom). Quotations should be interesting and punchy — the written equivalent of a 'sound bite'. Use them to increase the credibility of the story. Remember that most newspapers will only use one or two sentences of the quotes so make sure the first two are the best.

A news release must tackle a negative point head on and in plain language. However, it is often impractical or impolitic to lead with bad news. The best course may be to find a credible, positive point to lead on, but to tackle the awkward news quickly and clearly. Tackling bad news always tests the author of a news release. Do not bury the negative in the body of the release. It *will* be spotted and some one may take it as the headline.

A good news release should have a clear purpose, message, and target audience, and overwhelming relevance to the reader, in content and form. It must command credibility by being

- timely,
- properly structured,
- clear,
- succinct,
- unambiguous, and
- complete.

Some organizations also produce news releases on audiotape for radio stations — audio news releases (ANRs), or on videotape — video news releases (VNRs), for use by television. ANRs and VNRs can be shipped to the media on a tape, or they can be transmitted electronically via telephone line, 'wire service', or satellite transmission. Like the press release ANRs and VNRs should follow the news media style and format of radio and television news respectively with the aim of being used 'as is'.

Distribution

Governments have their own specialized news release networks but commercial and non-commercial organizations also can resort to distribution systems that are on hire. Many also maintain their own distribution networks. The tricks of the trade used in distribution and placement include:

- telephone tip-offs for specialists and news-desks;
- Electronic News Distribution Service (ENDS) to equipped newsrooms;
- multi-fax systems for other media;
- e-mail;
- Web publication of news release and documents;
- hard copy for the paper-dependent people.

Delivery systems such as ENDS and publication on the Web can make information available very quickly. However, it is not enough to simply press the button. There is no substitute for a timely phone call, tipping off journalists to news breaking on a screen near them.

Some public relations practitioners operate like news release factories, churning out as many releases as possible and distributing all of them to all possible media, even to the extent of sending copies to several reporters who worked for the same organization. For many it is just a matter of playing the percentages and thinking that the more they send out, the more likely they were to have at least some of them used. Others justified blanket distribution as a matter of fairness, saying they do not want to appear to be playing favourites by sending releases to some media but not to others.

Many practitioners think in terms of tailoring their releases to fit specific media. For some, this meant cutting down their distribution lists to selectively targeted media and distributing fewer copies of each release. For others it meant preparing and distributing multiple, slightly different copies of each release that could be selectively sent to different media without reducing the total number of media to whom they sent releases.

Some US practitioners using the latter approach simply prepared a print media version of the release using AP style guidelines and a separate broadcast version using RTNDA (Radio and Television News Directors Association) style guidelines that might include sound bites and/or B-roll video. It also meant preparing several localized versions of a release instead of a single version meant for general distribution.

Practitioners who applied targeted approaches found that they really worked. They experienced a marked increase in the percentage of releases they issued that were actually used by the media, and they often found that the media's stories were longer and more favourable. For some, personal relationships with reporters and editors were also enhanced with targetting. This is sometimes called a surgical media strategy.

Audio News Release (ANR) or Radio News Release

A Radio News Release, also called an audio news release (ANR) is a radio news story that communicates a public relations message to radio news outlets. It is a ready to use radio news item supplied to radio news outlets as a press release should be for print press. The story is marketed and distributed to target radio news media via the telephone for their free and unrestricted use.

When properly produced and distributed, the radio news media may include the story in the bulletin. The main advantage of a radio news release is the ability to target audiences by specific cultural and economic demographics, as well as geographic location. Like the press releases, the more the story meets the criteria of a good radio news story, the more likely it will be used in news programming. A good Radio News Release is usually made of a one-minute feed including an anchor lead-in, a sound bite and an anchor tag-out. In most cases, the radio media will re-voice the anchor lead-in and anchor tag-out and utilize the sound bite as if they had conducted the interview themselves. Radio News Releases are sometimes marketed and distributed by one-on-one media marketing calls to designated radio news contacts. If the story is found newsworthy, it is immediately fed over the telephone.

Looking at the need of radio another format has evolved which is known as a Radio Media Tour. It connects a spokesperson directly to radio newsrooms via a telephone conference call. One-on-one consecutive interviews are conducted allowing the spokesperson to communicate the public relations message. Radio news producers and reporters may broadcast spokesperson's interview, whole or in part, live or on tape. Radio Media Tours allow the spokesperson the additional flexibility of participating from any location with telephone access. For a successful Radio Media Tour, the message must be highly newsworthy and timely. The spokesperson should be articulate enough to transmit the message while maintaining news value. The audio from the spokesperson's interviews can be edited and distributed as a Radio News Release to interested media contacts who were not able to participate.

Video News Releases (VNR)

A Video News Release is a television news story produced and then distributed via videotape or satellite or digitally to the news media for their broadcast use. A VNR is the TV version of a press release. It is a ready-made television news story that communicates a public relations message. It is marketed and distributed to the television news media via satellite or videocassette for their free and unrestricted use. When properly and professionally produced and distributed, television producers may include it in news programming.

The production process for VNR begins with a consultation in which the client agrees on a concept, a timeline and a production budget. The producer prepares a script, schedules a camera crew, edits the videotape and submits it for client approval prior to distribution. VNR distribution involves notification — the process of informing newsrooms how and when the story will be available, the reporters and producers covering a specific beat or topic. Distribution of VNR involves delivering it by satellite or videotape. While satellite feeds are the most cost-effective way to reach all broadcast television newsrooms, videotape distribution is the most effective way to obtain broadcast placement. The best distribution plans should include a combination of both methods depending on target media outfits and broadcast journalists.

News Release Businesses

Many businesses have come up just to harness the news release market, linking various stakeholders.

News release distribution and placement was seen as a service industry and companies like PR Wire came into being. Later news agencies (also called wire agencies) that have been bulk suppliers of news to media have diversified into this business as well. Here are a few examples of such varied services available to PR professionals:

PA Mediapoint

In the UK the domestic wire agency the Press Association distributes press releases directly into editorial newsrooms through the same lines and satellite links as its editorial. This means that PA Mediapoint, the press release distribution service, is unique. Like PA news and sport, PA customers' press releases can be seen on thousands of editorial screens across the UK.

This service has been selected by the Government News Network, and serves all the English Regions, Scotland and Wales, to deliver more than 6,000 releases every year from government departments, official agencies and the Royal Family.

One can buy this service direct from PA and it is also sold by press release distribution companies. These companies are: PR Newswire, Business Wire and na europe.

PR Newswire

PR Newswire Association LLC provides electronic distribution, targeting, measurement, translation and broadcast services on behalf of some 40,000 corporate, government, association, labour, non-profit, and other customers world-wide who seek to reach a variety of critical audience including the news media, the investment community, government decision-makers, and the general public with their up-to-the-minute, full-text news developments. Established in 1954, PR Newswire has offices in 14 countries and routinely sends its customers' news to outlets in 135 countries and in 30 languages. Utilizing the latest in communications technology, PR Newswire content is considered a mainstay among news reporters, investors and individuals who seek breaking news from the source. PR Newswire is a subsidiary of United Business Media plc of London.

Business Wire

Business Wire disseminates full-text news announcements from thousands of companies and organizations worldwide (their members) to news media, financial markets, disclosure systems, investors, information websites, databases and other audiences. It claims more than four decades of experience and the most comprehensive news network ever assembled. With access to more than 60 leading news agencies throughout the world, Business Wire ensures that news is delivered to audiences in each market via their preferred mode of delivery and in their preferred language. 'Our members direct where they want their news disseminated, specifying the geographic markets, industry audiences and editorial desks most appropriate for the announcements. Our network delivers news simultaneously and in real-time directly into the news-room editorial systems at newspapers, wire services, television and radio programs, magazines and online news services.' Business Wire is used by public relations and investor relations professionals to disseminate news releases, photos, multimedia, regulatory filings and other information. News release subjects include breaking news, earnings results, product announcements, mergers and acquisitions, public policy, legal issues, webcasts, press conference advisories and more.

na europe

na europe is the largest and first truly dedicated European newswire service for corporate and marketing communications professionals.

A division of news aktuell, the distribution arm of dpa, the national news agency in Germany, na europe harnesses the power and reach of major national news agencies in the UK, Germany, Switzerland, Austria, Belgium, France, Italy and Spain among others.

na europe, with its own offices in London, Hamburg, Frankfurt, Berlin and Zurich, uses digital, satellite, e-mail and fax to deliver text, audio and video releases, photographs and graphics straight to the point of use in newspapers, magazines, radio and television stations and internet data bases.

The full na europe network, reaching more than 150,000 newspapers, radio and TV stations, online publications and individual journalists comprises:

- UK — Press Association, Britain's national news agency
- Germany — dpa (Deutsche Presse-Agentur GmbH), German Press Agency
- France — CompanynewsGroup, a subsidiary of Agence France Presse
- Belgium — Belga Press Agency
- Switzerland — na Schweiz, a joint venture with SDA (schweizerische depeschenagentur), the Swiss News Agency
- Austria — APA (Austria Presse Agentur), Austrian Press Agency
- Italy — ANSA, Italian News Agency
- The Netherlands – ANP (Algemeen Nederlands Persbureau), national news agency

- Spain – Europa Press Communications

In addition, the network reaches all the main Central European media outlets in Poland, Hungary, Bulgaria, Czech Republic, Slovenia, Estonia, Latvia, Lithuania and Russia. na europe's staff, experienced in European media and public relations, advise clients on country translations and help them devise media distribution plans. The service is so flexible and client friendly that each story can be targeted at individual media in any one country or to any region around the world.

Clients can also go global with na europe. With more than 25 partner news agencies worldwide the service can reach the widest possible spectrum of media across the United States, Latin America, Asia, Africa and the Middle East.

AsiaNet

AsiaNet's news distribution network via 14 Asia-Pacific news agencies and five worldwide affiliates connects communications professionals managing a multinational audience with delivery channels to international media for their media releases and images.

Formed in 1995, the consortium taps into the established infrastructure of its news agency and affiliate backbone to reach over 5000 media outlets across 34 countries and regions. Mainstream, specialist trade press, broadcast and online media are targeted, while versatile delivery via newswire, fax, e-mail and the Internet ensures that media releases and images are planted in the immediate passage of journalists, editors, corporates, the investment and financial community. The vast online exposure gained on scores of websites and databases also earns clients an additional opportunity to have their material cited for story backgrounding, industry contacts and educative purposes.

Clients choose a circulation-package, circuit or single-country destination, and the time they wish to distribute thei news. Narrow industry-targeted options or broad general news selections are available, with precision delivery guaranteed.

Translation services — often handled by the agencies' in-house journalists — are provided inclusive, optimizing access for companies whose media relations could otherwise be handicapped by language and cultural barriers. Instantaneous electronic delivery likewise supersedes any geographical and temporal barriers to communication.

Television News Release

Television New Release (TNR) is the UK's most highly regarded supplier of broadcast services for corporate communications. Owned partly by The Press Association, TNR perfectly straddles the worlds of business and the media. Since its establishment in 1999, TNR has provided award-winning commissioned TV news releases for companies, charities and other organizations. TNR are experienced in the whole process including proposing TV communication strategy, pre-production filming, editing, and distributing footage to all relevant broadcasters in the UK or internationally.

By using a Radio News Release, it is also possible to conduct a series of radio interviews for a company's spokesperson with any number of stations in the UK from the PA's London studios.

TNR can also produce video material for all types of promotional and presentational needs, for example for conferences, training or many different types of sales or marketing activities.

Medialink

The company was founded in 1986 as Video Broadcasting

Corporation, now provides production and satellite distribution of video and audio news, multimedia webcasting services, press release newswire distribution, photography production and digital distribution, and strategic corporate communications consulting. Medialink also provides media monitoring and analysis and public relations research to help clients determine return on investment from their communications efforts. Based in New York, Medialink has offices throughout the United States and an international hub in London.

Press Release Network

Press Release Network has been in the news distribution business since 1996. It has strategic partnerships with the following newswire services:

- Prime Zone
- M2 Communications
- Internet.com
- Newszoid
- Reuters

Press releases distributed by Press Release Network have been published by AFP, Associated Press, Bloomberg, CBS MarketWatch, Dow Jones Interactive Publishing, Excite News, Internet Business News, Market Wire, Lexis-Nexis, Newszoid, Prime Zone, Reuters, Yahoo News, M2 Presswire, Internet.com, Google News and many other global newswires and online services. Several multinational organizations around the globe use Press Release Network's services. Their media database now includes over 20,000 editors of newspapers and magazines and journalists of TV, radio and broadcast stations.

eReleases

eReleases was founded in 1998 with the idea that press release writing and targeted press release distribution shouldn't be out of the reach of small business owners.

Broadcast Connection

Broadcast Connection, LLC formed in February 1999 is a full-service broadcast public relations and multimedia company. It offers video production and customized distribution services. Clients are corporations and organizations seeking to spread their news and information to audiences utilizing the power of television, radio, print and the Internet.

These are just some examples of various types of news release distribution businesses and their services. Though ANRs and VNRs are available options the most widely used workhorse of public relations is still the good old press release.

Press Conferences

Besides news releases there are several other formats organizations use to communicate with the media. Some need speaking to media persons. They include interviews, press or media briefings and press or news conferences. In all these a spokesperson speaks to representatives of the media. Neither a news conference nor an interview opportunity is newsworthy in and of itself — unless it is with a head of state, or someone of comparable importance. It becomes newsworthy and worthwhile for the media only when something new and important is said.

News conferences: Traditionalists and the newspaper-minded persist in calling them press conferences, which are often criticized for their theatrical nature. However, for individuals, organizations, and government departments, press conferences serve important public relations function. They are the most popular and most standardized media opportunity and can be effective means of organizing and disseminating newsworthy information to the public.

Professionals generally agree that, as a public relations tool, press conferences should be used sparingly, reserved for circumstances that are truly newsworthy. Such occasions often call for a personal presentation by the organization's chief executive officer, a celebrity, a dignitary, etc. In the general realm, business organizations use press conferences to announce the introduction of major corporate changes such as new product lines, takeovers, or mergers. But press conferences also have been utilized to organize and manage information in crisis situations or to respond to accusations of wrongdoing. Some practitioners say that when the boss is pushing for a press conference, it can be tough to resist. The boss who is pushing so hard for the press conference, and who may envision him/herself taking centre stage to banter with reporters, may slip up and make a mistake. Calling unnecessary news conferences about non-newsworthy topics may get attention the first couple of times, but it is counter-productive in the long run.

A press conference these days usually means an on-camera event open to all news media. It is high profile, but has the difficulty of being treated like theatre by everyone. It therefore requires firm control to achieve effectiveness. In addition, the party on the podium has to cope with knowing that every word and grimace is being recorded as they tackle complex questions. The objective of a press conference is to provide the best possible platform for an announcement.

Although in the business sector press conferences are not viewed as a routine means of public relations, major government agencies employ them on a more regular basis. Indeed, press conferences are a principal component of governmental and political communications. They are relied upon by bureaucrats and politicians as a way of providing important information to the public and shaping public opinion and by correspondents as a means of obtaining such information and examining the opinion shaping process.

In the US, Theodore Roosevelt (1858–1919)[1] was one of the first American presidents to use the press as a frequent means of communicating with the public. Although he did not hold formal press conferences in their contemporary sense, he realized that the media could be used to shape public opinion and established close relationships with journalists. Woodrow Wilson (1856–1924)[2] was the first president to hold regular and formal press conferences.[3] Not only did he view the press as a means of influencing public opinion, but he also believed that communication via the press was a chief duty of democratic leaders. Since the Wilson administration, all presidents have held formal press conferences. However, the decision to grant a press conference is always made by the White House,

1. Twenty-sixth President of the United States, 1901–1909.

2. Twenty-eighth President of the United States, 1913–1921.

3. An unverifiable leak and an activist president combined to give birth to the White House Correspondents' Association on 25 February 1914. Rumours had leaked that the Congressional Standing Committee of Correspondents would be asked to decide which reporters to invite to an unprecedented series of regularly scheduled press conferences planned by Woodrow Wilson.

Horrified by this intrusion on their turf, 11 reporters formed the WHCA, decreeing that its 'primary object shall be the promotion of the interests of those reporters and correspondents assigned to cover the White House.'

The leak proved unfounded. The WHCA lay dormant until 1920 when the organization held its first dinner. In 1924, Calvin Coolidge became the first of 13 presidents to attend the dinner.

Until World War II, the WHCA controlled the issuing of White House credentials. The annual dinner was an entertainment extravaganza, featuring singing between courses, a homemade movie and an hour-long, post-dinner show with big-name performers. In the 1990s, the association has focused primarily on coverage-related issues affecting regular White House correspondents, including access to the president and efforts to reduce the costs that news organizations face covering the president on the road.

The WHCA established a site on the World Wide Web in conjunction with the annual dinner on 1 May 1999, to help keep members abreast of developments. The site has an awards section that provides biographies of winners of the WHCA scholarship and the annual journalism awards, and direct access to the journalists' winning entries.

and press conferences have varied in frequency and format with each administration.

Although President Dwight D. Eisenhower (1890–1969)[4] regularly used television as a means to address the American electorate, John F. Kennedy (1917–1963),[5] was the first to utilize television as a direct means of communication with voters via live press conferences. His successors have scheduled press conferences less frequently. They have also employed variations to the live-press conference format. The Carter, Reagan, and Bush administrations held mini-press conferences. President Bush also relied on impromptu daytime televised press conferences rather than the formal, prime-time gatherings. President Clinton used a variation of the press conference with his televised 'town meetings'. With these conferences Clinton managed to sidestep the White House press corps and address questions asked by average citizens. There has been a tradition of a photo opportunity with visiting dignitaries for photographers. With the arrival of television most photo opportunities are converted into joint mini-press conferences of the president with the visiting dignitaries at the White House.

Prime Time / National Press Conference

Thus there are several versions of Press Conferences used by heads of state and government. Most important but least frequent in the US is the prime time press conference of the President. The parallel to this in India is the Prime Minister's National Press Conference. It is interesting to compare the 13 April 2004 prime time press conference of President Bush with

4. Thirty-fourth President 1953–1961.
5. Thirty-fifth President of the United States 1961–1963.

the National Press Conference addressed by the Indian Prime Minister, Dr Manmohan Singh on 4 September 2004. Both were broadcast live. President Bush began by saying, 'Before I take your questions, let me speak with the American people about the situation in Iraq.' He utilized the live broadcast to his advantage and spoke about 2,000 words very well written for the time. Here is how he began:

THE PRESIDENT: Good evening. Before I take your questions, let me speak with the American people about the situation in Iraq.

This has been a tough week in that country. Coalition forces have encountered serious violence in some areas of Iraq. Our military commanders report that this violence is being instigated by three groups: Some remnants of Saddam Hussein's regime, along with Islamic militants have attacked coalition forces in the city of Fallujah. Terrorists from other countries have infiltrated Iraq to incite and organize attacks. In the south of Iraq, coalition forces face riots and attacks that are being incited by a radical cleric named al-Sadr. He has assembled some of his supporters into an illegal militia, and publicly supported the terrorist groups, Hamas and Hezbollah. Al-Sadr's methods of violence and intimidation are widely repudiated by other Iraqi Shias. He's been indicted by Iraqi authorities for the murder of a prominent Shia cleric.

Although these instigations of violence come from different factions, they share common goals. They want to run us out of Iraq and destroy the democratic hopes of the Iraqi people. The violence we have seen is a power grab by these extreme and ruthless elements . . .

President Bush ended his about 2,000 word statement, which almost became an address to the nation as well with:

> A desperate enemy is also a dangerous enemy, and our work may become more difficult before it is finished. No one can predict all the hazards that lie ahead, or the costs they will bring. Yet, in this conflict, there is no safe alternative to resolute action. The consequences of failure in Iraq would be unthinkable. Every friend of America and Iraq would be betrayed to prison and murder as a new tyranny arose. Every enemy of America and the world would celebrate, proclaiming our weakness and decadence, and using that victory to recruit a new generation of killers.
>
> We will succeed in Iraq. We're carrying out a decision that has already been made and will not change: Iraq will be a free, independent country, and America and the Middle East will be safer because of it. Our coalition has the means and the will to prevail. We serve the cause of liberty, and that is, always and everywhere, a cause worth serving.
>
> Now, I'll be glad to take your questions. I will start with you.

Here is how Dr Manmohan Singh began:

> Ladies and gentlemen, ever since I assumed the office of the Prime Minister, I have received several requests from distinguished ladies and gentlemen of the Press to interview me. Unfortunately, because of my other preoccupations, I have not been able to accede to these requests. But, nevertheless, I have been very keen to meet all of you, even though I am told that a conference of this type at the level of the Prime Minister has not been held for at least, a decade. I recognize there are risks, but I am ready to throw the pigeon among the cats.

I have a prepared text by way of introductory remarks, but I thought the best way to use this time is to give you all the time and attention and this statement can be taken as read. So, that will give you more time to ask me questions that you would like me to answer.

This shows complete lack of understanding of the use of this major PR tool in the PR team of the Indian Prime Minister. Dr Singh did not use the opportunity like President Bush who retained control from the beginning. There was another problem. First it was announced that the written statement of the Prime Minister will be distributed after the Press Conference, but then at the request of journalists the distribution started after a few minutes of the beginning. Dr Singh said, '. . . the best way to use this time is to give you all the time and attention and this statement can be taken as read. So, that will give you more time to ask me questions that you would like me to answer.' He had to prolong the press conference, as many journalists had not finished with their questions. However, it was found that answers to most of the questions were in the statement. So did the Prime Minster save the time or utilize that properly? He also lost an opportunity to address the people at large in the beginning and giving a direction to questions, as President Bush did.

Now let us look at the ends. The Indian Prime Minister in all answered 51 questions the last one was:

Q51: Mr Prime Minster it is being said in certain quarters that the threat to Dr Manmohan Singh comes not from the Left or from the Opposition, but from Dr Manmohan Singh himself and that if you are pushed against the wall and compelled to do things that go against your grain in the course of keeping the coalition together, you might just decide to put in your papers. Could such a thing happen?

PRIME MINISTER: Well, Madam, I believe our Government is going to last for full five years, and let there be no doubt or ambiguity about this. Therefore, this misconception that I can be pressurised into giving up is simply not going to materialize.

MEDIA ADVISOR: Ladies and Gentlemen, I am sure you will all agree that this is a brilliant note to end this session. I am sure all of you have lots of questions. Please bear with me. Another opportunity will come by. You have been very graceful and extremely polite and thank you very, very much. Thank you, Sir.

President Bush had to reply not even half the number of questions compared to Dr Singh, thanks to his initial statement. The last question he faced was:

Q. I guess I just wonder if you feel that you have failed in any way? You don't have many of these press conferences, where you engage in this kind of exchange. Have you failed in any way to really make the case to the American public?

THE PRESIDENT: I guess if you put it into a political context, that's the kind of thing the voters will decide next November. That's what elections are about. They'll take a look at me and my opponent and say, let's see, which one of them can better win the war on terror? Who best can see to it that Iraq emerges as a free society?

Don, if I tried to fine-tune my messages based upon polls, I think I'd be pretty ineffective. I know I would be disappointed in myself. I hope today you've got a sense of my conviction about what we're doing. If you don't, maybe I need to learn to communicate better.

I feel strongly about what we're doing. I feel strongly that the course this administration has taken will make America more secure and the world more free, and, therefore, the world more peaceful. It's a conviction that's deep in my soul. And I will say it as best as I possibly can to the American people.

I look forward to the debate and the campaign. I look forward to helping — for the American people to hear, what is a proper use of American power; do we have an obligation to lead, or should we shirk responsibility. That's how I view this debate. And I look forward to making it, Don. I'll do it the best I possibly can. I'll give it the best shot. I'll speak as plainly as I can.

One thing is for certain, though, about me — and the world has learned this — when I say something, I mean it. And the credibility of the United States is incredibly important for keeping world peace and freedom. Thank you all very much.

President Bush was informal with the questioner 'Don' while Prime Minister Singh was formal with 'Madam'. This can be attributed to personality traits. Bush was aware that the Press Conference was being broadcast live and used this opportunity to address the American people and their values. Before ending the press conference with 'Thank you all very much,' Bush said a few last lines: 'One thing is for certain, though, about me — and the world has learned this — when I say something, I mean it. And the credibility of the United States is incredibly important for keeping world peace and freedom. Thank you all very much.'

The Indian team behaved as if they were unaware of the live broadcast. The Media Advisor to the Prime Minister promised the journalists, 'Another opportunity will come by.' But the next National Press Conference of the Prime Minister did not happen soon. 'You have been very graceful and extremely polite and thank you very, very much.' What did he expect them to be?

Indira Gandhi used to have a National Press Conference once a year. This tradition has not been followed by her successors for various reasons. Thus in India, this tool is underused compared to many other countries.

The British Prime Minister, Tony Blair, holds a monthly press conference at 10 Downing Street, there is no fixed date. For example the monthly press conference of March 2006 took place on 16 March while the April 2006 one took place on 24 April. The PM's Press Conferences allows regional, national and international journalists to ask Tony Blair questions on any aspect of government policy.

Every press conference started with an opening statement. In the press conference in March the British PM spoke about the government's public sector reform agenda during his opening remarks to the conference (about 1,500 words). He was then asked about Iran, education, free bus travel and pensions among other subjects. In April Tony Blair's monthly press conference was dominated by the current debate in the National Health Service. The opening remarks was of about 2,000 words. He also answered questions on the Middle East Peace Process and Al-Qaida.

The monthly press conference for May 2006 took place on 8 May 2006. Tony Blair spoke about the Government's future policy agenda during this press conference. He was asked questions about the Cabinet reshuffle, his leadership, foreign prisoners, Guantanamo Bay and Iran. The opening statement was of more that 1,000 words, beginning with, 'Good morning everyone. Before starting I would like to express my deep condolences to the families of those killed in Basra on Saturday and once again pay tribute to the heroism, commitment and professionalism of our Armed Forces.'

And then he went on to make a comprehensive opening statement:

> This week we are now one year from the last election and a new Cabinet is charged with continuing delivery of the commitments that we made when we won that third term, and you might be forgiven for thinking over the past few days that there isn't actually a busy government agenda, but there is.
>
> Later in May, John Hutton, Gordon and myself will publish the proposals to deliver a new long-term pensions framework which will be about implementing the Turner Commission report.
>
> Before the end of the summer, the Department of Trade and Industry, under the new leadership of Alistair Darling, will complete the review of Energy Policy, vital to providing affordable, secure and sustainable energy to British business and British families. The Department for Transport will continue its analysis of long-term transport funding which will be complemented by important work on the future of planning and housing that will be announced by Ruth Kelly.
>
> On Public Service reform too, in the coming period of course, together with Patricia Hewitt, I will be working on the essential reforms of the National Health Service.
>
> Indeed, in the coming weeks we will see the final stages of the Education and Inspections Bill with its far-reaching

> package of measures to improve standards, tackle discipline and give new freedoms and opportunities to schools. Alan Johnson and his team will be underlining the way these measures can benefit all schools and pupils and benefit the least-advantaged most. . . .

Blair ended his opening statement with:

> I have said there will be a stable and orderly transition to a new leader, I will see that this is done because it is in the interests of the country, but it is also in the interests of this country that in the meantime we get on with the business of governing, carrying through the reforms of pensions, schools, the National Health Service, our Criminal Justice System and focus resolutely on the jobs and living standards of the British people, because that is what they expect us to do having elected us for a third term.

And then opened the floor for questions with:

> Nick, which part of the government programme would you like to ask me about?

Transcripts are put on the 10 Downing Street website as soon as possible.'Sometimes it is necessary to edit the transcripts. This is either because in accordance with long-standing practice under the Ministerial and Civil Service codes, government websites cannot carry party political content, or because the audio quality has made it impossible to transcribe.'

President Bush also addresses press conferences but not with fixed periodicity. There is also another term 'press availability' used these days. For example on 28 April 2006, President Bush discussed the economy with media participating in Press Availability. Dates of press confernces addressed by him in the White House are 21 March 2006, 26 January 2006, 19 December 2005, 9 October 2005, 31 May 2005, 28 April

2005, 16 March 2005, 17 February 2005. It is not monthly, as in case of Tony Blair.

Photo-Op and Joint Press Conferences

In recent years whenever a head of state or government has visited the White House, the President has posed for photographs with him for the press. In the era of television each such Photo-Opportunity is turned into a mini-press conference. For example, on 25 May 2006, President Bush and Prime Minister Tony Blair of the United Kingdom participated in Joint Press Availability at the East Room, White House. For all practical purposes it was a joint press conference by two heads of Governments. It lasted about an hour (from 7:30 P.M. to 8:24 P.M. EDT). President Bush began his 900 word opening statement with, 'Thank you all. Good evening. I want to thank Prime Minister Tony Blair for coming to Washington to discuss his recent visit to Iraq. The Prime Minister met with key leaders of the new Iraqi government that represents the will of the Iraqi people and reflects their nation's diversity. As Prime Minister Blair will tell you, Iraqi Prime Minister Maliki outlined an aggressive agenda to bring security to the Iraqi people, to improve electricity and other essential services, and to pursue a strategy for national reconciliation.' His opening statement ended with, 'Our coalition will seize this moment, as well. I look forward for continued in-depth discussions with Tony Blair, so we can develop the best approach in helping the new Iraqi government achieve its objectives. The new government of Iraq will have the full support of our two countries and our coalition, and we will work to engage other nations around the world to ensure that constitutional democracy in Iraq succeeds and the terrorists are defeated.' With this Bush handed the floor to Mr Prime Minister who made a 920 word opening statement before taking questions.

A similar White House event took place when the Indian Prime Minister Manmohan Singh was there on 18 July 2005:

The East Room

11:08 A.M. EDT

PRESIDENT BUSH: Thank you. I'm proud to stand here today with Prime Minister Singh, the leader of one of the world's great democracies. Mr Prime Minister, welcome to America. I applaud your vision and I applaud your leadership. Laura and I are honoured to welcome you and Mrs Kaur to the White House.

We just had a great discussion, a very frank and open discussion. And tonight we look forward to welcoming you for a little family dinner.

India and the United States share a commitment to freedom and a belief that democracy provides the best path to a more hopeful future for all people. We also believe that the spread of liberty is the best alternative to hatred and violence. Because of our shared values, the relationship between our two countries has never been stronger. We're working together to make our nations more secure, deliver a better life to our citizens and advance the cause of peace and freedom throughout the world.

The governments of India and the United States are working together to safeguard our people. We are charting new steps in our defence relationship through the recently signed new framework that will help our two nations work toward common security objectives. We're working together on counter-terrorism to help protect our people and make the world a safer place. We're also committed to increasing the prosperity of the people of India and America alike. Today, we announced the completion of the next steps in strategic partnership. Completing this partnership will help us further enhance our cooperation in the areas of civil nuclear, civil space and high technology commerce.

Last month, we launched a reinvigorated US-India economic dialogue to focus high-level attention on trade, finance, investment and the environment. Prime Minister Singh and I are about to meet with business leaders from both our nations who have joined us here today for the inaugural meeting of the CEO Forum. The expertise of these private sector leaders will help our two governments build trade and increase investment for the good of our peoples. Cleaner energy resources, including nuclear power, are vital for the future of both our economies. We have begun a bilateral energy dialogue to find ways to work together in this important area. Our two nations also have a common interest in bettering the lives of people around the world. We are launching a disaster response initiative to better respond to future disasters, just not in Asia, but around the world.

I appreciate Prime Minister Singh's leadership. He's a man who's committed to peace and liberty. I look forward to working with you, Prime Minister. I thank you for coming. The podium is yours.

PRIME MINISTER SINGH: Thank you very much, Mr President. Ladies and gentlemen of the press, I would like to begin by thanking President Bush for the warmth of his hospitality and the wide-ranging discussions that we've had this morning with him. These discussions have been, indeed, very productive and focused on the future direction of a transformation in our multifaceted relations. I am happy that the President and I share the common goal of making this one of the principal relationships for each of our countries. The President's personal commitment to this relationship is deeply admired by the people of India. The support and goodwill of the friendly people of the United States in managing the transition from a developing country to a fast-expanding economy is something we greatly welcome and greatly appreciate. The President's assurance to me that India's sustained economic growth has his strong support and support of the United States means a lot to us.

The joint statement that we have agreed upon lays out the full potential of our multifaceted cooperation. The President has accepted my invitation to visit India at the earliest, and we are confident that the results of the understanding that we have reached today would be fully evident by then.

Our partnership is one between rigorous and vibrant democracies, and we have agreed today to give expression to our shared values in a variety of ways. The President's steadfast determination and leadership in meeting the challenges of international terrorism is widely appreciated by us, in particular, by all the world, all civilized men and women all over the world. There can be no cause that justifies the killing of innocent and defenceless civilians. There must be an international norm of zero tolerance for terrorists.

Meeting global challenges requires credible and effective global institutions. Today the world is debating the reform of the United Nations. In our talks, the President and I were of one mind that contemporary reality must be fully reflected in the central organs and decision-making processes of the U.N. India has a compelling case for permanent membership of the Security Council. We are convinced that India can significantly contribute to U.N. decision-making and capabilities.

A growing Indian economy, with an accelerated growth rate averaging about 6 to 7 per cent in recent years, and its integration with the world economy would expand the scope for commerce, investment and technological cooperation between our two countries. Shortly, after this press interaction, the President and I will spend a few minutes with corporate leaders from both countries of the first meeting of the CEO's Forum. This forum includes some of the best business minds of our two countries. We have announced today a series of other initiatives designed to build a long-term, knowledge-driven partnership between India and the United States. These reflect the vision that the President and I have of our shared future.

We also discussed the importance of ensuring adequate energy and affordable supplies at a time when oil prices remain high. Both of us recognize that civilian nuclear energy has a greater role in meeting global energy demands. We in India have an ambitious and attainable national road map in this regard. We look forward to President Bush's strong leadership on these important issues.

I must once again thank you, Mr President, for the warmth of your welcome and for your deep and abiding personal commitment to the building of our partnership.

I would now be glad to take your questions.

PRESIDENT BUSH: Hold on a second. The way this is going to work, the way this will work is I'll call on somebody from the American side, and then the Prime Minister will do so; and then I'll call somebody, and the Prime Minister will do so. We'll answer two questions apiece, starting with Terry.

Q. Mr President, you said you don't want to talk about an ongoing investigation, so I'd like to ask you, regardless of whether a crime was committed, do you still intend to fire anyone found to be involved in the CIA leak case? And are you displeased that Karl Rove told a reporter that Ambassador Joe Wilson's wife worked for the Agency on WMD issues?

PRESIDENT BUSH: We have a serious ongoing investigation here. (*Laughter.*) And it's being played out in the press. And I think it's best that people wait until the investigation is complete before you jump to conclusions. And I will do so, as well. I don't know all the facts. I want to know all the facts. The best place for the facts to be done is by somebody who's spending time investigating it. I would like this to end as quickly as possible so we know the facts, and if someone committed a crime, they will no longer work in my administration.

Q. My question is to President Bush. The question relates to the line of control in Kashmir, Mr President. President Clinton had made clear the US policy that in the interest of peace, the sanctity of the line of control must be maintained by every side.

Would you, Mr President, like to reaffirm the US stand that the sanctity of the line of control cannot be violated by anyone in future in the interest of the peace? Mr President.

PRESIDENT BUSH: Well, US policy has not changed. This problem will be solved by India and Pakistan. And our role is to encourage the leaders from both countries to work in good faith to solve this long-standing problem. And I am pleased with the progress being made, as should the people of India. I think the people of India ought to applaud strong leaders that are willing to work to achieve peace. And I think — I think we have an opportunity to help facilitate the dialogue on this long-standing issue.

But the truth of the matter is, in order for there to be a solution, the Prime Minister, representing the great people of India, and President Musharraf, representing the people of Pakistan, are going to have to come to a mutually acceptable agreement. To the extent we can help, we're more than willing to try to help. But we're not a party to the agreement, of course. I'm hopeful — I'm hopeful — I'm hopeful that the progress achieved thus far can be continued. And I applauded the Prime Minister in my private meeting with him for taking a step toward peace.

Adam.

Q. Thank you.

THE PRESIDENT: Yes, thanks.

Q. Thank you, Mr President. We understand you are now close to a decision on a Supreme Court nominee.

THE PRESIDENT: Really? (*Laughter*) It's amazing how Washington works, Mr Prime Minister. (*Laughter*)

Q. Have you narrowed down the list and met with finalists? Will you now share the list with Senate leaders to avoid a confirmation battle, as the Democrats have proposed?

THE PRESIDENT: Well, thank you for telling me where I am in the process. I appreciate that. We've consulted with the Senate. We will continue to consult with the Senate. I, of course, am the person that picks the nominee, and they get to decide whether or not the nominee gets confirmed. That's the way it has worked in the past. That's the way it's going to work in this administration.

And of course I'm reviewing a different candidate. I'm reviewing their curriculum vitae, as well as their findings. I will sit down with some and talk to them face-to-face, those who I have not known already. You know, we've got some people that — perhaps in contention that I've already spent time with, that I know; in other words, I'm familiar with some of the people that are being speculated about in the press. And so I don't need to interview those. But of course I'm going to take a very thorough approach.

What they're referring to is a Supreme Court vacancy. And this is a really important decision. And I'm going to take my time and I will be thorough and deliberate. But make no mistake; we have heard a lot of suggestions from members of the United States Senate — a lot. It turns out, many of the senators have got strong opinions one way or the other. And of course we're listening to them.

But my desire, Adam, is to get this process moving so that someone will be confirmed, whoever he or she is, will be confirmed by October. And if that's the backstop, we're working back to try to accommodate the Senate and their desire. Part of the consultation was to ask the senators, what's it take to get somebody in place by the October session?

And thank you for your question, and thank you for telling me how close I am to — or at least indicating what others think. (*Laughter*)

Q. Mr Prime Minister, you have sought the removal of restrictions on nuclear and high technology supplies to India.

After the meeting with President Bush, how do you see the prospects in this area?

PRIME MINISTER SINGH: Well, I think we have had a very constructive and productive meeting. And as you will see from the joint statement, this issue has been addressed in a manner which gives me great satisfaction. And I thank the President for his personal role and interest in facilitating a solution to this complex problem.

PRESIDENT BUSH: Mr Prime Minister, thank you. Very good job. Well done. Thank you, sir.

END 11:24 A.M. EDT

Look at the way President Bush took charge when Prime Minister Singh ended his statement with 'I would now be glad to take your questions.' President Bush jumped in with, 'Hold on a second. The way this is going to work, the way this will work is I'll call on somebody from the American side, and then the Prime Minister will do so; and then I'll call somebody, and the Prime Minister will do so. We'll answer two questions apiece, starting with Terry.' Prime Minister Singh, did well by making a 578 word opening statement.

A similar event took place in New Delhi on 2 March 2006 during the visit of President Bush at Hyderabad House:

Hyderabad House
New Delhi, India

12:26 P.M. (Local)

PRIME MINISTER SINGH: Shall I start?

PRESIDENT BUSH: Please.

PRIME MINISTER SINGH: Mr President, ladies and gentlemen of the press: President Bush and I have completed very cordial and productive discussions this morning. We reviewed the status of our cooperation, including the agenda that was set on 18 July 2005. The joint statement that will be shared with all of you today contains a number of announcements and initiatives that underline the significant progress in our relationship.

Many of the areas that our cooperation now covers are essential to India's national development. They include energy, agriculture, science and technology, trade and investment, high technology, health and a clean environment. This is a highly ambitious agenda, one that is befitting our growing strategic partnership. When implemented they will make a real difference to the lives of our people.

The President and I had an opportunity to review the global situation in our talks. As you're all aware, India and the United States are working together increasingly on global issues. This is not just good for our two countries, but also benefits the international community, as we can complement each others' capabilities and share responsibilities. President Bush is admired for his strong position on terrorism. And I was particularly pleased that we agreed on the need to root out terrorism, of which India has been a major victim.

I'm particularly pleased that we have reached an understanding on the implementation of our agreement on civil nuclear cooperation of 18 July 2005. I have conveyed to the President that India has finalized the identification of civilian facilities to which we had committed. I was also happy to hear from the President that he now intended to approach the U.S. Congress to amend U.S. laws and the

Nuclear Supplier Group to adjust its guideline. We will discuss with the International Atomic Energy Agency in regard to fashioning an appropriate India-specific safeguards agreement. You will appreciate I cannot say more now, while our parliament is in session.

Before concluding, I would like to express my warm appreciation for the personal interest shown and the leadership role that President Bush has played in the transformation of our ties. I have met the President a number of times, and on each occasion, I have admired his vision, his resolve, and his commitment to strengthening our bilateral relations. Our discussion today make me confident that there are no limits to the Indo-US partnerships.

May I invite you, Mr President, now to make your remarks.

PRESIDENT BUSH: Mr Prime Minister, thank you very much. It's a joy to be here. Laura and I are really thankful for your hospitality, and I appreciate the lengthy and constructive dialogue we just had on a wide range of issues. I particularly thank the CEOs from both the United States and India who have worked hard to help develop a way forward to make sure our relationship is constructive and long-lasting.

India and America have built a strategic partnership based upon common values. Our two democracies respect religious pluralism and the rule of law. We seek to foster economic development through trade and advancing the entrepreneurial spirit in both countries. We're working as partners to make the world safer. India and America both suffered from terrorist attacks on our home soil. Terrorists attacked New Delhi. We're sharing information to protect each other. We have a common desire to enhance the security of our peoples. We're cooperating on the military front. We worked as partners in responding to the tsunami. I was struck, and so were the American people, that the Indian Air Force delivered Hurricane Katrina aid to an air force base in Little Rock, Arkansas. And for that, Mr Prime Minister, thank you.

We are committed to promoting democracy worldwide. We are leaders in the United Nations Democracy Fund, which provides grants to help young democracies develop civil institutions in a free society. I particularly want to thank the Indian people and the Indian government for supporting the new democracy in the neighbourhood, and that being the democracy in Afghanistan, where you've pledged $ 565 million in reconstruction aid, plus $ 50 million for the new national assembly building.

On Burma, we agree on the deplorable state of human rights in Burma, and all nations to seek the release of Aung San Suu Kyi. In Nepal, we agreed that the Maoists should abandon violence, and that the King should reach out to the political parties to restore democratic institutions. In other words, our discussions are more than just friendly handshakes. We discuss important international relations. We're partners in peace. And that's in the interests of our own people, as well as the interests of people around the world.

On trade and investment, ties are growing. We're partners in expanding global trade. The United States is India's largest trading partner, and India is one of the United States' fastest growing export markets. That's one of the reasons we met with the CEOs today, is to how to further trade and how to further commerce and how to further opportunities.

And, oh, by the way, Mr Prime Minister, the United States is looking forward to eating Indian mangos. Part of liberalizing trade is to open up markets. And as a result of your leadership, and our hard work, we are opening up markets. Our agricultural knowledge initiative is an important initiative for both countries, where we'll fund joint agricultural research projects.

Prime Minister Singh and I established a trade policy forum to address bilateral trade issues. One of the areas we discussed today is how we can work together to make sure that the Doha negotiations end on a positive note. Trade is important. Trade is important for our peoples. Trade is important to help nations develop ways forward, help nations overcome poverty. And I appreciate your understanding of that, Mr Prime Minister. I'm looking forward to working with you.

As the Prime Minister mentioned, we concluded a historic agreement today on nuclear power. It's not an easy job for the Prime Minister to achieve this agreement, I understand. It's not easy for the American President to achieve this agreement. But it's a necessary agreement. It's one that will help both our peoples.

Again, I applaud you for your courage and your leadership. I'm looking forward to working with our United States Congress to change decades of law that will enable us to move forward in this important initiative.

Also we talked about the advanced energy initiative that I'm proposing in my own country. Listen, the whole purpose of the advanced energy initiative is to end our dependence on oil, and as we develop technologies that will enable us to do so, we look forward to working with India so we can achieve the same objectives. Dependency upon fossil fuels causes, particularly during times of shortage, causes prices to rise in both our countries. And it's in our interests that we share technologies to move away from the era of fossil fuels.

India and Pakistan have an historic opportunity to work toward lasting peace. Prime Minister Singh and President Musharraf have shown themselves to be leaders of courage and vision. And I encourage them to continue making progress on all issues, including Kashmir.

India and America are partners in addressing other global issues like HIV/AIDS and pandemic flu. In other words, this partnership of ours is substantive and it's important and it's strategic. And I thank the Prime Minister for working with me to advance this relationship in such a way that we can define our previous meetings and today's meeting as historic in nature. I'm confident that the relationship between India and the United States is good for the United States of America. I hope it's good for the people of India, and I know it's going to be good for laying the foundations of peace in this world of ours.

So, Mr Prime Minister, thank you very much for having me.

PRIME MINISTER SINGH: It's a great honour, Mr President, to have you.

Q. Thank you, Mr Prime Minister. Thank you, Mr President. Sir, since you have said that India-US nuclear cooperation agreement is on, what we would like to know from you that how are you going to ensure India's concerns and Indian scientific community's concerns regarding non-stop supply of fuel, and also protecting India's three-phased nuclear research programme.

And excuse me, sir. Mr President, I have a question for

you, too, sir. Sir, you know, everybody is saying that India and the United States are natural allies. And you have also said many times that our strategic partnership is based on common values, shared values. Sir, then why the largest democracy of the world is reluctant or not forthcoming to support — the oldest democracy of the world is not supporting the largest democracy of the world to have a permanent membership of the United Nations Security Council? This is an issue India would like to hear from you more, sir. Thank you. Thank you, Prime Minister.

PRIME MINISTER SINGH: You have asked me about the nuclear agreement. As I mentioned, we have reached a mutually satisfactory understanding with regard to carrying forward the process that was outlined in the 18 July statement which I and President Bush signed.

An important step forward is the preparation of a separation plan, a separation plan which separates the civilian nuclear programme from the military programme. That phase has been successfully completed. Now it is for the United States to go to the Congress for necessary amendments in US laws. Also, the US will approach the members of the Nuclear Supplier Groups, and thereafter we'll also have to go to the International Atomic Energy Agency for India-specific safeguards.

So we have made very satisfactory progress. And I thank the President for his initiative. But for his leadership this day would probably have not come so soon.

PRESIDENT BUSH: Thank you for your question on the U.N. Security Council. I'm not surprised you asked it. As a matter of fact, I gave an interview to a person from the India media in Washington, D.C., prior to my trip, and that was one of the questions asked.

My answer hasn't changed, by the way, which is this. One, we support United Nations Security Council reform, and we're interested in different ways to reform the United Nations Security Council. My concern all along, however, is that if we only stick to the United Nations Security Council reform, we miss an opportunity to reform the United Nations overall. And so our position is, let's make sure reform overall moves forward, as we think about the best way to reform the Security Council.

The United Nations is a very important international body. It's one that does, however, require better accountability and — accountability on how we spend money and accountability on getting results. One such area, for example, is the Human Rights Commission. The Human Rights Commission needs to be reformed in a way that actually is able to achieve significant results on behalf of the world.

And so we're open-minded and we're listening. But what we don't want to do is have a Security Council reform measure that causes the other reforms not to go forward.

Suzanne: You probably need a microphone, unless you want to belt it out.

Q. I'll try. Thank you, Mr President. There are reports of multiple bombings out of Karachi, Pakistan, outside of the US consulate, as well as the Marriott Hotel. What can you tell us about this? Will this impact your trip, your visit to that country? And how does this speak to Pakistan, or even Musharraf's ability to contain terrorists?

PRESIDENT BUSH: First of all, I've been briefed on the bombings. We have lost at least one US citizen in a bombing, a foreign service officer, and I send our country's deepest condolences to that person's loved one and family. We also send condolences to the people from Pakistan who lost their lives. Terrorists and killers are not going to prevent me from going to Pakistan. My trip to Pakistan is an important trip. It's important to talk with President Musharraf about continuing our fight against terrorists. After all, he has had a direct stake in this fight — four times the terrorists have tried to kill him.

The Prime Minister and I talked about the need to continue working together to fight the scourge of terrorism. People — these terrorists will kill innocent life just like that. They have no conscience. You can't negotiate with them, you can't reason with them. They must be brought to justice. The bombing that took place prior to my trip is an indication that there are — that the war on terror goes on, and that free nations must come together to fight terrorism.

The way to defeat terrorism in the short run is to share intelligence and to take action. The way to defeat terrorism in the long run is to defeat the ideology of hate with an ideology of hope. And that's democracy. The great thing about being here in India is it's a perfect opportunity to remind the world that it is possible for people of different religions to live peacefully together. That's precisely what this grand democracy has shown the world.

And my resolve has never been stronger about protecting our own people by working with other nations, to answer the call to history and the call to history now is to stand strong in the face of these terrorist attacks. And we will.

Q. President Bush, two questions for you. First —

PRESIDENT BUSH: Only two? That's good.

Q. First, on the nuclear deal, how do you plan to sell the agreement to a very powerful non-proliferation lobby in

Washington which has opposed the deal? And second, on the issue of terrorism, in the context of today's bomb blasts in Karachi, how do you propose to work with India on terrorism, considering India considers that the epicentre of terrorism is in Pakistan?

PRESIDENT BUSH: Well, one way we work together on terrorism is to make sure intelligence services share information. The way you defeat terrorists is you — in the short-term — is you anticipate and react to their motives and their actions through good intelligence.

We're involved in a different kind of war. This is a war where people hide and plot and plan and then all of a sudden emerge and kill. And so it requires a different response. And part of the response is to commit our intelligence services to sharing information. We spent some time talking about that issue today.

As well, I will send — bring the same message to President Musharraf that we will continue to work with the President to share information to bring terrorists to justice. Terrorism is not prevalent only in this part of the world. It's prevalent in the Middle East, as well. In the long run, terrorism will be defeated by giving people hope and opportunity, as opposed to systems of government which breed resentment and provide — and as a result of that resentment, provide opportunity for these killers to recruit.

In terms of convincing the Congress, the first thing I will say to our Congress is that our relationship is changing to the better. You know, sometimes it's hard to get rid of history, and short-term history shows that the United States and India were divided. We didn't have much of a relationship. And as a result, there are laws on the books that reflect that. Now the relationship is changing dramatically. People in the United States have got to understand that trade with India is in our interests, that diplomatic relations with India is in our interests, that cultural exchanges with India are in our interest.

One of the things that helps make that case, of course, is the — there's a lot of Indian Americans making important contributions to our country. And we welcome those contributions. I think there needs to be more student exchanges between our countries. I think we ought to expand H1B visas for Indian scientists and engineers and physicists and people in our country.

In other words, what I'm trying to explain to you is that it's a changing relationship, and part of that change is going to be how to deal with the nuclear issue. Now, proliferation is certainly a concern and a part of our discussions, and we've got a good faith gesture by the Indian government that I'll be able to take to the Congress. But the other thing that our Congress has got to understand, that it's in our economic interests that India have a civilian nuclear power industry to help take the pressure off of the global demand for energy.

Obviously, nuclear power is a renewable source of energy, and the less demand there is for non-renewable sources of energy, like fossil fuels, the better off it is for the American people. Increasing demand for oil from America, from India and China, relative to a supply that's not keeping up with demand, causes our fuel prices to go up. And so, to the extent that we can reduce demand for fossil fuels, it will help the American consumer.

And so there are several ways for me to make the case, which I'm kind of laying out for you now, so that — but this is what I'll be telling our Congress.

Axelrod.

Q. Mr President, Mr Prime Minister, following up on this just a touch, what kind of message, sir, does it send to the world that India, which has been testing as late as 1998, nuclear testing, and is not — has not signed the Nuclear Non-proliferation Treaty — is this a reward for bad behaviour, as some critics suggest? And what kind of message does it send to other countries that are in the process of developing nuclear technology? Why should they sign the NPT if India is getting a deal without doing so, sir?

PRESIDENT BUSH: What this agreement says is things change, times change, that leadership can make a difference, and telling the world — sending the world a different message from that which is — what used to exist in people's minds.

I — listen, I've always said this was going to be a difficult deal for the Prime Minister to sell to his parliament, but he showed great courage and leadership. And it's difficult for the American President to sell to our Congress, because some people just don't want to change and change with the times. I understand that. But this agreement is in our interests, and therefore, Jim, I'm confident we can sell this to our Congress as in the interest of the United States, and at the same time make it clear that there's a way forward for other nations to participate in a — in civilian nuclear power in such a way as to address non-proliferation concerns.

India has charted a way forward. You heard the Prime Minister talk about going to the IAEA. That group exists to help safeguard — safeguard the world from proliferation.

Listen, I proposed reprocessing agreements — that

stands in stark contrast to current nuclear theology that we shouldn't reprocess for proliferation concerns. I don't see how you can advocate nuclear power, in order to take the pressure off of our own economy, for example, without advocating technological development of reprocessing, because reprocessing will not only — reprocessing is going to help with the environmental concerns with nuclear power. It will make there — to put it bluntly, there will be less material to dispose.

And so I'm trying to think differently, not to stay stuck in the past, and recognize that by thinking differently, particularly on nuclear power, we can achieve some important objectives, one of which is less reliance on fossil fuels; second is to work with our partners to help both our economies grow; and thirdly is to be strong on dealing with the proliferation issues.

Well, Mr Prime Minister, it's been a joy.

PRIME MINISTER SINGH.: Thank you very much, Mr President. We have made history today, and I thank you.

PRESIDENT BUSH: Thank you, sir. Thank you.

END 12:55 P.M. (Local)

As we see here, Prime Minister Singh spoke about 400 words in his opening statement, while President Bush used more than 900 words in his opening remarks. There are no points to guess who dominated the question answer session. However, one can analyse these events to pick up some tricks of the trade, like identifying correspondents by name and limiting the number of questions by giving long answers to useful questions.

Example from Europe

Let us take an example from Europe. The British Prime Minister Tony Blair held a joint press conference with the German Chancellor Gerhard Schroeder and the French President Jacques Chirac following talks in Berlin on 18 February 2004. Here is a transcript of the press conference:

CHANCELLOR SCHROEDER: Ladies and Gentlemen, I would like to extend a very cordial welcome to all of you here in the Federal Chancellor's office and I appreciate the fact that you have turned up in such great numbers. We have had a very intensive discussion for about two and a half hours. You are aware of the system. We focused very much in our discussion today on how we can provide new impulses to what was decided in Lisbon. In Lisbon we decided to make Europe the strongest growing market in the world, the most competitive market in the world, and of course that presupposes certain measures. What we are talking about first and foremost here is that we have to be quite clear about the fact that prosperity for the people in our countries, prosperity for Europe and for Europe's citizens can only be guaranteed in the long run if we succeed in, when it comes to implementing knowledge and implementing it into new products and thus creating new jobs, if we continue to be top when it comes to this matter, and in those areas where we are not yet top, try to become top, which is to say that more than ever before we have to focus on innovation. Innovation, that is to say we have to increase our efforts in the field of R&D so that new products and new products can evolve from this and new jobs can develop in these fields.

But that is only one face of the coin about which we talked today and on which we reached agreement. The other face of the coin is to do with the fact that in view of the completely new economic framework for all the countries in Europe, for the countries in the world, a readjustment of the social security systems that have evolved and have been established in Europe, not in order to bring them down or to destroy them; rather the opposite, only through change can we maintain them, only by changing them can we make them affordable. And it is this necessity that we can trace back to two trends in development and these affect all our countries. On the one hand we have, and the term globalisation is very often used to describe that, a general change in economic development in the world, this affects the competitiveness of individual countries, competition becomes more tense, that does have positive effects but it also affects the labour markets. And then a second trend that is noticeable, we have societies in which people grow . . . positive trend basically, but the result of this development is that the payments out of the social transfer system, function payments, but also health payments, have to cover longer periods in time, have to be paid over longer periods in time and thus create a greater burden on the system of a country, and that is why we have to adapt and to adjust our social security systems to the new conditions that become especially visible in the economies of our countries. We also have to adapt them in order to free up resources that we need to invest in other areas, like in those areas that are the areas of the future and we have defined them together.

That is what we focused on today, and in our discussions one thing became quite clear and that is that we are indeed facing quite a number of similar problems and that we also can draw similar consequences from that. The reform processes that are necessary are under way in our three countries, the adaptation of the social security system to the new economic conditions, the differences really aren't all that noticeable, and the problems don't really differ from one country to the other, and there is a common will in the countries we are talking about to define the future field for innovation and to increase our efforts, material efforts too in those fields. And what we have decided upon today, and what we have agreed upon today will affect the developments of our countries, it will at the same time also affect the development of Europe. It cannot be kept separate. The positive developments in the countries here represented will have a positive effect on Europe and therefore it is quite clear that by providing fresh impulses, fresh impetus, we also provide fresh impetus to developments in the European framework. In the direction of achieving the goals of Lisbon we are quite convinced that that is what we want to achieve.

I would like to leave it at that, and Ladies and Gentlemen for the time being, as I said, we have reached common agreement, we have drawn up a common letter that we want to send to the Commission and the Irish President, and of course to our colleagues in the European Council as the outcome of our meeting here today. I myself will, at least that is what we have seen, brief the Presidency about the discussions we have had here today simply in order to make it quite clear that these discussions are discussions that have taken place in an open atmosphere and that are open and public.

President Chirac: I would like first and foremost to thank very warmly the Chancellor for taking this initiative. He organized this meeting in a very, very positive fashion. I think he has already given you an overview of what we have done, but this meeting has in fact enabled us to pool ideas, pool thoughts, and we will be able to share our views with the Commission and the Irish Presidency in the run-up to the spring Council. We, as the Chancellor said, have focussed on the need for an increased level of research and further education. We have also said that we need a more structured momentum on global economic issues, and we also need to make our reforms and make them positive in our societies to make sure that our entire communities do not collapse and end up in worse situations if we do not embark on this programme of reform. We also all know that we have to deal with the issue of population ageing, and draw all the appropriate conclusions from it. What I am trying to tell you is that I fully endorse what the Chancellor has just said and I fully agree with the conclusions that he drew from our talks this afternoon.

There is one point that I am sure though the French press will be very much interested in, and I am sure the Chancellor will allow me to make this comment, and our foreign colleagues will not mind too much I hope, and I just wanted to say that we have come to a conclusion on our talks bilaterally to bring the VAT levels in the food industry, or rather in the restaurant industry, down to 5 per cent and we will do so in 2006. I know you are smiling. You shouldn't smile in that way, you should realize that in France this is something that people had pinned high hopes on. So what I wanted to do is to make this announcement and thank very warmly the Chancellor and the German authorities for their understanding *vis-à-vis* this very specific labour-related issue in France.

PRIME MINISTER BLAIR: First of all can I thank Chancellor Schroeder for arranging today's meeting, which has been immensely constructive and I think it is a very timely meeting because it comes in advance obviously of the European Summit on economic reform and it is very much in line with the efforts that have been made by the Irish Presidency, excellent efforts I might say, to make sure that we give some impulsion back into the whole process of economic reform that was started at the Lisbon Summit four years ago. And I agree entirely with what President Chirac and Chancellor Schroeder have just said on the content of the letter that we are going to write, and on the general nature of our discussions, and I would just simply add this thing, that really what this is about is trying to say to our people in our own respective countries, but also in Europe as a whole, there is an economic world that as people know is changing very rapidly, globalisation is changing it, technology is changing it, the ageing population is changing the basis of it very, very fast. And what this means is that the response of government, both at a national and a European level, has to be equally quick and equally able to adapt to the changing circumstances. And whether it is in how we move people from welfare and benefits into work, how we give people the skills they need, how we develop the businesses of the future, particularly focusing on areas like research and science and innovation, or whether it is how we adapt our social security systems and healthcare systems to this modern changing world, whether it is in any of these areas the basic position remains the same, that we want the highest possible security for people, and opportunity for people, in a world that is changing so rapidly. And that is what this whole discussion is about. And we know that out there people in Europe are worried about insecurity, they are worried about lack of job opportunities, they are worried about the consequences of globalisation, and our discussion on economic reform is an attempt to say both to our own countries, but also to Europe as a whole, there are real changes that we have to make in order to equip our citizens for this world of change, and that is what it is about and it builds on the work obviously that has been done over the past few years, but I think it is particularly important that we have been able to come to such clear agreement on the way forward on this issue because I think it is of tremendous importance for the future of our people in the early part of this century. And again, many thanks to my colleagues for participating in it with me.

Q. I would like to put a question to all of you gentlemen. There are quite a few critics across Europe who are looking at this meeting and who have got the impression that you are trying to dominate Europe. So what is your answer to those critics?

CHANCELLOR SCHROEDER: Well it is very easy, we are not trying to dominate anybody, let alone Europe. This is not the first time that we are meeting as a threesome here, we have met in September last year and I personally think that we have given important impulses for Europe in the field of foreign and security policy, those were adopted by the Council unanimously mind you thereafter, otherwise it wouldn't have been possible, and we can only point to the fact that the discussion that we have now got into is a discussion that is important in the one or the other aspect for all European nations. I mean they all have slightly different structures, but in a nutshell problems are indeed similar in all of the European countries and the scenarios that we have elaborated as answers to those questions and that will hopefully be implemented in our countries, and if possible also in Europe, are meant to help the people in our countries and in Europe and are by no means directed against or versus anything or anybody, and that is why we are quite confident that even those who feel slightly critical will understand it in this very way.

President Chirac: If you will allow me, I would just like to make one short comment in that respect. I must say I do not understand what people are criticizing, unless of course they are embarking in controversy, but I wouldn't even dare start thinking it is all about controversy. Now there are meetings across Europe in different formats and there always have been. The Nordic countries meet together regularly, the countries of Benelux do the same. In the same way we have meetings of the Weimar (phon) Triangle, or the Visegrad group. Yes I think we have these meetings, there are constant regular Franco-German meetings at all levels of government. And as the Chancellor rightly pointed out, it is not the first trilateral meeting we are having. We have said, and made it known very clearly that we wanted to be involved in discussing issues that affect everybody in Europe, and that we wanted to pool ideas and share these views with our colleagues in the run-up to the spring Council through the Irish Presidency, and the Presidency has understood that and welcomes it as far as I know, and we will share these views with the Commission. So I must say I can't see what anyone would hold up against us, in all honesty.

Q. The summit has been talking about economic reform, part of that of course is labour force flexibility. Why then is it necessary to impose curbs on workers coming in from the accession states from the east, and if it is necessary why is Britain imposing those curbs rather later in the day than your colleagues?

PRIME MINISTER BLAIR: Well first of all, as you know there is going to be an announcement made on this issue on Monday and I am not going to pre-empt that, if you will forgive me. But I do just want to emphasize this about the importance of economic reform, and the importance of this to Britain in a European context. There are literally today millions, millions of British jobs that depend on Europe. Sixty per cent of British trade is with Europe. Now it matters to us that the European economy functions well. And so the importance of having a meeting like this on economic reform is that given that relationship between the British economy and the European economy, and given the fact that we represent such a large part of the European economy together, it is important that we make the changes necessary to give our people the best chance of still having jobs and security and rising living standards in the new world in which we live, and that is why it is important that it is not, you know I think sometimes people can see this in too political a sense, it is a very, very important economic priority for our country and for the wider world.

Q. Federal Chancellor, Prime Minister, M le President. Good Evening, could I maybe ask you whether you consider, gentlemen, that you should have regular meetings in this format similar to what is being done in the Blairtime (phon) format in the Franco-German relationship?

PRESIDENT CHIRAC: Well any meeting that would enable us to develop together vision and understanding of tomorrow's

Europe, and drawing the appropriate consequences in terms of reform, is a positive meeting. We will therefore go on working along those lines. Now talking about the so-called Blairtime format is inappropriate. I think everybody will understand, and knows, that the Franco-German relationship is very specific, that it is not something that you could transpose or export in the short term, it is a very — how shall I put it — intense relationship that is illustrated by regular contacts, not only in the Blairtime format. We have, dare I say it, almost daily contacts between government officials and public officials between France and Germany, so I don't think it is quite the right example. However, I think coordinating views between France, Britain and Germany, and in due course expanding that to all our colleagues is very positive, and again I would like to thank the Chancellor for taking such an initiative.

Q. Federal Chancellor, did you also talk about how to institutionalise these considerations, how to find an institutional guarantee so to speak, this idea of a Super Commissioner we read about?

CHANCELLOR SCHROEDER: Well I wouldn't use that term of a Super Commissioner really, but in the letter that will be distributed to you at the end of this press conference there will be a proposal in this direction, we not only talked about it, we also took a common decision on this.

Q. I wonder if we could slightly anticipate your next session? One of the reasons why perhaps people are suspicious about the formation of a triumvirate directorate if you like is because of the breakdown which there was in December with no constitution for the future of an enlarged Europe. I wonder what each of your thoughts are, whether you agree on the way ahead on that, whether you think it is an urgent priority to get the new constitution, or perhaps it should be put aside until at least after the British general election?

PRIME MINISTER: I am sure we will continue to work on the European constitution and the Irish Presidency is, as you know, having a series of discussions with people at the moment about it. If I can just say a word though about this, what you were saying about the three countries co-operating together. There will be all sorts of different relationships in Europe and I totally agree with what President Chirac has just said about the French-German relationship, that is a very special specific relationship for France and Germany. We came together however as three counties, and let's be frank about this, we came together after a very difficult period in international relations when we were on different sides of a particular issue, but we came together and worked at European defence in a way that in the end was to the advantage of all of Europe. When the three Foreign Ministers from our countries engaged with Iran, the result was of enormous benefit, not just to Europe in this instance but to the wider world, and if these countries, which comprise almost half the population in Europe, but actually over half the wealth of Europe that is generated by Europe, if we can come to clear agreement on the way forward to make our economies work better for the future, that is a good thing for our three countries, but also it is a good thing for Europe, and there shouldn't be any, in my view, sensitivity about this or any sense of exclusivity, people will continue to work in different formats, the French-German relationship will continue to be an immensely strong relationship, I happen to think that is a good thing for Europe too. But we are going to be finding, and should be finding, ways the whole time of making Europe work more effectively for our people, that is what this whole exercise is about. As I said a moment or two ago, it shouldn't be as a piece simply of politics or diplomacy, it has got to result in specific things that do good for people in Europe. That is what people want to hear, they want to hear what are we going to do to protect them in a very difficult changing world with the challenge of globalisation there, they want to know we are working together to do that, and that is what this is about and I don't think we need be apologetic in any shape or form about it, or defensive about different relationships. We will all carry on working in our different ways with different relationships, but I think just as we did with defence, so that we can do with the question of economic reform, we can do good for our own countries but also for Europe.

Q. A question concerning international politics directed to all of you. Did you touch upon the issue of an arms embargo towards China, have you reached agreement there?

CHANCELLOR SCHROEDER: This subject has not yet been raised, but I believe that it will be raised later on today during dinner where we have the opportunity to talk about European issues, again without taking any formal decisions here, it will no doubt play a part there. The position on this question, and I think the position of the French President and my position on this issue, it is clear that position has not changed.

OFFICIAL: Thank you Federal Chancellor. Mr President, Mr Prime Minister, we will now sign the joint letter of the Federal Chancellor, the President, the Prime Minister.

Press Briefing

Then there is another variety called a press / media briefing. Here is one from the White House:

16 April 2004

Press Briefing by Scott McClellan
The James S. Brady Briefing Room

2:41 P.M. EDT

SCOTT MCCLELLAN: Good afternoon, everybody, and 'welcome' to our new White House correspondents. I will go straight to your questions at this point.

Q. Scott, can I try you again on this intelligence post? Is it fair to say this idea of creating a new director of national intelligence is being discussed — aside from the 9/11 Commission?

SCOTT MCCLELLAN: Steve, I think that is premature to start making that suggestion at this point. The President made it very clear that he wants to look at other ways we might be able to reform and revamp our intelligence services, beyond the significant steps that we are already — that we have already taken in the aftermath of September 11th.

Remember, in the wake of that terrible day the President made a number of significant changes in the way we protect the homeland. He created the Department of Homeland Security. We worked to create to Terrorist Threat Integration Center. That was very important to making sure that we improved our intelligence gathering capability and our intelligence sharing capability. And, most importantly, he was taking the offensive and taking the fight to the enemy.

So we have made significant changes in the aftermath of September 11th. But we always should be looking at what more can we do to better protect the American people. And the President very much looks forward to the recommendations from the September 11th Commission and from the Silberman Commission, which is focusing broadly on our intelligence capabilities related to weapons of mass destruction.

Q. I think there had been some talk on the Hill about creating a domestic intelligence agency — maybe Senator Edwards or some others are backing that idea. Is that a good idea?

SCOTT MCCLELLAN: I think it's just premature to get into what specific steps we may want to look at. Let's let the commissions do their work. They are carrying out very important work that can help us better prepare in the future. Certainly, we have already taken a number of steps to make sure that we are prepared to prevent attacks and respond to attacks if they may come.

Most importantly, the — well, the number one thing we can do to prevent these attacks from happening in the first place is take the fight to the enemy and win the war on terrorism. We have many dangerous threats in this day and age, and we should always be looking at ways we can better protect the American people.

Q. Scott, the President said he couldn't recall whether it was in November 2001 when he asked Secretary Rumsfeld to draw up war plans for Iraq, and he said he was going to check and try to refresh his memory. Do you know whether it was — that's the correct date, November?

SCOTT MCCLELLAN: First of all, I think what he was referring to was the September time period in the immediate aftermath of the September 11th attacks, and when he was meeting with his national security team. And at that point in September, all our focus was on Afghanistan and removing the Taliban regime from power and taking away the safe harbour for Al-Qaeda that existed in Afghanistan.

Certainly, late November it was becoming increasingly clear what direction things were headed in Afghanistan. It was clear that the Taliban was no longer going to have a hold on Afghanistan. We began combat operations in Afghanistan in the earlier period of October, and by November and early December things were winding down. And the President did talk to Secretary Rumsfeld about Iraq. But there is a difference between planning and making a decision.

Q. So he did ask him to draw up invasion plans in November of 2001?

SCOTT MCCLELLAN: You're talking about the late period of November, when things were winding down in Afghanistan. He did talk to Secretary Rumsfeld about planning related to Iraq.

And the question and answers continued the last being:

Q. It's someone who was previously taken hostage and now there's apparently a video of it.

SCOTT MCCLELLAN: And I don't have any confirmation on that, nor am I aware of any such.

Q. Thank you.

SCOTT MCCLELLAN: Thanks.

END 3:09 P.M. EDT

It is a question and answer session like the press conference, but the difference is that here the Press Secretary is briefing the press and not the President. The number of media persons present is usually less than at a press conference. The briefing is also less formal than the press conference. In this example there is no statement and just after the welcome the questions start. But if the spokesperson or the official briefing the press has something to say he can make a statement or announcement in the beginning. Many institutions have regular press briefings on a time fixed everyday or every working day and if there is no briefing then the correspondents covering that beat are informed. In the above example the first question indicates continuity from an earlier briefing by the same person. 'Scott, can I try you again on this intelligence post? Is it fair to say this idea of creating a new director of national intelligence is being discussed — aside from the 9/11 Commission?'

The White House also uses another term 'press gaggle'. It is used for briefings that are on record, but where videography is not allowed but transcripts are made available. The nickname stems from the idea that these more freewheeling press sessions, where the talk is much more rapid and free-form, are like a 'gaggle of geese' honking.

Here is a typical press briefing of Indian External Affairs Ministry spokesman Navtej Sarna on 29 May 2006:

Official Spokesperson: To begin with, we have two press releases. One is on the meeting of the Foreign Ministers of TEAM-9 in Accra where the Indian delegation was led by Shri Anand Sharma. The second is the press release on Minister of State Shri E. Ahamed's visit to Laos for the 5th India-Lao Joint Commission meeting in Vientiane. Both press releases are available on the website.

We had briefed you last week on the release of Pakistani fishermen through the Attari-Wagah border which was scheduled for today. I understand that this has now been done. Fifty-nine Pakistani prisoners have gone back to Pakistan. We have also been informed by Pakistan that they would be releasing 71 Indian fishermen through Wagah.

Arrangements are being made to receive these fishermen — this is expected to be done tomorrow — and send them to Gujarat. We have requested Pakistan to release the other 242 Indian fishermen whose nationality has been confirmed. We are also expediting the confirmation of nationality of the remaining 192 Indian fishermen in Pakistani custody. President Dr A.P.J. Abdul Kalam and Prime Minister Dr Manmohan Singh have sent messages of condolences to the President of Indonesia Dr Susilo Yudhoyono on the tragic loss of life and damage to property resulting from the disastrous earthquake that struck Yogyakarta and the adjacent areas in Indonesia.

The Government of India has, in keeping with the friendly relations with Indonesia, dispatched humanitarian relief material consisting of tents, blankets, medicines, milk powder and rice. An IAF IL-76 aircraft carrying the relief supplies is departing for Jakarta today. A naval vessel, INS Rajput will be reaching Jakarta port tomorrow with a medical team and additional relief supplies. We remain ready to provide any further assistance that may be required in the aftermath of this tragic natural calamity.

Q. India-Pakistan talks are taking place in Islamabad. Do you have something?

Official Spokesperson: After the talks . . . I can also tell you the talks between the Culture Secretaries are going to take place in Delhi on 1 and 2 June. The two delegations will be led by Mr Badal Das on the Indian side and Mr Jalil

Abbas, Secretary, Ministry of Culture, Government of Pakistan.

Q. On Saturday Mr Eric Solheim said that Norway has been passing messages from India to the LTTE that they should return to the peace process. I wonder whether you can confirm this?

Official Spokesperson: As you know, we have, for several years, been sharing our assessments with the Norwegians about the developments in Sri Lanka and the peace process. This does not amount to sending any messages to the LTTE or any other party. The Norwegian Minister for International Development and Chief Negotiator for Sri Lankan Peace Process, Mr Erik Solheim, visited Delhi on 27 May 2006. He met NSA and other officials of the GOI. The visit was part of the traditional briefing by Norway to GOI about the delicately-poised peace process in Sri Lanka. Norway is continuing in its efforts to bring both parties to the table for a political dialogue. We support Norway in its efforts and express the hope that talks can resume at the earliest. We conveyed to Mr Solheim our well-known view that there must be a peaceful, negotiated settlement that is acceptable to all sections of Sri Lankan society which preserves the unity, sovereignty and territorial integrity of Sri Lanka.

I can add that the Co-Chairs meeting i.e., US, EU, Japan and Norway is scheduled to take place in Tokyo on 30 May 2006. As in the past, a representative of the Indian Embassy in Tokyo will receive a briefing after the Co-Chairs meeting.

Q. Any word on the NSG plenary which is supposed to take place today? Will there be any observer from the Indian side?

Official Spokesperson: Not to my knowledge, but what happens in the meeting we will see.

Q. Two officials from the American consulate in Mumbai met the Chattisgarh government and apparently offered help in dealing with Maoist insurgency there. Can Americans offer such help? What is the . . .

Official Spokesperson: Well, I understand prominent sections of the press, including IANS, have already carried a denial. I do know that this question has been raised by the MEA with the US Embassy whether there was any such offer and I understand that the MEA has been told that no such offer was made. Sections of the press have already carried something — part of it — issued by the US Embassy.

Q. In the talks between Culture Secretaries would a formal permission for Bollywood films by Pakistan be taken up?

Official Spokesperson: In the talks on culture and friendly exchanges one of the possible CBMs has always been greater freedom for Indian programmes and Indian films to be shown in Pakistan. Whether or not it comes up in these two days I cannot guess, but certainly it is one of the issues which we have been pointing to as one which has the potential of strengthening people-to-people contacts.

Q. There are reports that PM might visit Nankana Sahib . . .

Official Spokesperson: I have no information. Thank you.

In press briefings, correspondents regularly covering the organization or department usually take part. They know the rules of the game. However, some organizations put this information on their websites, for example the US State Department.

The State Department Spokesman, or the alternate, generally briefs the State Department press corps ON THE RECORD, ON CAMERA each workday afternoon in the Carl T. Rowan Press Briefing Room, room 2209 in the Harry S. Truman building of the US Department of State. A mult box[6] is available. While most video camera positions on the risers are assigned, two unassigned positions are available on a first-come, first-serve basis. TV lighting is available. The official transcript of the briefing is posted on the Department's website later that day. Reporters who wish to attend can confirm that a briefing will be held and at what time through the Daily Appointment Schedule (provided on the website). Special Press Briefings are announced in the Daily Appointment Schedule. Camera set-up times and final access time for press are included, as are pick-up times for events that require an escort to and from the site. Transcripts of on-the-record briefings are released on the day of the briefing.

Checklist

Even in the Government the workhorse is a briefing, press conferences are used less, in the corporate world it is more so. When public relations practitioners remember to look at their goals and interests through the eyes of the media and the media's audiences, and when they use these insights to relate to the media people with whom they work, they are more successful. Here is a checklist for success:

6. A mult box is a distribution amplifier which has multiple connections for reporters to connect their voice or video recorders to. The major benefit is that members of the press do not have to put their microphones on the podium to get a good audio signal.

Decide between a conference and a briefing

A Press Conference is a big show. Sometimes if not the press release a press briefing can do the job. It has to have real news value. Even the President of the United States uses other options. But if it is finally decided to hold a press conference then do it well.

Time the trailing announcements and invitation ring-rounds well

The press conference should be timed to ensure best possible news coverage. For press conferences the invitation ring-round must be in good time. It is a chance to stimulate constructive background filming by TV news and to set the context of the announcement for people unfamiliar with the subject. Reactions to the invitation and subject matter should help inform the content of the press pack. Trailing announcements during the previous weekend can also help set the context and stimulate interest.

Consider when you are going to hold the press conference and accordingly build interest in the media. Make some announcements that lead to the big event. Carefully decide who all are invited depending on the subject. Just an invitation is not enough. Ring up to find out who is coming, your persuasive skills may be required to enthuse some who you think are important for you. Also check up if there are other events on the same time that may require the correspondents you have invited. Avoid a clash of time, if the competition is significant from news angle.

Encourage relevant interest groups that support the announcement to endorse it publicly

If the announcement is significant, then find out relevant

interest groups who can support it publicly. These groups may not be part of your show but could separately communicate to media their support to the announcement.

Prepare press packs; consider a video news release

A properly prepared written briefing is essential. For a major announcement, journalists should be given the main message in a news release; background material; a chronology of former references; a copy of any associated publications; and graphical and/or tabular material in hard copy and on disk if possible. They should have a reasonable opportunity to read the material before the briefing or conference, but copies of any opening statement should be issued at the end of the discussion.

To use a press conference effectively it is essential that a proper pack be prepared containing enough background material. Besides printed matter like annual reports, brochures, FAQs, etc., a press release containing the main announcement should also be given in the press pack. This will most likely be the main source when the journalists starts working on the story. Copies on disk of graphical or tabular material may be useful in a press pack.

For those television journalists who failed to reach with the camera team, a video news release of the press conference may be very useful. It should be considered with cost benefit considerations.

Provide backdrops, lectern, voice reinforcement and lighting

Press conferences today mean the presence of television, radio, press photographers and each of them have to be provided for. Good visual backdrops illustrating the issues, or branding is essential for television, a lectern with branding for the opening statement is useful. Take care to provide space for news photographers in the front and rear staging for TV camera crews. A broadcast-quality voice-reinforcement system, with distribution amplifier facilities is necessary for broadcasters. For press conference venues these days you should have installed TV lighting to avoid crews cluttering up the room with their own lights. A computer-driven presentation system (for example PowerPoint) to highlight main themes is useful. Arrangements should be made for parking broadcasting vans nearby.

Provide regionalized material, briefings, interviews

If the announcement has a regional impact, it is advisable that those correspondents who represent media of specific regions be provided regionalized material. After the event specialized briefings or interviews can be very effective. Television teams sometimes insist on separate bites to be exclusive. Arrange interview rooms for broadcasters which may be used just after the conference. Sometimes separate briefings are useful to editorial writers, if the announcement is very significant. It can be arranged just after the press conference.

Ensure policy / technical officials are on hand to help with detail

Policy and other relevant specialist officials should be on hand during and after the conference or briefing to help with detail. While the press conference is addressed by the top man, a lot of homework should be done before the event, it is advisable that those officials who deal with the details should be at hand with the details. It is useful if a tricky question is asked, this official can take the floor with details.

Monitor news media to determine the need for follow through

The whole range of news programmes and bulletins immediately after the event should be monitored to determine the need for follow through. Short-term tracking of coverage is necessary to ensure that the case is accurately reported and inaccuracy rebutted. After the event it is essential to monitor the content of media resulting from it. If there are any distortions or mistakes, which need correction, immediate effort will be required. In the wake of a major announcement it is often helpful to have somebody stationed in the press office to help with telephone enquiries. Also quickly put all relevant material on the department or corporate website.

Embargoes

It is essential to deal with the point of embargo. Sometimes it is helpful to issue publications to journalists and/or hold press events under embargo. The key consideration in these days of 24-hour news and heavy competitive pressure is to keep the embargoes short.

Key components of both, press briefings and press conferences include high-quality written material, a constructive opportunity for questioning, facilities for broadcast interviews, and good backgrounds for photography. Attention should also be paid to ensure that relevant interest groups are briefed on the announcement. If they support it, they should be encouraged to endorse it publicly.

Background Briefings

Sometimes separate background briefings can also be arranged with officials. Usually terms need to be agreed before the briefing takes place. For example, sometimes it is agreed that quotes should be attributed to the unnamed spokesperson, not to the official. These briefings are used to give invited journalists more background details on what the department / company is doing and often offer them an opportunity to question senior officials on an un-attributable basis.

Digital Public Relations

When the current century began it was called the Internet Century. Despite the dot-com bust the Internet has emerged as the most powerful communication medium in the world and has revolutionized how people communicate, think, learn, behave, and conduct business. PR professionals have to proactively tap the Internet strategically or tactically. Every company and government department is going online and has a website. Today, there are many progressive leaders in the PR profession innovating in the online PR field or cyber PR. Some new digital tools in their online PR include e-mail pitching, online newsrooms, webcasts, online contests, and discussion group monitoring and participation. As time passes and the Web evolves further, a whole new host of strategies and tactics will materialize. For example, e-mail, wireless, and instant messaging, all using an Internet protocol, will change the online PR game as they evolve in popular use and as technology matures.

The Internet is an international network of interconnected computers that enables millions of people to communicate with one another in 'cyberspace' (the invisible space in which the Internet operates) and to access vast amounts of information from around the world. Unlike online services, which are centrally controlled, the Internet is decentralized by design. Each Internet computer, called a host, is independent. Its operators can choose which Internet services to use and which local services to make available to the global Internet community. There are a variety of ways to access the Internet. Most online services, such as America Online offer access to some Internet services. It is also possible to gain access through a commercial Internet Service Provider (ISP).

The Internet is at once a world-wide broadcasting capability, a mechanism for information dissemination, and a medium for collaboration and interaction between individuals and their computers without regard for geographic location. The invention of the telegraph, telephone, radio, and computer set the stage for this unprecedented integration of capabilities. The Internet represents one of the most successful examples of the benefits of sustained investment and commitment to research and development of information infrastructure.

The Internet and the Web are not synonymous. The *Internet* is a massive network of networks, a networking infrastructure. It connects millions of computers together globally, forming a network in which any computer can communicate with any other computer as long as they are both connected to the Internet.

Information that travels over the Internet does so via a variety of computer languages known as protocols.

The *World Wide Web*, or simply the *Web*, is a way of accessing information over the Internet. It is an information-sharing model that is built on top of the Internet. The *HyperText Transfer Protocol* (HTTP) is the method used to make hypertext documents readable on the Web. Web servers and clients (user computers) communicate with each other using HTTP, and don't require users to know anything about its intricacies. Users access Web documents called Web pages that are linked to each other via hyperlinks using programmes called browsers, such as Internet Explorer, Netscape, Opera, Firefox amongst others. Web documents can contain graphics, sounds, text and video.

The Web is just one of the ways that information can be disseminated over the Internet. The Internet, not the Web, is also used for e-mail, which relies on *Simple Mail Transfer Protocol* (SMTP). This protocol tells each system how mail messages are to be formed for transmission between two computers. So the Web is just a portion of the Internet, but the two terms are not synonymous and should not be confused.

The Beginnings

In 1957 USSR launched Sputnik, the first artificial earth satellite. In response, the US formed the Advanced Research Projects Agency (ARPA) the following year, within the Department of Defense (DoD) to establish an American lead in science and technology applicable to the military. ARPA changed its name to Defense Advanced Research Projects Agency (DARPA) in 1971, then back to ARPA in 1993, and back to DARPA in 1996.

The first recorded description of interactions that could be enabled through networking was a series of memos written by J.C.R. Licklider of the Massachusetts Institute of Technology (MIT) in August 1962 discussing his 'Galactic Network' concept. He envisioned a globally interconnected set of computers through which everyone could quickly access data and programmes from any site. Licklider was the first head of the computer research programme at DARPA, starting in October

1962. Leonard Kleinrock at MIT published the first paper on packet switching in July 1961 and the first book on the subject in 1964. Kleinrock convinced MIT researcher Lawrence G. Roberts of the theoretical feasibility of communications using packets rather than circuits, which was a major step along the path towards computer networking. The other key step was to make the computers talk together. To explore this, Roberts working with Thomas Merrill in 1965, connected the TX-2 computer in Massachusetts to the Q-32 in California over a low speed dial-up telephone line. The result of this experiment was the realization that time-shared computers could work well together, running programmes and retrieving data as necessary on the remote machine, but that the circuit switched telephone system was totally inadequate for the job.

ARPANET

In late 1966 Roberts went to DARPA to develop the computer network concept and quickly put together his plan for the ARPANET, publishing it in 1967.

At the conference where he presented the paper, there was also a paper on a packet network concept from the UK by Donald Davies and Roger Scantlebury of National Physical Laboratories (NPL). Scantlebury told Roberts about the NPL work as well as that of Paul Baran and others at RAND.

The RAND group had written a paper on packet switching networks for secure voice in the military in 1964.

It happened that the work at MIT (1961–1967), at RAND (1962–1965), and at NPL (1964–1967) had all proceeded in parallel without any of the researchers knowing about the others work. The word 'packet' was adopted from the work at NPL and the proposed line speed to be used in the ARPANET design was upgraded from 2.4 Kbps (Kilo bits per second) to 50 Kbps. By the end of 1969, four host computers were connected together into the initial ARPANET, and the budding Internet was off the ground. In December 1970 the Network Working Group (NWG) working under S. Crocker finished the initial ARPANET Host-to-Host protocol, called the Network Control Protocol (NCP). In October 1972 Kahn organized a large, very successful demonstration of the ARPANET at the International Computer Communication Conference (ICCC). This was the first public demonstration of this new network technology to the public.

Electronic Mail (e-mail)

It was also in 1972 that the initial 'hot' application, electronic mail, was introduced. In March, Ray Tomlinson at BBN Technologies wrote the basic e-mail message send-and-read software, motivated by the need of the ARPANET developers for an easy coordination mechanism. In July, Roberts expanded its utility by writing the first e-mail utility programme to list, selectively read, file, forward, and respond to messages. From there e-mail took off as the largest network application for over a decade.

TCP/IP

The idea of open-architecture networking was first introduced by Kahn shortly after having arrived at DARPA in 1972. Kahn decided to develop a new version of the protocol which could meet the needs of an open-architecture network environment. This protocol would eventually be called the Transmission Control Protocol/Internet Protocol (TCP/IP). In the spring of

1973, after starting the internetting effort, he asked Vint Cerf (then at Stanford) to work with him on the detailed design of the protocol. Cerf had been intimately involved in the original NCP design and development and already had the knowledge about interfacing to existing operating systems. So armed with Kahn's architectural approach to the communications side and with Cerf's NCP experience, they teamed up to spell out the details of what became TCP/IP.

In 1976, Kleinrock published the first book on the ARPANET. It included an emphasis on the complexity of protocols and the pitfalls they often introduce. In March 1978 the original TCP was split into two protocols, the simple IP which provided only for addressing and forwarding of individual packets, and the separate TCP, which was concerned with service features such as flow control and recovery from lost packets. TCP/IP was adopted as a defence standard in 1980. The transition of the ARPANET host protocol from NCP to TCP/IP became effective as of 1 January 1983.

DNS

Widespread development of LANs (Local Area Networks), PCs and workstations in the 1980s allowed the nascent Internet to flourish. Originally, there were a fairly limited number of hosts, so it was feasible to maintain a single table of all the hosts and their associated names and addresses. The shift to having a large number of independently managed networks (e.g. LANs) meant that having a single table of hosts was no longer feasible, and the Domain Name System (DNS) was invented by Paul Mockapetris of the Information Sciences Institute of the University of Southern California (USC/ISI) in (1984) The DNS permitted a scalable distributed mechanism for resolving hierarchical host names (e.g. www.acm.org) into an Internet address.

Backbone

In 1986, the US National Science Foundation (NSF) initiated the development of the NSFNET which, today, provides a major backbone communication service for the Internet. With its 45 megabit per second facilities, the NSFNET carries to the order of 12 billion packets per month between the networks it links. The National Aeronautics and Space Administration (NASA) and the US Department of Energy contributed additional backbone facilities in the form of the NSINET and ESNET respectively.

In Europe, major international backbones such as NORDUNET and others provide connectivity to over one hundred thousand computers on a large number of networks. Commercial network providers in the US and Europe are beginning to offer Internet backbone and access support on a competitive basis to any interested parties.

Tim Berners-Lee

In 1989 Tim Berners-Lee proposed a global hypertext project, to be known as the World Wide Web. Based on the earlier 'Enquire' work, it was designed to allow people to work together by combining their knowledge in a web of hypertext documents. He wrote the first World Wide Web server, *'httpd'*, and first client, *'WorldWideWeb'* a what-you-see-is-what-you-get hypertext browser/editor which ran in the NeXTStep environment. This work was started in October 1990, and the programme 'WorldWideWeb' first made available within CERN in December, and on the Internet at large in the summer of 1991.

Through 1991 and 1993, Tim continued working on the design of the Web, coordinating feedback from users across the Internet. In 1994, Tim founded the World Wide Web Consortium at the Laboratory for Computer Science (LCS) at the MIT. Since that time he has served as the Director of the World Wide Web Consortium which coordinates Web development worldwide, with teams at MIT, at the Institut National de Recherche en Informatique et Automatique (INRIA) in France, and at Keio University in Japan. The Consortium's goal was to lead the Web to its full potential, ensuring its stability through rapid evolution and transformations of its usage. In 1999, he became the first holder of the 3Com Founders chair at LCS. The Lab merged with the AI lab to become 'CSAIL', the Computer Science and Artificial Intelligence Laboratory at MIT.

What is a Website?

A website is an electronic 'piece of information' that is hosted on a computer that is permanently connected to the Internet, allowing 'browsers' to view that information. Produced in full colour, it can have animation on it, pictures, products, you can even buy items directly from it. There is virtually no limit to what can be displayed on a website but it is often at the expense of 'download time' (i.e., the more a website displays, the longer it will take to appear on a viewers screen).

Domain Name

A domain name is a way to identify and locate computers and resources connected to the Internet. No two organizations can have the same domain name. Every company or organization that wants to be on the Internet will register a domain name for use as their online identity or name that clients (customers, all Internet users) will use to access online services such as the organization's website or e-mail system.

Server

A server is the name given to a computer that is permanently connected to the Internet for the purpose of displaying websites. One thing to be aware of is that you need the server to be fast and to have a high speed telecommunications connection so that your website will download quickly and appear on the viewers screen as quickly as possible.

Web Hosting

The term Web Hosting means that looking after or 'hosting' your website on a computer or 'server' that is permanently connected to the Internet. This is necessary in order for people to be able view your website. You need it to be hosted on a fast, efficient server.

Maintenance of Website

The maintenance of a website can be split into two areas: (a) keeping the contents of website accurate and up to date, (b) keeping it up to date from a technical point of view. To find something on the Internet, often people will type their enquiry into a search engine to try and locate it. Once a website has been built and uploaded to the Internet, submit it to the major search engines: Yahoo, Excite, Infoseek, Alta Vista, Google, Dmoz, Hotbot, Fast, Ask, Mamma, MSN, etc.

Reading is Dominant

People spend most of their time on the Web reading. They read a web page (it is called a 'page').They read search results. They read their way through a purchase process. They read a discussion forum. They read their way through 'chat'. They read the instructions that allow them to download audio and video.

Web-design Function

If reading is the primary activity on the Web, then readability is a primary function of web design. Another primary activity on the Web is search and navigation. Therefore, the organization of content to make it easily searchable and navigable is a primary function of web design.

The online reader

- Gathers content: They know broadly what they are looking for but not exactly.
- Scan reads: They are practical, impatient, in a hurry.
- Is sceptical and suspicious: They know there's an awful lot of junk on the Web.
- Is conservative: Once they find a website they like, they'll stick with it.

If the fundamental activity that people carry out on the Web is to read, then any design must make sure that it is as easy as possible to read (black text on white background, reasonable font sizes, and so on).

Focus and Clarity

What makes a great website is focus and clarity of purpose. A great website is unpretentious. It doesn't pretend to be what it is not. It never wastes your time because it always gets to the point. A great website helps you to act.

Look versus Text

The look 'n' feel of your website is important. However, it is the text-based content which is of prime importance. In most commercial websites, the role of the traditional graphic designer is relatively minor. The role of the information architect is central. The role of the editor and author is critical.

Key Questions

If you want to know if your website is well designed, ask yourself the following questions:

- How quickly does it download?
- How easy is it to navigate?
- How well does the search work?
- How readable is the content?

The Brochure Mindset

Too many websites are still being designed as if they were some once-off brochure. It was natural with the first websites. The brochure mindset fundamentally misses the point of what a website is for. A website should take you beyond brochure-speak.

Awful Websites

Many website designers tend to design awful websites because they are obsessed with getting attention. When someone comes to your website, you have already got their attention. They want details. They want facts. The thing they value most is their time. So don't waste it.

Simplicity

The days of the Web as a frontier for pioneers are over. In a growing number of countries, the Web reflects the society at large. Ebay, AOL and Yahoo have long designed websites that are simple and easy-to-use. Web design needs to focus on ordinary people who are relatively unfamiliar with the

Internet. Simplicity of design is the number one characteristic of website design that works.

What People Want

People who use the Web want pages that download quickly. They want websites that are full of useful information. They want to be able to customize these websites so that they can get to the information they want as quickly as possible. Some websites still don't get it. They behave as if broadband had already arrived, delivering large graphics, video, audio and animation. The reality is that for the average consumer broadband access is far away, and they are still accessing the Web over a 56 KB modem.

Three Columns

A website requires a flexible, rather than a fixed design. The three-column layout is a flexible design. The left column contains navigation, the centre contains key messages, the right contains features. The web page can easily stretch up and down depending on what content is required at any particular point in time. A great many websites now use the three-column layout. Black text on a white background dominates. Where is all the multimedia? We saw more websites offering video in 1999 than today. Why? Because it didn't work.

Directory

The Web is all about publishing content in an organized manner. All the great websites are driven by great directories that allow people to quickly find the content they want. Those websites that fail are those that frustrate the reader. They don't classify their content well. Their search doesn't work well. Their navigation is poor. Their pages are full of big graphics that take ages to download.

Boring?

Classification (directory) design is the science of organizing large quantities of content in an efficient and intuitive manner so that people can find what they're looking for quickly. Directories will always have some sort of an A to Z classification structure. The reason that people will never get bored with an A to Z directory design is the same reason they never get bored with street sign design. The classification system is not what interests the reader; it's the content that the classification holds that's of interest.

Road-signs?

People see the Web as one huge place. What they learn through navigating around one website, they like to bring with them to another website. The original design for hypertext was blue for un-clicked and purple for clicked. People like it because they're used to it. So when they see a blue link, they know that's a part of the website they haven't been to. When they see a purple link, they know that's a part of the website they have visited. Changing the colour of the hyperlinks just confuses people. It's like having red and green traffic signals in one part of town, and orange and yellow in another.

Newspapers and the Web

If we were to lay out the front pages of ten of the world's biggest-selling broadsheet newspapers in a row, they would be almost identical from a layout point of view. There would be a masthead, a lead story, several smaller stories, a large picture, some features running across the top, and perhaps an ad near the bottom.

What makes newspapers different is not their layout. The

difference is in the content. So too should it be on a website. The Web is an even more limited design environment than a newspaper. It's harder to read from a screen than from paper. The average screen page is much smaller than a newspaper page.

In theory, you can have audio, video, and animation, but bandwidth restrictions severely limit these multimedia options. Within this limited layout environment, a small number of layout conventions are emerging.

Emerging Web Conventions

Global navigation: This relates to a small selection of essential links that are presented on every page. This global navigation begins with a link to 'Home'.

Masthead: This is the top-of page area. It contains a logo on the left and a search box on the right or on the left, directly underneath the logo. Mastheads are getting very slim to maximize the amount of space for the presentation of content.

Three-column layout: Designers have found that the optimal way to lay out the maximum quantity of content and navigation with the maximum readability is the three-column approach. The left column contains navigation, the middle recent content, the right features.

Footer: Every page should have a footer containing global navigation, contact details, copyright and privacy links.

Iterative Design

Iterative design is a popular approach to website design. It generally involves getting something up quickly, analysing the results and making improvements based on that analysis. This can make sense in an environment that little is understood about. That is no longer the case with the Web.

Truly 'Cool'

An essential focus of web design is the effective communication of text-based content. Web design that is truly 'cool' seeks to organize and communicate information in innovative and useful ways. Quality web design is concerned with getting the right content to the right person at the right time and at the right cost.

Re-design?

The desire to 're-design' your website just because it looks 'out-of-date' may not simply be unnecessary but may also be counterproductive. Your most loyal customers will have got used to the layout and structure of your website. Launching a major new design risks confusing and alienating them.

Web design is primarily concerned with the organization and presentation of text-based content. This requires metadata, classification, navigation, search, layout and graphic design skills.

Metadata

Metadata is 'data about data'. For example, a library catalogue is metadata, since it describes publications or specifically in the context of this specification 'data describing Web resources'. The distinction between 'data' and 'metadata' is not an absolute one; it is a distinction created primarily by a particular application, and many times the same resource will be interpreted in both ways simultaneously. Examples of metadata that will be exchanged using RDF include 'Title', 'Author' (or 'Creator'), 'Publisher', and 'Format'.

The Resource Description Framework (RDF) as its name

implies, is a framework for describing and interchanging metadata. RDF provides interoperability between applications that exchange machine-understandable information on the Web. RDF emphasizes facilities to enable automated processing of Web resources.

Metadata is the 'who, what, where, when, and how' of a particular website. Think about it as an extension of grammar. Metadata is about classifying your content in a directory structure that will help the reader navigate to it easily. Metadata also collects keywords and other information on your content such as author name and date of publication. This sort of information makes the search of your website much more efficient.

Without quality metadata, you are lost on the Web. Metadata makes it possible to create quality navigation and search, which are the foundations on which all websites are built. Navigation deals with how readers move through a website, search is how readers search for something specific. The larger the website gets, the more critical navigation and search become. This is where the complexity and elegance of web design comes into play.

Navigation and Search

Navigation design is about providing a variety of logical paths through the content, such as allowing the reader to navigate by geographic sector or by subject matter. It's about letting the reader know where they are (by using prominent section headings), where they've been (by using correctly coloured hyperlinks), and where they're going (by using self-explanatory classification names) at all times.

Navigation is about following web convention — going with what the reader is familiar with — such as having the

'Home' link as the first link on your global navigation running across every page on the site. Designing a quality search is about making sure that you have quality metadata for every web page so that search can be at its most efficient. It's also about having a search box on every page of your website. Don't hide your search behind a link.

DCMI

The Dublin Core Metadata Initiative (DCMI) is an organization dedicated to promoting the widespread adoption of interoperable metadata standards and developing specialized metadata vocabularies for describing resources that enable more intelligent information discovery systems.

The original workshop for the Initiative was held in Dublin, Ohio in 1995. Hence the term 'Dublin Core' in the name of the Initiative. Since that time there have been a total of eleven workshops held in England, Australia, Finland, Germany, Canada, Japan, United States, China and Spain.

Design for People

A great number of the people who design for the Web think that the average person who uses the Web is like them. What this means is that far too many websites are designed by designers for designers. The same problem has afflicted poetry over the last half a century.

We live in a world where change and complexity are forced on us at every turn. The world is hitting back. People are yearning for simplicity. People are tired of technology that constantly overcomplicates things, that is poorly designed and that is full of bugs.

If you were to place the world's 100 biggest selling English-language newspapers in a row, you would find no more than

2–3 layouts for the front page. There are only so many ways to properly lay out content, whether in a newspaper or on the Web.

Saving Time

Current web design is framed by the central concern of saving time. The online reader belongs to the time-starved generation and any design which wastes their time risks losing them.

Media Friendly Websites

Though we have a wider variety of avenues to reach our target audience than ever before, the increase in messages each individual is receiving is resulting in a logjam in our relationship-building efforts. The media, often frustrated with today's information overload from PR professionals, are looking for one-stop sources that can deliver comprehensive information on demand. To this end, corporate websites can be powerful communication tools if optimally constructed.

As the corporate website becomes the de facto centre of communications efforts, PR practitioners should make sure that their company's site effectively supports the media relations.

Here are some strategies to ensure a media friendly website:

Make sure the Press can find your site

If possible, a website name should be the company or organization's name followed by ' com' or '.org'. Try to register all possible names for your company. Make sure your meta tags include critical key words for your organization, and ensure that your home page title includes both your company name and major category. For example, the page title for Company X, which is an accounts software vendor, might read: 'Company X: Delivers Accounts Software Solutions to Businesses Worldwide'. In addition, include your website address on everything — business cards, product literature, press releases, e-mail signatures, etc.

Organize site information based on the tasks of your visitors

Reporters will turn to your site if they find information quickly and easily. Provide a link directly from the home page entitled 'Press / Media Room' which will lead to media contacts, press releases, success stories, and a calendar of the organization's upcoming events.

Keep it simple

The home page should be simple, composed of a brief explanation of the organization (and a telephone number) with clearly labelled section headings, such as, 'About the Company', 'History', 'Products and Services', 'Contact Information', 'Press Room', and 'Site Map'. These will provide a sufficient starting point for website users.

Serve as an information resource

Include articles of information written by company executives and industry analysts, links to research on your industry, as well as links to appropriate industry organizations. Offer value-added content beyond marketing rhetoric.

Include downloadable artwork

Photographs can increase the amount of space devoted to your story and add an element of visual interest, increasing retention. Include product shots, action-based artwork to accompany success stories, as well as your company logo and photographs of key company executives.

Enable interaction

When appropriate, include a product demonstration. Perhaps a video clip of a customer talking about the results they have achieved with your product, or a 'request an interview/request a product to review' form. Include key questions on the form such as the outlet, topic of discussion and questions, familiarity with the company, and if they have a specific individual with whom they would like to speak.

Include a press guest book

Invite reporters to register online to be included on the press list. Keep the request form brief to encourage reporters to take the time to reply: Include fields for name, outlet, phone, fax, and e-mail.

Revise and refresh

If the last release on your site is dated six months ago, your corporate image will be stagnant. Ensure releases are posted and corporate/product information is updated.

The media has traditionally provided the public with news in a clear, concise manner using the inverted pyramid style placing the most important details in the beginning of a story, followed by the supporting information. Press-friendly websites should be designed keeping this format in mind the home page should provide quick, easy reference points to efficiently lead the press to the information they need.

Despite the current dot-com doom and gloom, the Internet is here to stay. Thus, it is imperative that future PR professionals understand how to leverage the Internet, alongside broadcast, print, and radio. To do so, PR pros must redefine their roles within their organizations and learn new skill sets given that the Internet is blurring the lines between PR and other disciplines. To truly harness the power of the Web, the new PR pros toolkit will combine new skill sets from various disciplines such as consulting, publishing, direct marketing, market research and Web marketing.

Briefing Websites

Though IT experts or vendors may ultimately do the technical work for the website, the content should be the responsibility of PR professionals. They should decide what they wish to communicate. Decide whether you can use existing websites to meet your specific PR campaign objectives. If you need to set up a new site, first decide what your website will do. This will determine what technology it uses. This is a highly complex area, involving a range of technical issues. If there is anything you don't understand, or you have no experience of buying IT, you will need a technical expert to specify the requirements and help choose suppliers.

Your website will be hosted on a server computer — the choice of server determines how secure and reliable your site is and what it can do. Your website will need a new, easily remembered electronic address (called the Uniform Resource Locator, or URL). It is important that the URL be registered in time to appear on ads and publicity.

Your brief should specify:

- your aims for the website within the campaign;
- the audience and its needs;

- server technology or specifications of the server your suppliers should find for you;
- how much of the text, photography and videos you expect your suppliers to create, and how much you will provide;
- a clear description of how the supplier is to test and debug programmes;
- who is monitoring/updating the website after the supplier's role is over (for example, after delivery of the launch version);
- all services you want (for example, reporting back on access statistics, promotion advice); and delivery date and other key stages.

The Web page can add in-depth or up-to-date information to a campaign. It can also provide services such as the ability to order free publications or to book an appointment by e-mail.

Other Digital Tools

Given below are just some of the ways that new or digital media can add value to campaigns:

CD-ROMs / DVDs

CD-ROMs or DVDs can quickly and reliably get large files like databases, software, videos or heavily interactive games onto the audience's own computers.

Decide how you want the audience to use a CD-ROM/ DVD. This is especially important if you plan to distribute in schools, where educational use is paramount. Consider how much time you expect people to spend using the CD-ROM/ DVD. Make sure this informs your decision on content and length.

If you plan to recover costs through sales make sure you have a good business case and marketing plan. Be clear about distribution — that will tell you how many copies of the CD-ROM/DVD you want produced.

Unlike other software, CD-ROMs/DVDs can't be updated. If material needs frequent updating, consider linking the CD-ROM/DVD to your website.

You should specify your aims for the CD-ROM/DVD within the campaign; the audience and its needs; the level of technology and platforms on which you want the CD-ROM/DVD to run; how much of the text, photography and videos you expect your suppliers to create, and what you will provide; a clear description of how they are to test and debug programmes; how long before the information on the CD-ROM/DVD needs updating; packaging; print run — for CD-ROMs/DVDs and packaging; and delivery date and other key stages.

Kiosks

Kiosks can get interactive information to people. They are useful in exhibitions and places such as offices and libraries. Clarify what value the kiosk will add to your communication strategy. Decide if you need to be able to print out information, have a link to your website, or use a touch-screen or keyboard for input. If the kiosk is for a touring display rather than permanent use, it will have to be durable and transportable.

Consider the setting — how do you want people to use the kiosk and how will they find their way to it?

Kiosks need to be protected and managed. Their programmes need updating. You will also need to have a service contract for repairs. Decide whether you want replacement machines on hand as back-up.

Mobile Communications

Mobile communications can send short messages electronically to mobiles, pagers, fax and voice systems. Mobile communication is an immediate, personal and guaranteed way to reach a targeted audience with a short message. Decide what part the Short Messaging Service (SMS) could play in your communications strategy. The message can usually be up to 150 characters long.

Here is a checklist of questions you should consider:

- Will the SMS deliver an update, alert to a change, request a response or signpost to further information?
- Does your organization already have mobile numbers on a database, or will you need to collect them via your Internet site, mobiles or forms?
- What incentive, if any will you offer for your audience to give their mobile numbers?
- Do you want the message delivered only to mobile phones, or will it go to e-mail addresses, pagers, fax and voice systems.

Resolving these questions will determine the technology that you use. The delivery of your message will probably be processed by IT called a hosting environment, which organizes and manages the 'mailing' process.

Mobile numbers can be obtained from mobile networks. But using numbers without the users' permission is discouraged. Unsolicited messages (or spam), like junk mail, are irritating and can damage your relationship with your audience. The best practice is to gain your audience's individual permission. Having opted into receiving information, they are more likely to respond positively to your SMS communication when it is sent.

Mobile messaging is developing rapidly from SMS to EMS to MMS. The Enhanced Messaging Service (EMS) gives the ability to send a combination of simple media such as ring-tones, pictures, sounds, animations and text for display on an EMS compliant handset. The Multimedia Messaging Service (MMS) gives the ability to send messages comprising text, sounds, images and video to MMS capable handsets. The type of messaging service you choose should be determined by your audience's access to the different levels of service as well as the message you want to transmit.

You have to specify your aims for the text message within the campaign. The audience and its needs, plus any other information you have collected to enable segmentation of the audience. You may need to ask for advice on the most suitable technology for your message delivery (will the message be delivered over SMS, Wireless Application Protocol (WAP), General Packet Radio Service (GPRS) or 3rd Generation (3G) technology?)

The outlets you would like your message delivered to, e.g. SMS/WAP mobile phones, the web, e-mail, pager, fax, and voice systems have to be identified.

As a PR professional you have to decide the content, date and time you would like the message delivered and also how text message/e-mail responses from your audience will be handled and what feedback information you want for evaluation of the exercise.

Cyber and digital tools have to be understood and used depending on how various publics are using them. The key to success is usefulness and user-friendliness. A simple, clear and concise message is the key to success as it is in other forms of communication.

Communication in Crisis and War

Crises are a fact of life. Every company, organization, or government has to deal with a crisis. It's never simply a question of: Will one happen? But rather: When? Observe the market-place, the social and economic environment, understand public opinion, identify what will make for success and what will make for failure and then, courageously, share that understanding. By identifying issues during their earliest stages and before they grow into a crisis situation, PR can play a very important role in shaping organizational values and behaviour.

True crises are almost always the result of mismanaging the early phases of an issue or incident. How a company responds is much more important than the details of the response, but few companies focus on this critical factor.

A crisis is a critical or crucial situation whose outcome will determine whether extremely negative consequences will follow or not. Regardless of how traumatic things are during a crisis, the ultimate outcome can be positive or negative.

Crisis communication is something public relations practitioners need to know about, but they should know that it is different from crisis management. In good times and in bad, PR professionals are responsible for maintaining and improving their organizations' relationships by effectively communicating with their target audiences. A crisis merely increases the intensity of the communication and induces stress in all parties and in their relationships. Public relations' goal during a crisis is to get the organization through the situation with as little damage to its reputation, credibility, and key relationships as possible.

Every company faces a range of problems that can escalate into a public crisis at any time. Management must be on a constant alert and prepared to respond to any and all the serious issues that could, under the glare of public and media scrutiny, damage corporate, product or personal reputations.

Every company should have a detailed crisis plan to guide them through difficult and trying times. Such plans instil a feeling of security and preparedness. Crisis planners conduct a review of risks and threats, evaluate internal crisis procedures and draft new plans as needed. Crisis management may involve: managing victims; reducing litigation; recovering reputation; healing corporate wounds; dealing with organized opposition; selectively engaging the media, influencing employee attitudes managing community, and public attitudes.

Crisis preparedness and response is a necessity — anticipate, prepare for and manage complex situations. How an organization behaves and communicates during a crisis can be as important as the crisis itself. Organizational preparedness is first and foremost about the creation of a 'crisis mind-set' among those in charge. Since this environment is alien to anything previously experienced, this mind-set is often counter-intuitive and even painful. But failure to train managers to adopt the proper attitude is likely to result in all other efforts coming to naught. Companies must contend with two potential crises in parallel — the actual issue or problem, and the fallout if the situation is not addressed swiftly and effectively.

Dr Daniel Kahneman, a Princeton psychologist and the co-winner of the 2002 Nobel Prize in economics, has uncovered a few simple, but disconcerting truths about how *rational* we human beings are:[1]

- First, losses are more powerful than gains in determining how we form opinions, which means that accusations of harm will always win over responses about benefits. You must address people's perceived losses or injury first. Numerous scientific studies have found that people won't hear anything you say until you deal with what's uppermost in their minds.
- Second, first impressions shape subsequent judgements regardless of the evidence against them. Get into the debate early. Set the context. You won't have all the information you need, but conflicting, inadequate information is endemic to every crisis. However, if you let your opponents set the stage, you're by definition on the defensive.
- Third, vivid impressions are a greater factor in decision making than more abstract but more accurate information.

Crisis preparedness must include learning how to diffuse intense, blinding emotions. The crisis team must accept that they too are under extreme emotional stress, which affects their judgement, and they need extensive training to successfully handle hostile audiences.

1. Quoted in 'On Profit, Loss and the Mysteries of the Mind', by Erica Goode, *New York Times*, 5 November 2002.

In the court of public opinion, a charge is considered proof, and you're guilty until proven innocent. Because you're 'guilty', you have no credibility. It's simply a part of human nature that explains why executives have trouble changing their approach when disaster strikes. Initial responses set the stage for what comes later, but many managers under stress succumb to emotion and respond as they always have, not realizing that their actions often create more tension, suspicion, and anger.

Responsible Communication

When a situation arises that could be a crisis, the first thing is to contact your CEO and the chief of the public relations department. These two should assemble a crisis communication team as quickly as possible, including key officials of the departments where the crisis has occurred or being handled. This team may have legal, security, financial and technical department heads depending upon the nature of crisis. It has to come up with a plan of action and decide who the spokesperson should be. It should also determine the appropriate positioning or message to address the emergency.

Spokespersons

One individual should be designated as the primary spokesperson to represent the Company, make official statements and answer media questions throughout the crisis. If there are many locations of crisis there could be more spokespersons but they should coordinate with the primary spokesperson. A backup to the designated spokesperson should also be identified to fill the position in the event that the primary spokesperson is unavailable.

A spokesperson should be: comfortable in front of a TV camera and with reporters, preferably, skilled in handling media, skilled in identifying key points, able to speak without using jargon, knowledgeable about the organization and the crisis, able to establish credibility with the media being sincere, straightforward and believable. The spokesperson should be accessible to the media and to internal communications personnel who will facilitate media interviews and should be able to remain calm in stressful situations.

Rules of the Game

- Select a place to be used as a media centre.
- Time for regular briefings by spokesman should be fixed.
- At the end of a briefing, the time for an update briefing should be announced if needed.
- Decide rules of the game and don't change them during the crisis.
- All media should be treated equally. What is given to one (such as access to an area affected by the crisis) should be available to all media.

Prepare Answers

- A crisis situation is always difficult when dealing with the media. Therefore, tough questions and rehearsals are necessary to help the spokesperson prepare.
- It is important, at the onset of the crisis, that the spokesperson, backup and advisors spend some time rehearsing prepared statements and answers to possible 'tough' questions that may be asked by reporters.
- If possible, similar rehearsals should be conducted prior to each media interview, briefing or news conference.

- It is also important to anticipate and practice new questions as the story evolves.

Prepared Statement

- If you don't communicate immediately, you lose your greatest opportunity to control events.
- You must have a prepared statement on hand that can be used to make an initial general response to the media when knowledge about the crisis first becomes known.
- Your first news release should include at a minimum the who, what, when and where of the situation.
- You must give the facts that have been gathered from reliable sources and confirmed.
- If you do nothing more than show concern for the public and for your employees in your first media interaction, you are already on the right track.

Off the Record

- As the crisis progresses and new information and facts become available, it is also advisable to develop prepared statements to be made by the spokesperson at the onset of any media interview, briefing or news conference.
- However, don't overreach and don't speculate. There is a limit to your role. To exceed that limit is a mistake.
- Don't volunteer information unless it is a point the company wants to make and the question hasn't been asked.
- Don't talk off the record. Do not say anything which you do not want to be carried by media.

Use the Fax, Phone, e-mail

- These prepared statements also can be read over the

telephone to reporters who call to request information but are not represented at news conferences or briefings.

- Those who are answering phones for the CEO and PR chief should have copy of latest press release and prepared statement.
- The statement or press release can also be sent by fax or e-mail upon request.

The Internet

- These days the Internet is also being used in PR in a big way and should be used in crisis communication.
- In the US a study found that many companies dealing with a crisis use their websites to address the issue or crisis, but they did it by simply posting a traditional press release, often embedded with other news.
- Only a few companies actually designated special sections exclusively devoted to communicating crisis information.
- Most companies posted crisis information in inconspicuous locations — too often, too deep inside the website. This made the information virtually inaccessible.
- There were actually some companies that chose to ignore the crisis making no mention of the controversy on their site.
- Few CEOs addressed the crisis or issue online.

Best Internet Practices

- The study also found examples of how some companies effectively used the Web.
- They made their case, addressed internal and external audiences, and kept website visitors informed and engaged.

- Made sure they mentioned relevant positive news and took responsibility for any transgressions for which they were responsible.
- Some CEOs took personal responsibility for problems. Some posted their personal responses on the company website and asked for comments and feedback. They understood how the Internet could be used. They recognized that it was not just an online version of other communications.
- It was different. It had to be managed. It could be a device for speed, candour and solidifying relationships.

Goal

- The first and foremost communication goal in a crisis situation is protecting the integrity and reputation of the Company.
- If you ignore the situation it will only get worse.
- The cause of almost all crises fall into two broad categories: Overt acts and acts of omission.
- Try to view the crisis from the eye of the public or those affected or involved in the crisis.

Keep it Simple

- No matter how deep the crisis is, think first of what information your audience truly needs to hear.
- Keep it simple, keep it relative, keep it up and — above all else — keep it personal, or exclusive to the audience.
- It's simple in concept but difficult in execution because there are a thousand things that can knock you off track.
- Mantra of simplicity, relativity and repetition.
- Do unto others as you would have them do unto you.

Mary Matalin the keynote speaker at the 2003 PRSA International Conference in New Orleans said that on 11 September 2001, she was huddled with Vice President Dick Cheney and other senior government officials in a bunker beneath the White House trying to determine what President Bush would say to the nation: The President needed to say only three things to the people — your government is intact, we're dealing with the crisis and, for those who need it, help is on the way.

At the time of a crisis, besides the outside world PR also has to deal with internal publics, employees in particular. Let us look at the communication of AOL Time Warner management dealing with crisis related to its trouble with Securities and Exchange Commission (SEC) aimed at damage control. On 14 August 2002 the Company issued a press release to deal with external publics and also issued an internal memo to all working in AOL Time Warner. Here is the press release:

For Immediate Release

AOL TIME WARNER ANNOUNCES CERTIFICATION OF ITS FINANCIAL RESULTS

NEW YORK, August 14, 2002 — AOL Time Warner (NYSE: AOL) today announced that its Chief Executive Officer Richard Parsons and its Chief Financial Officer Wayne Pace have certified the Company's financial reports, in compliance with both Securities and Exchange Commission (SEC) Order 4-460 and the Sarbanes-Oxley Act of 2002.

The Company also disclosed in its Form 10-Q for the second quarter of 2002 that, based on information that it learned within the past 10 days, the Company had identified three transactions involving its AOL unit with respect to which the Company may conclude, after further investigation, that consideration received by AOL from third parties may have been inappropriately recognized as advertising and commerce revenues. The advertising and commerce revenues recognized in connection with these three transactions totaled approximately $49 million occurring over a period of six quarters. While these amounts are an insignificant portion of the Company's revenue during these reporting periods, the Company stated that it is further reviewing these, as well as other, transactions involving the AOL division relating to advertising and commerce revenues. After completing its internal review, the Company will determine whether its accounting for any transactions was not appropriate, and if so, what action, if any, is appropriate with respect to its reported financial results.

Mr Parsons said: 'I consider the accuracy of AOL Time Warner's financial reporting to be one of my most important responsibilities, and I am committed to giving investors accurate and transparent information about the Company. Consistent with that commitment, we disclosed in our Form 10-Q today that we have very recently learned of information that raises some questions about the accounting for a small number of transactions involving our AOL division relating to advertising and commerce revenues. I am committed to completing our internal review and resolving those questions on a thorough and timely basis, and we are moving forward to implement additional internal controls at AOL. I am also committed to conducting the operations of all of our AOL Time Warner businesses with the utmost integrity and responsibility.'

About AOL Time Warner

AOL Time Warner is the world's leading media and entertainment company, whose businesses include interactive services, cable systems, filmed entertainment, television networks, music and publishing.[2]

Caution Concerning Forward-Looking Statements

This document includes certain forward-looking statements within the meaning of the Private Securities Litigation Reform Act of 1995. These statements are based on management's current expectations or beliefs, and are subject to uncertainty and changes in circumstances. Actual results may vary materially from those expressed or implied by the statements herein due to changes in economic, business, competitive, technological, strategic and/or regulatory factors, and factors affecting the integration of the businesses of AOL Time Warner Inc. More detailed information about these factors may be found in filings by AOL Time Warner with the Securities and Exchange Commission, including its most recent annual report on Form 10-K and its most recent quarterly report on Form 10-Q. AOL Time Warner is under no obligation to, and expressly disclaims any such obligation to, update or alter its forward-looking statements, whether as a result of new information, future events, or otherwise.[3]

Contacts:
Edward Adler
(212) 484-6630

Tricia Primrose
(212) 484-7450

2. This information forms part of every press release around this time.

3. This is also a general notice attached to every press release, to avoid legal problems.

On 14 August 2002, the CEO Richard Parsons issued the following memo:

To All AOL Time Warner Colleagues:

Today we are announcing that Wayne Pace, our CFO, and I have certified the company's financial statements with the SEC. Wayne and I have always considered the accuracy of AOL Time Warner's financial reporting to be one of our most important responsibilities, and we are committed to giving investors accurate and transparent information about the company.

Consistent with that commitment, in the Form 10-Q (which is our regular quarterly filing that we filed with the SEC today), we have also disclosed that some additional facts have recently come to light that raise some questions about the accounting for three transactions involving online advertising at the America Online division. While the amount of revenue at issue in the three transactions is relatively small — totaling $49 million over six quarters, which is less than one half of one percent of the AOL division's revenues during that period — and while we are still reviewing the accounting for these matters, the mere existence of questions regarding these transactions requires that we take appropriate action.

Accordingly, we are conducting an internal review of the accounting for certain online advertising and e-commerce transactions involving the America Online division. We hope to complete this review by no later than the end of the third quarter. This review should not affect the vast majority of our company's employees, or even the vast majority of those who work at the America Online division. But such a review is an important part of ensuring that we have the organization and business practices in place that puts every part of the company above reproach. In addition, with Don Logan and Jon Miller, our new Chairman and

CEO of America Online, we are putting some enhanced controls in place. And, as we separately announced last week, Don and Jon are reviewing the America Online organization, and we plan to put a new structure in place in a few weeks.

As I said in a memo to you a couple of weeks ago, it is not enough merely that our accounting, disclosure, or other business practices are legal or appropriate. We must hold ourselves to a higher standard. I am dedicated to making sure that this company not only produces value for our stockholders, but also abides by the values for which this company stands — including integrity, accuracy, and public responsibility. The value we create for our stockholders depends on the values we live by. And, of course, there is no room at this company for any unethical behavior. So let me remind you that, if you have any questions or concerns about conduct at this company, I would encourage you to contact your supervisor, or your division's Human Resources Department, Law Department, or Compliance Officer.

I'm sharing all this with you because the more you know, the better you will be able to put things in their proper perspective. Most of our divisions are performing in a spectacular fashion and America Online, which remains the premier company in the Internet space, is in the process of regaining its footing under new leadership. As we move forward, it will be important that we stay focused on our businesses and that we continue to deliver superior performance in a manner that lives up to our core values. We've all got to continue to produce and distribute the best information, entertainment, and communications services of any company in the world.

Thank you for your dedication and hard work. As always, I would welcome all comments any of you wish to share.

Dick Parsons

In normal times, information is a tool controlled by management to gain a certain strategic advantage. In a crisis, many managers continue to believe that they have that advantage. Enron, Andersen, WorldCom, Tyco, and a host of others had control over when and how much information they would provide. Meanwhile, their critics dominated the news with vivid images and explosive charges. Failing to provide information or at least opening lines of communication creates ambiguity and all ambiguous behaviour is perceived negatively. If there is an information vacuum out there, someone will fill it. Rapid response does not mean giving away everything, but as a general rule, speculation and suspicion feed controversy; information quiets speculation and alleviates suspicion.

In a demanding era there is no substitute for complete disclosure, integrity and speed. The mandate is: *be honest, leave nothing out, genuinely care for others and get there first with the news.* There are some very new elements — the most critical is speed and it is here that the Internet plays a very powerful role. Rapid response is essential. Should a crisis occur or an issue emerge.

Dealing with Activist Publics

There has been some research in crisis communication relating to activist publics which need mention here. Activist groups, which have mastered the art of public relations, have coined a new term for it. media advocacy. Head of the Advocacy Institute Michael Pertschuk, defined it as 'the strategic use of mass media for advancing a social or public policy initiative,' Rose (1991).[4] This usually means that activists should use

4. Merrill Rose, 'Activism in the 90s: Changing Roles for Public Relations', *Public Relations Quarterly*, 36, 1991, pp. 29, 31–32.

research and frame data so that it is interesting and understandable to the media and the general public.

There are several solutions that public relations practitioners can and should consider when dealing with activist publics. According to Murphy and Dee (1992),[5] many public relations practitioners generally assume that the solution to dealing with activist publics lies in negotiation and compromise: The solution is a redefinition of the relative roles in a non-adversary climate, no matter what it takes. The rule makers are not evil, capricious, unthinking people, but more likely hard-working public servants. They can, with some sense of community, engage in a dialogue . . . (to) balance the conflicting needs of employment and the environment. This type of solution is based on the two-way symmetrical model of public relations. It is here that organizations uses communication and research in order to cooperate with activist publics, instead of trying to persuade them. This model seeks to promote mutual understanding and respect between the organization and the activist public(s).

Another type of public relations solution that practitioners may use in resolving conflict with activists publics according to Rose (1991)[6] is to consider the following options:

1. *Know who you're up against.* Activists of the 1990s are of a different breed. Public relations practitioners must do research to find out 'if the group you're dealing with has a large grassroots membership base or just a few important sounding names on the letterhead.' Organizational public relations should find out

5. Priscilla Murphy and Juliet Dee, 'Du Pont and Greenpeace: The Dynamics of Conflict Between Corporations and Activists Groups', *Public Relations Research*, 4 (1), 1992, pp. 3–20.

6. See note 4 on previous page.

if the group has public relations professionals that they can deal with in order to more effectively deal with the conflict.

2. *Be an advocate for alternative solutions to the problem.* When an organization is caught in a struggle with an activist, it should think long and hard about something that it may be able to advocate that will demonstrate the organization's responsiveness to the activist(s) concerns.

3. *Put a face on the issue.* Although facts and figures are always necessary to support the organization's point of view, personal stories bring issues alive while simultaneously capturing the attention of the media and policymakers. It is important to talk in terms of what the issue means to the activists, instead of solely focusing on the organizational bottom line.

4. *Put your words in someone else's mouth.* Research has shown that business and industry are not always held in high esteem in the eyes of the public. Oftentimes when an organization attempts to advocate a good image, it is not supported or accepted by the public because it knows who the organization is. Organizations must realize that they are not immune from potential credibility problems. In realizing this, organizations must seek the help of other credible institutions to re-establish its credibility.

Lesly (1992)[7] noted that an organization must have expertise in five areas which are: (1) knowing the situation and the

7. P. Lesly, 'Coping with Opposition Groups', *Public Relations Review*, 18 (4), 1992, pp. 325–34.

climate, (2) knowing your people, (3) knowing your adversaries, (4) knowing what to do, and (5) knowing how to do it. It is here that Lesly established a list of guidelines to carry out the function of 'coping with opponents': Establish a process for monitoring what is developing among the publics that may have an impact on the organization. Establish liaison with public-interest groups and the public. Get the highest calibre of input from one or more experts outside the organization. Set up a process for watching the general media to see what subjects arise and show signs of becoming issues. Set up guidelines to make leaders of the organization accessible and knowledgeable for the media.

Ryan and Martinson (1983),[8] felt that responsible corporations must sometimes give up some profit in order to protect the well being of the public. By honestly doing so, the public usually perceive the organization as being more socially responsible. They suggested that organizations should, 'Represent the public to your management, and the management to your public'. Corporations hire public relations practitioners to act as the social conscience for the organization. Thus, it is important that the public relations person is allowed enough freedom to act as the 'corporate conscience' in order to do the job properly. This job usually entails getting complete information to the public(s).

According to L.A. Grunig (1992)[9] there are six propositions that deal with the aspects of two-way symmetrical communication as a way of dealing with activism.

8. Michael Ryan and David L. Martinson, 'The PR Officer as Corporate Conscience', *Public Relations Quarterly*, 28 (2), 1983, pp. 20–23.

9. Larissa Grunig, 'Activism: How it limits the effectiveness of organizations and how excellent public relations departments respond', in James E. Grunig (ed.), *Excellence in Public Relations and Communication Management*, Hillsdale, NJ: Lawrence Erlbaum Associates, 1992.

1. Organizations need two-way communication to learn the consequences of what they are doing on all of their relevant publics — not just their owners, their employees, and their associates.

2. Organizations need two-way communication to tell the publics what they are doing about any negative consequences. This means that public relations practitioners should be flexible and consider adopting new strategies or new messages in order to effectively deal with activist groups. These new strategies/messages should be made depending on the need and predispositions of the activists opposing the organization(s). 'Involving the public relations staff in a joint organization-activist committee also would help transform the perception of public relations from corporate mouthpiece to advocate for understanding.'

3. Continuous efforts at communicating with activists are necessary to contend with their shifting stances. The two-way symmetrical approach to public relations is an on-going process. It has been shown that interest groups are willing to trust organizations but at other times, they appeal either to the government or the media for satisfaction.

4. An on-going, balanced and proactive programme of constituency relations must acknowledge the legitimacy of all constituent groups — regardless of their size. Organizations should never underestimate the power and influence an organization has, based on its size. Studies show that smaller organizations are able to get more done versus medium or large ones.

5. Conducting a two-way symmetrical communication programmes hinges on employing people with the necessary background and education.
6. Organizations must learn to measure their effectiveness in terms of more than simplistic, short-term gains or losses.

This means that public relations persons should implement a continuous programme of evaluation. Analysing piggyback questions from polls, counting clips and media impressions, and profit increase provide minimal evidence as to how the publics perceive the organization. Thus, it is important that public relations utilizes environmental scanning and two-way communication in order to effectively monitor the public's perception of the organization.

Communication in War

War is the ultimate crisis for Governments. Communication during a war is very critical. We have seen that many pioneers of PR were part of Government communication during the wars. Propaganda was once a good word, but maligned during the war. Even Harold Lasswell's model of communication was invented for the purpose of war communication.

Presidents Woodrow Wilson and Franklin D. Roosevelt knew their communication challenges were more than those in government could handle in times of war. The Creel Committee in World War I and the Office of War Information in World War II — both led by journalists, scholars, press agents and editors from the private sector. Elmer Davis, who led the war information office for Roosevelt, was a journalist and

Rhodes Scholar who spent 15 years as a novelist and freelance writer, 10 years as a *New York Times* reporter, and three as a radio commentator. In both cases, the PR campaigns were successful in promoting the sale of war bonds and in obtaining media support for other wartime needs, including secrecy regarding troop movement and weapon development.

Military commanders serving at all levels are responsible for informing their troops and the public about their mission and how that mission supports national defence policy. What's more, with the exception of national security matters, commanders have an obligation to inform their publics of actions they're taking to accomplish their mission. This is not a new concept for the military. During World War II, the late General Matthew Ridgeway, who became the Army's Chief of Staff after leading US forces in Normandy, told peers that, except for valid security reasons, any action that cannot be explained to the troops, Congress and the public, should be regarded as suspect and thoroughly examined.

However, news management has become an essential part of any war. In the First World War fake stories of German soldiers bayoneting Belgian children finally convinced the US to join the fray. During the Gulf War the public were enraged and galvanized their support for Operation Desert Storm when they heard a tragic — but fictional — tale from a tearful woman who claimed to have seen Iraqi soldiers throwing Kuwaiti babies out of incubators.

C.P. Scott, the legendary editor of the Manchester *Guardian* said at the end of World War I, 'If people knew the truth the war would be stopped tomorrow. But of course they don't know, and they can't know.' During that war, the Chief of the British Military Intelligence was asked to describe the ideal war correspondent. 'He is a man', said the general, 'who writes what he is told is true, or even what he thinks to be true, but never what he knows to be true.' A well-known correspondent of that war, Sir Phillip Gibbs, described the situation even better, 'There was no need of censorship, for we were our own censors . . . The problem was nobody believed us.' Patriotism plays a major role as Walter Lippmann put it, 'We must remember that in time of war what is said on the enemy's side of the front is always propaganda, and what is said on our side of the front is truth and righteousness, the cause of humanity and a crusade for peace.' Winston Churchill, the British Prime Minister during World War II, is credited with, 'In wartime, truth is so precious that she should always be attended by a bodyguard of lies.'

A legendary news-agency man, Kent Cooper, wrote in his autobiography how the US Government used the Associated Press, 'President Wilson and Secretary of State Lancing gave the AP an exclusive, which was a propaganda "plant". A German coded message was intercepted by the British intelligence service, which gave it to President Wilson. It asked Mexico to seek adherence and military support from Japan for a Mexican-Japanese attack on the US from the Southwest if America went to war against Germany. Lancing in his memoirs written several years later, confirmed that he and Wilson secretly schemed to use the AP solely to incite public demand for a declaration of war. The 'cold-blooded proposition' of Germany's Secretary of Foreign Affairs in one day accomplished a change in sentiment and public opinion that would have required months to accomplish. From the time that telegram was published, the United States entry into the war was assured since it could no longer be doubted that it was desired by the American people from Maine to California and from Michigan to Texas.'

Kent Cooper's comment on this episode is also revealing, 'I never thought that American Government would ever secretly scheme to plant propaganda for war in the news here at home. I was wrong. In 1912, our own Government followed the German lead (Kaiser's Government used the Wolff Bureau, its national news agency, by turning news into propaganda to create a jealous rage against anything not German). It was done so effectively that for the first time in history a Government incited its people by propaganda to ask for a declaration of war before they were ordered headlong into it and became the second in the history successfully to use news to incite the people to demand war.' Another important fact about this episode is that the AP agreed not to disclose the source and thus the AP and not the US Government stood sponsor for the accuracy of the fake German message.

Since then the technology and sophistication in news manipulation have increased manifold. In fact, the use of mass media as an additional weapon of war assumed significance during the First World War and it reached a level of higher sophistication in the Second World War. The use of radio in particular and news agencies for management of information and disinformation became very significant in the Second World War period. The word propaganda assumed its current negative meaning during that period, as it was a positive word before that.

Now, war by media is categorized as low intensity warfare alongside subversion, insurgency and psychological sabotage. Propaganda theorists say that in effect the human being should be considered the priority objective in a political war. And conceived as the military target of a guerrilla war, the human being has his most critical point in his mind. Once his mind has been reached the 'political animal' has been defeated, without necessarily receiving bullets. In Central America, the US doctrine of low intensity warfare against Nicaragua was based on the accumulated experience of the Germans in World War II, the British in Malaya, Kenya and Ireland, the French in Algeria and specially the US in Vietnam. Andrew Messing of the National Defense Council of the United States called the region an 'accessible laboratory' for the study of low intensity conflict. However, the use of media in the Gulf War, Yugoslav War, Afghan War and Iraq War appears to be that of a force multiplier. Coverage of these wars by global media like CNN, BBC, AP and Reuters has once again highlighted the importance of the media in modern warfare.

The Vietnam War was the first to have the use of television and perhaps it could not be managed so well by the US generals and is usually blamed for the US defeat in Vietnam. There had been lot of controversy about the coverage of Falkland War and also about the US invasion of Grenada when the media were not allowed to go to the war theatre with the invading troops. In the war in the Gulf in 1991 the media management was much improved and perhaps played a major role in projecting mainly the story of the US led forces. In fact, media have been turned into weapons of psychological warfare, which can justify a war and can continue the war of minds without even a formal declaration prior to, during and even after the actual war.

During the Vietnam War, the propaganda was that it was a conflict of Vietnamese against Vietnamese into which the US threw their weight on the side of democracy and freedom. This assumption pervaded the media and was in fact quite false and dishonest like the Nazi propaganda when the Germans were overrunning Czechoslovakia. But it was so insistent and so powerful and insidious that a great many people believed in the fundamental goodness of the US mission. There appeared to be saturation media coverage of the Vietnam War but the big story of the war was not reported until it was virtually over. In the Vietnam War atrocities were neither isolated, nor aberrations. But this was seldom judged to be news and therefore seldom told. With the assumption that the war was right, atrocities were reported as 'mistakes' which were 'blundered into'.

The British term 'pacification', which they used in relation to Ireland gained currency in Vietnam and became familiar to newspaper readers and television viewers in the West, but whose real meaning was seldom understood. Pacification meant killing as many people as possible in a given area within a given period of time. In 1971 the US Ninth Division killed 11,000 people in a pacification campaign named 'Operation Speedy Express'. Two diligent *Newsweek* reporters discovered that almost half of these were civilians and this was a mass slaughter condoned and covered up. The reporters wrote the story but six months later a watered down version appeared and no one was made responsible. In this sense even in Vietnam the management of media was quite a success.

The ultimate failure of the Vietnam enterprise (1961–1975) became undeniable by April 1975 when Saigon fell to North Vietnamese troops. So painful was the Vietnam experience that both the US Army and civilians seemed to want to put Vietnam out of memory. Many thought that journalists should not have been allowed at all and tried to put the blame of defeat on war coverage. Perhaps the Vietnam controversy led to the decision by the Reagan administration refusing permission for reporters to cover the US invasion of Grenada (25 October 1983).

Furious protests from the media led to a negotiated pool

plan for coverage of future military actions. In the NBC Nightly News Commentary John Chancellor termed the invasion 'a bureaucrats dream: Do anything. No one is watching.' General John W. Vessey Jr., Chairman of the Joint Chief's of Staff appointed a commission to consider future press-military relations headed by retired General Winant Sidle. The result was the 'combat-correspondent pool' under which a small handful of physically fit reporters would be taken to combat zones. During the 1989 Panama invasion the scheme failed miserably as the pool was flown to Panama late, then virtually barred from witnessing any fighting for fear that details of civilian casualties would be reported.

By the 1991 Gulf War a lot more thought and preparation went in and twelve media combat pools were formed. Two of them, of 18 reporters each, specifically covered US Army and Marine Corps' ground combat activities; eight others, of seven reporters each, split their coverage among the four US armed services. There was a five-member pool to observe naval activities, and there was a 'quick reaction' pool sent to areas of hostility on a quick basis. Guidelines established by the Pentagon sought 'to keep the public informed while protecting the safety of armed forces personnel in combat.' Under these rules, reporters covered US combat activities as part of a group, or media 'pool', and were escorted to those areas by a Department of Defense (DoD) official. The escort officer on the scene had to approve any written or broadcast report before it was released to the other reporters covering the war. Most of the pool reporters covering US forces were those who worked for the US news organizations, although there was a slot for a Saudi reporter and another for a foreign journalist in each of the 18-member combat pools. If there was a disagreement about the contents of a pool report the report was sent immediately to public affairs officials at the JIB in Dhahran for review by them and the appropriate media organization. If no agreement was reached at that level, the disputed item was to be sent to Pentagon for review there by DoD officials in conjunction with the reporter's supervisor.

The opportunity to impartially record what happened in the Gulf War was lost; since almost all news came from military sources, independent reporting was virtually impossible and some of the most respected war photographers, including Don McCullin, were not given pool credentials to cover frontline activities.

Only journalists who signed an agreement to abide by US Defense Department restrictions on the coverage of the war were chosen to work in military pools; attempts to move independently were impeded by military roadblocks. Some of the correspondents have complained that they had been accompanied constantly even to the bathroom when on a warship to prevent unsupervised conversation with marines or pilots. Most of the journalists were lodged in a hotel in Riyadh from the outbreak of war and were entirely dependent on military personnel for transportation and access to news. The detention of a *New York Times* journalist and confiscation of his credentials demonstrated the imposed constraints of 'pool' coverage after he interviewed local residents in a small border town in Saudi Arabia.

The use of propaganda and the disinformation during the Gulf War was widespread and effective in achieving its purpose. The Coalition forces succeeded in giving and maintaining the impression that it was a 'clean' war in which the use of high-tech weapons resulted in negligible human casualties. For this purpose wide use was made in press briefings of video films demonstrating the accuracy of the new weapons, military spokesmen avoided discussion on the human cost of the war and a new kind of jargon was introduced (using phrases such as 'collateral damage' for civilian casualties). In spite of the fact that up to 100,000 Iraqi soldiers and unknown number of civilians were killed in the war, there has been little coverage in the media of the unpalatable aspects of the war. There were other uses of media coverage of the Gulf war. It was serving as advertising to promote new weapons. The Patriot missile was advertised and was later sold to the South Koreans who had enough money to pay for the deployment of this weapon system.

Another interesting feature, which got consolidated during the Yugoslav and Afghan wars and was also used to great success in Iraq war were multi-point briefings: official briefings from different centres of power. Central Command, Pentagon and White House gave briefings at different times so that television news channels could broadcast all these briefings live, and CNN, BBC and Fox could take this one sided message around the world. During this war even British Parliament became such a centre where Tony Blair and his defence minister could speak on the subject and get live coverage on news networks.

Particularly in the 24-hour rolling news networks the general coverage was a mesh of glorious take-off's launching into battle, examples of the high precision bombing equipment that was 'bringing Milosevic to his knees', and the victims — distraught and dishevelled Kosovar-Albanian refugees. The TV news channels churned out the NATO briefings complete with selective footage, becoming a part of the campaign itself and certainly simplifying a complicated history. On occasions, during the live transmission of NATO briefings, one could be forgiven for believing that British Foreign Secretary Robin Cook or NATO spokesman Jamie Shea had changed careers and become TV anchors. They played host, bringing in their guests to comment, popping up questions to echo the NATO sentiment, while the cameras rolled on.

While the Milosevic regime was evidently guilty of systematic human rights abuses, practically no mention was made of the fact that the KLA had been involved in a bloody secessionist war employing tactics such as 'ethnic cleansing'. Jake Lynch, a *Sky News* correspondent, noted 'as Kosovo was beginning to make a serious impact on the news agenda, throughout 1998, virtually no Western media reported the ethnic cleansing of 90 villages in the province by the KLA — an estimate made by the UNHCR.'

The Kosovo News and Propaganda War published by the Vienna based International Press Institute (September 1999) examines and challenges the media's coverage of the conflict; questions the sources of information; outlines the obstacles that were erected to impede free reporting; asks where and how the truth got lost or distorted. In his introduction to this publication Peter Goff from IPI says, 'Officials on both sides pursued their goals of dominating coverage through sheer volume of information, although much of it was inaccurate and of little relevance. Journalists were invited to mounds of propaganda but a dearth of information. Those covering the NATO briefings felt an escalating sense of frustration and irritation that the events were primarily platforms to disseminate sound bites and NATO propaganda aimed at consolidating the alliance. Rhetoric, it was felt, was king and facts the poor relation.'

Examples: NATO reported on 29 March1999, that Fehmi Agani and four other well-known Kosovo Albanians had been murdered by Serbian troops. Air Commodore Wilby said the report came from a 'very reliable source' in Kosovo, which his department had checked carefully. The reports turned out to be totally false. The 'very reliable source' was the London-based Kosovo Information Centre, which is run by Kosovan exiles. They also reported without any basis that Ibrahim Rugova's house had been burned down and that he was in hiding.

The Pristina football stadium had been turned into a concentration camp for 100,000 ethnic Albanians; 20 school-teachers had been killed in front of their pupils; President Slobodan Milosevic's family had fled the country — all false. These false reports, however, received extensive media coverage and helped to strengthen the unity of the 19-member alliance at critical times. It is difficult not to conclude that the alliance used stories — which it knew were not adequately corroborated and were often coming from sources with a vested interest in intensifying the conflict — to justify the bombings to an unconvinced public.

Every effort was made to question the credibility of any development that did not serve NATO's purpose. For example, when the moderate Albanian leader Ibrahim Rugova, who was said to be in hiding, turned up on Yugoslav television condemning the NATO bombing, it was insinuated that the pictures were faked, or that he had been drugged, coerced, blackmailed, or at least misquoted.

Officials persisted with the line that 'we are not at war with the Yugoslav people,' despite the claims from various sources which say the alliance killed approximately 2,000 civilians and wounded 6,000, destroyed 300 factories, 200 schools and colleges, 20 hospitals, 30 clinics, 60 bridges and 5 airports.

'NATO called its devastating air war against Yugoslavia a "humanitarian intervention", a historic battle between good and evil to stop "ethnic cleansing" and return Kosovo Albanians to their homes', wrote Paul Watson of the *Los Angeles Times*, 'But from inside Kosovo, it rarely looked so pure and simple. It seemed more like calling in a plumber to fix a leak and watching him flood the house.'

The 'embedding' of media persons with US forces is the latest in the use of media in the Iraq war. The public affairs guidance on embedding of media during possible future operations/deployments in the US Central Command (CENTCOM) area of responsibility was ready on 3 February 2003. The policy paragraph 2.A says, 'The Department of Defense (DoD) policy on media coverage of future military operations is that media will have long-term, minimally restrictive access to US air, ground and naval forces through embedding. Media coverage of any future operation will, to a large extent, shape public perception of the national security environment now and in the years ahead. This holds true of the US public; the public in allied countries whose opinion can affect the durability of our coalition; and publics in countries where we conduct operations whose perceptions of us can affect the cost and duration of our involvement. Our ultimate strategic success in bringing peace and security to this region will come in our long-term commitment to supporting our democratic ideals. We need to tell the factual story — good or bad — before others seed the media with disinformation and distortions, as they most certainly will continue to do. Our people in the field need to tell our story — only commanders can ensure the media get to the story alongside the troops. We must organize for and facilitate access of national and international media to our forces, including those forces engaged in ground operations, with goal of doing so from the start. To accomplish this, we will embed media with our units. These embedded media will live, work and travel as part of the units with which they are embedded to facilitate maximum, in-depth coverage of the US forces in combat and related operations. Commanders and public affairs officers must work together to balance the need for media access with the need for operational security.'

The media representative and the organization he or she represents before embedding sign an agreement. By paragraph 4(a) of this agreement the media employee agrees to 'participate in the embedding process and to follow the direction and orders of the Government related to such participation. The media employee further agrees to follow Government regulations. The media employee acknowledges that failure to follow any directions, order, regulation, or ground rule may result in termination of the media employee's participation in the embedding process.'

In the Iraq war there were about 500 embedded journalists giving out the US version from different theatres of war and this gave additional support to already established media manipulation practices. It is clear that the news management effort is not to allow media to give the real picture of the war but to give the impression that enough is being told. However, many journalists also became tools of the authorities in making sure that the US led forces also won the media war.

A study released in March 2004 by the University of Maryland's Center for International Security Studies concluded that much of the pre-war coverage about Iraq and weapons of mass destruction 'stenographically reported the incumbent administration's perspective', and provided 'too little critical examination of the way officials framed the events, issues, threats, and policy options.' This aspect of the use of the media by those in authority needs investigation and media in other parts of the world also need to be careful about.

A study published in February 2004 in *The New York Review of Books* by Michael Massing, a *Columbia Journalism Review* contributing editor reached a similar conclusion. 'In the period before the war, US journalists were far too reliant on sources sympathetic to the administration. Those with dissenting views — and there were more than a few — were shut out.' There was vigorous debate inside intelligence circles about the veracity of many of the defectors' claims, but not much of this reached the reader. Instead, defectors on the Pentagon's payroll repeatedly duped media. Even when reporters did good investigative work, it often got buried. *Post* staff writer Walter Pincus told Massing that his paper's editors 'went through a whole phase in which they didn't put things on the front page that would make a difference.'

Knight Ridder journalists Jonathan Landay and Tish Wells found that the main Iraqi exile group, the Iraqi National Congress, fed the *New York Times*, the *Washington Post*, the Associated Press and other media numerous unsubstantiated allegations about the Iraqi regime that resulted in over 100 articles worldwide.

The day after Powell's big show at the United Nations, an editorial in the *Post* titled 'Irrefutable' declared it 'hard to imagine how anyone could doubt that Iraq possesses weapons of mass destruction.' The *Post's* news pages, and those of other élite publications, seemed to have been operating under that assumption for months, but Powell's performance sealed the deal. Most mass media weren't interested in drawing too much attention to weaknesses in Powell's case or in doing further investigative work to scrutinize the Secretary of State's claims. Instead, they played it safe and geared up for war.

The president of Poland, Aleksander Kwaniewski, who sent over 2,000 troops in Iraq, said 'I certainly feel uncomfortable as we were being misinformed as to the weapons of mass destruction.' It's now clear that the major media helped navigate for the White House during that long trip to Europe.

Because there is so much of media today, people tend to believe that they are given more information and they can find the truth. This is not so. The media is managed to the disadvantage of the truth, particularly more so in times of war and to win the war at home and internationally. However, the war is fought in the name of high principles. Naturally media-haves have advantage over the media have-nots in this area of modern warfare where media become force multiplier.

The reality is that in all systems different stakeholders to further their own ends use the media. Government is not behind in this race. Western Democracies are no exception. The difference between the Western Democracies on one hand and the Socialist and Totalitarian regimes on the other in relation to media has been that of manipulation and direct control. It has been proved that manipulation is more effective than control. Thus the global dominance of Western media serves the interests of their governments and businesses. BBC seems to be the ultimate model where the British establishment uses it beautifully during a war and then a crisis between BBC and the British Government emerges to repair the damage to the credibility to make it fit for use in future.

The Indian Experience

The experience in India shows that for Governments in the developing world openness pays. During Operation Blue Star conducted by the Indian Army to clear terrorists from the premises of the Golden Temple[10] in June 1984 no person

10. The Goldent Temple, one of the holiest of the Sikh shrines is located at Amritsar, in Punjab. The western part of Punjab, which has gone to Pakistan, has many important Sikh shrines including one near Lahore at Nankana Saheb where the first Guru of the Sikhs, Guru Nanak was born. He started the Sikh Panth as a reform and reconciliatory movement between

representing the foreign media was allowed to be present in Amritsar. This proved counter-productive. The lesson was learnt.

A few years later in 1988, Indian security forces in full view of media carried out Operation Black Thunder, which had the same aim as Operation Blue Star. Even during the operation, there was no restriction on media persons if they dared to go into the Golden Temple Complex. Some did and had a change of heart. Media were allowed to go into the Complex with officers of the civil administration after the surrender of the terrorists. Even after the operation was over security forces just did not enter the Golden Temple Complex. The result was just the opposite of the Operation Blue Star as the media could describe at first-hand how the shrine was being misused and desecrated by the terrorists. In fact, initially the order was that nobody would be allowed within 300 metres of the Golden Temple for security reasons. But fearing the consequences like the Operation Blue Star the media persons were exempted from this restriction. Even outdoor broadcast vans with TV cameras had no restrictions. This openness paid off as people around the world and also in Punjab could see what was happening and any attempt to distort the facts did not bear any fruits. Doordarshan got international awards for the coverage of Operation Black Thunder.

A comparison of the 1947 Kashmir war and Kargil war in

Hinduism and Islam. It continued to be so until the ninth Sikh Guru, Guru Teg Bahadur was beheaded on the orders of Emperor Aurangzeb as he refused first the request and then the order of the Emperor to convert to Islam. Aurangzeb was told by his advisors if Guru Teg Bahadur accepts Islam it would be easy to convert the Hindus of Kashmir to Islam. Guru Teg Bahadur's son, the tenth Sikh Guru, Guru Gobind Singh raised a fighting force from among his followers and gave the present form to the Sikhs. After that it became a tradition in Punjab that the eldest son of a Hindu family would become a Sikh.

1999 is more or less similar to the two Golden Temple operations discussed above. At the time of Kargil War, which was almost a replay of events of 1947, there were enough media persons to tell the world what was happening. In 1947 Pakistan denied involvement and blamed it on tribal raiders.[11] The Maharaja of Kashmir, Hari Singh wanted to remain independent and had an agreement with Pakistan.[12] Communication links to Srinagar were from Lahore. Lord Louis Mountbatten was still the Governor General of India and did not want India to intervene unless the Maharaja joined the Indian Union, despite the appeals for help. There was direct involvement of the Pakistani Army in both the operations. They were tribal raiders in 1947 and they were Mujahideen in 1999.

The Indian establishment was caught napping in Kargil[13] and therefore they could hardly plan any media manipulation. Media persons were there and were reporting events as they saw them. Not only Indian media but even foreign media representatives were also there and enjoyed full freedom. The lesson had been learnt from Operation Blue Star and Operation Black Thunder. In case of Operation Blue Star, officials had asked the journalists staying in a hotel in Amritsar which organization did they represent? And if, the news organization was foreign the person was asked to pack-up and sit in the

11. In an editorial, 'Freedom's Battle in Kashmir', veteran journalist M. Chalapathi Rau wrote in the *National Herald*, Lucknow, on 8 November 1947, 'Can he (Pakistani Prime Minister Liaquat Ali Khan) or Mr Jinnah deny a plan or a programme? If aggression was not thought of, where from did the arms come? Why is there a plan in attack and defence? Why are ex-INA officers violating the sanctity of the pledge to Netaji Bose and Pakistan army officers, found among the leaders? How is there a directing brain behind the operation?'

12. It was called the 'Stand-Still Agreement' and was to maintain the status quo.

13. Everybody in the Indian establishment accepts it.

coach standing in the hotel compound and were taken back to Delhi. Media persons then missed the story and they were hostile. They believed whatever they heard and some even imagined,[14] things as they were denied the access to the event. In Operation Black Thunder they were allowed to go in and the reports were factual.

The difference between Kashmir 1947 and Kashmir 1999 (Kargil) was the huge presence of free media and the freedom enjoyed by them on the Indian side. Pakistan mostly kept them outside the war zone. The reports from the front clearly indicated who the aggressor was. It led to Washington identifying India as the good guy and then the US and world media turned the heat on Pakistan. Total transparency and maximum possible access to media made the difference. There were some wrong reports[15] but they were corrected in due course. In the end, media freedom paid.

It is still a fact that the Western media dominate the world. It is becoming more so with the mergers and strategic alliances among Western media corporations and companies. It is also a fact that they present a distorted picture of the world, which is unfair to the developing countries.[16] But even then for the countries of the developing world, despite fears of distortion, the best policy is to allow full freedom to the media. The Kargil case has proved this point.

14. Those days I was Special Correspondent of the news agency *Samachar Bharti*. We had a correspondent in Punjab who was close to Sant Bhindranwale. In the early stages of Operation Blue Star when some foreign media representatives started quoting him in their reports I asked to get through to him. After trying all the phone numbers he reported that if somebody is quoting him it's a lie.

15. Like three storied bunkers in the mountains.

16. It has been well documented during an NWICO debate, when UNESCO funding was available for such research. Things have not changed much since, though there is not much research now in that area.

Other Public Relation Tools

Many PR tools have been already dealt with in the earlier chapters. Some of them have emerged recently while others are old. Some of the older tools have modified their delivery with the use of new technologies. For example annual reports now can be delivered using websites.

Annual Reports

Annual reports are the most important PR tool a company has to communicate with its current and potential shareholders. An annual report gives a company an opportunity to offer an overview of its direction as it moves forward. Annual reports should be attractive, but not lavish.

Annual reports address two distinct publics. First, investors who focus on the front section and want basic information about the company and its products; and second, securities analysts who read both sections to obtain financial data to check for consistency with other data sources to see the image that management wants to convey and to gain insights into the management's thinking. Do not assume that these publics are familiar with your industry. Care should be taken to write in plain language and define unfamiliar terminology.

In fact, investors often want the most elementary information about the company. Many analysts, especially those who are unfamiliar with the company, may also find such basic information useful and expect it to be present.

Investors and analysts expect the company to put its best efforts in the annual report. Thus readers approach reports with great scepticism and are hypersensitive to wording omissions and any perceived discrepancies. Readers often magnify any problem that is mentioned. Take care to address challenges forthrightly without overstating them. Conversely, if no negatives are mentioned many readers will suspect an attempt to hide damaging information.

Annual reports are often skimmed rather than studied. Only few investors will read every word. Readers are generally impatient. They want to be able to extract key messages quickly and easily. Consequently layered presentations replete with bullet points, bold highlights, and other such devices are more easily digested.

Comprehension of the report is enhanced when key themes are emphasized throughout the report. 'Repetition with variation' is the classic tool of effective communication and is especially necessary for written material that tends to be skimmed rather than studied. However, it has to be done skilfully as too much overt repetition can sometimes bother those readers who closely review the report.

Satisfaction with an annual report is closely related to comprehension. If the document is difficult to understand the individual investor is likely to put it aside. For that reason technical terms should be explained. Charts, photographs, captions, and other graphic design elements are also powerful tools to improve comprehension, not just to make the publication look attractive. Annual report writers must strike a balance between the seasoned, knowledgeable investor and the novice, taking care to keep information sophisticated enough to please the former while simple enough to be understood by the latter.

Analysts and investors want the report to be easy to read and convenient to use. Readers easily get distracted and confused by cluttered, unimaginative layouts. Symbolism, irony, and puns are often missed or misunderstood. Both analysts and investors are mainly concerned with three things: profitability, products, and plans. All three issues are directed toward a company's future performance.

Investors and analysts want to know what a company produces and how that product affects them. Even for companies making intermediary products, annual report readers want to know what the final product is and how it impacts consumers.

The report should set up goals and explain how the company will use strategic objectives to meet these goals.

Annual reports are interpreted as reflecting the judgment of top management. The tone of the entire report not just the chairman's letter is thought to reveal much about the attitude and mind-set of the company's leaders. Annual reports should be direct, and clear and full of pertinent information.

Public Speaking

Delivering a speech is a very important PR tool. It still remains a powerful means of strategic communication even in this age of the Internet. There is still no equal to a speech as a vehicle for sharing one's thoughts with a live audience. Carefully prepared and skilfully delivered presentations are critical for helping the organization achieve their fundamental business objectives. To fully realize this potential, PR professionals must elevate public speaking opportunities to centre stage in an organization's overall communications strategy. Invitations to speak should be evaluated based on the opportunities they offer the organization to communicate with key audiences. Invitations then should be prioritized and assigned to appropriate individuals in the organization, or declined if they appear to offer little value. Speaking opportunities should be even solicited before audiences upon whom the success of an organization depends.

Remember every speaking engagement is fundamentally different. There is no presentation that you can develop and use at any occasion. One key difference concerns the situation of a speech. You could be giving a stand-alone talk, or a presentation as part of a panel. The two situations require different types of preparation. With stand-alone talks, you can focus solely on preparing and delivering your remarks. Other speeches at the same event don't directly determine what you say and how long you have to say it, although it's important to understand how your presentation fits into the overall event.

Panel presentations offer greater challenges because each speech must 'fit' into a designated theme. An effective moderator ensures that individual presenters are familiar with each other's prepared remarks so their comments overlap as little as possible, and that each speaker remain within the allotted timeframe. Many people are not skilled moderators, so it's incumbent on the individual speakers to communicate with fellow panellists prior to the event.

The audience also makes every speech unique. Each audience has its own collective expectations, values, and experience in relation to the topic. It is vital to incorporate this perspective into your remarks. Studying materials on the organization sponsoring the event is worthwhile. Secure a list of people attending to determine if there will be familiar faces (friendly or unfriendly) in the crowd. Contact some of them before the speech to gauge their expectations.

You also need to prepare and practice your presentation well in advance of the actual event. More important, make sure that the speech communicates your organization's business objectives clearly and succinctly, without appearing like a commercial. Input from other staff is helpful, especially when obtained far enough in advance of your talk to be effectively incorporated into it.

Preparation is also necessary for the question and answer session that follows a speech. You should prepare answers to questions most likely to be asked. Include difficult, even controversial questions as well as straightforward ones. Rehearse your answers beforehand so that you can give right answers. This preparation will enable you to use the question and answer session to expand on key messages in your talk, while solidifying your standing in the eyes of the audience as a knowledgeable, skilled communicator. Speaking engagements put your CEO in front of large audiences. Being part of an event can create an 'expert' reputation for your company or senior management. Such reputation may lead to an invitation to write a bylined article in a key trade publication which can bring more exposure. You can meet with the editors. Networking instead of exhibiting or advertising can reduce costs and possibly lead to better results.

Exhibitions and Road Shows

Exhibitions and road shows allow you to interact with your

audience face to face. Start by identifying exactly what you want to achieve. Your target audience should dictate your choice of approach. If your audience is specific, your best solution would be a specialist exhibition. To communicate a blanket message to a wide, diverse audience, a touring exhibition stand or promotional vehicle at a series of shopping centres or other 'through venues' may be the answer.

With your requirements identified, you should prepare a design brief and appoint a specialist designer.

The Exhibition Stand or Vehicle

- Designs should allow for any space limitations. Surprisingly, this is often overlooked.
- The design should be vibrant, attractive and reflect the corporate identity. The appearance should be graphically based. It should not be cluttered.
- Maximize interest by using interactive displays.
- Make sure all your logistical needs as well as IT, communications, storage, etc., are catered for.
- Make written messages clear by using bullet point text.
- The stand should be open — avoid too many exterior walls, as some people may feel trapped.
- The stand should conform to all fire and safety regulations.

Construction

Prepare technical specifications based on the design. Make this the basis of your construction tender documents. Select a company that is financially secure, with sufficient logistical support and personnel to fulfil the contract, and a track record in the type of event you are staging.

Promotional Literature

Provide hand-outs for the public. Make sure there is enough for the whole project and divide it between venues.

Sound project management is the key to a successful event. A badly staged event is worse than none at all as the public will associate any problems with your organization.

Videos

Consult all involved parties and agree to a concise statement of your objectives. This should define the target audience, where and how they will view the video, and what you want them to do, know or think as a result. It's worth taking time to get an agreement on all uses. Ensure that key communication priorities are not watered down by less essential ones.

Decide key content. Context and background material can also be very helpful. State any required references to other publicity material.

Check availability of your key people or areas that may be involved in making the video. Include these, and any restrictions on access, in the brief. Also include details of facilities you will provide and be sure you can deliver.

State start and delivery dates, giving as long a production period as possible. Indicate how long approvals are likely to take. Give a budget indication. Think through the marketing and distribution and investigate their associated costs.

Compile a short list of four or five production companies who have handled this type of project before — you might wish to allow one 'outsider'. Always ask to see examples of similar work and a list of recent clients.

In your written brief, give as much supplementary information as you can and offer an oral brief. State that you will need to approve scripts, rough-cuts, commentary and the finished video. Reserve the option of approving locations, contributors, artistes, graphics and music. Request an overall approach, a detailed treatment, itemized budget and fully detailed schedule. The payment schedule should be linked to your approval(s). Ask for a nominated producer, director and writer and full details of their recent work. Get company and financial details and state what intellectual property rights you require to be included in the price.

You can make initial judgments from written submissions with the treatment as the key element. Trust your response to the overall approach rather than an analysis of whether details are correct — these can be corrected in later drafts. You will be dependent on the abilities of the producer and director to realize the script, and it is usually best to meet them in person.

Your tender team can judge the producer's effectiveness from the presentation and their track record. A director's ability shows up in their show-reel but you will want to hear how they visualize the script and see evidence of enthusiasm. If you pay after approvals, only modest financial stability is required, but be alert to signals that the contractor will try for extra charges. Clarify queries the company may have about terms and conditions.

Making a video is an evolutionary process. At every stage of production, the creative and technical team can all add something positive or be restricted to a limited role. One key function for you is to provide clear feedback at all stages and to arrange sign-offs at agreed stages. Arrange for your experts to check scripts, and possibly shoots as well, for technical accuracy. Don't feel inhibited about challenging anything that does not seem right, and ask again if you do not understand the explanation. You will contribute most if you state what is not right rather than how to make it right and if you tactfully restrain the budding scriptwriters and directors among your colleagues.

Merchandising

Branded merchandise items are important for self-promotion and help raise awareness of particular messages with the target audience. The use of merchandise items is becoming more widely acceptable even for government campaigns and is a vital part of the promotions mix. Merchandise items are mainly used to communicate messages rather than generate sales and are usually used as giveaways.

Sales Promotion

Sales promotion covers the range of techniques used to attain sales/marketing objectives in a cost-effective manner by adding value to a product or service either to intermediaries or end users, normally but not exclusively within a defined time period

The application of sales promotion in government campaigns is not as extensive or appropriate as in the private sector. Sales promotion tends to focus attention on particular issues/ products at a particular time and place and provides the immediate incentive to buy. Objectives can include increasing loyalty, repeat purchase, widening usage, and creating interest and awareness. Sales promotion techniques that may be applicable for communicating government messages could include competitions, tie-ins with third parties, reader offers, advertising, promotions and promotional items (merchandise).

Advertising

Advertisements involve purchasing time or space in such mass media as television, radio, newspapers or magazines to explain, or to urge or to persuade the use or adoption of a product, service or an idea. Advertising, a Marketing Management function, has been defined by the American Marketing Association as 'any paid form of non-personal presentation and promotion of ideas, goals or services by an identified sponsor'.

PR departments are often asked to handle advertising directly or through ad agencies. There are two motives, one to use the communication expertise of PR professionals and the other to give them some leverage with media. There are times when advertising should be used as a PR tool so that the message is given as such and not as mediated by the editorial process of media.

The field of advertisement management is made up of a system of interacting organizations and institutions, all of which play a role in the advertising process. At the core of the system are advertisers, the organizations that provide financial resources that support advertising. Advertisers are private and public sector organizations that use mass media to achieve their respective organizational objectives.

Though the advertisers provide money, advertising agencies make things happen. Their importance has increased because the era of brand loyalty is almost a thing of the past. Ad agencies now create brand images for new products and resurrect those of the fading ones. The agencies vary in size, organization structure and services they offer. Large agencies have networks of branch offices in major cities. Advertising agencies do the planning for their clients, create advertisements, and select the appropriate media for placing them.

A mid-size agency has typically four core departments, viz., *client servicing*, *creative*, *media*, and *art production*, besides other support services, such as, finance and accounts.

The Client Servicing Department provides the link between the agency and the client on the one hand, and with other departments in the agency, on the other.

The Creative Department, which actually creates the advertisement, is perceived as the most glamorous one in an advertising agency. It engages two types of people — visualisers and copywriters. Visualisers are artists who are responsible for the layout and visual aspects of the advertisement. Copywriters, on the other hand, prepare the copy, i.e., the written part of the advertisement or scripts for TV commercials.

The Media Department is responsible for media planning and buying space or time. Media planning largely involves market research about, among others, media habits and preferences of consumers.

The Art Production Department is responsible for giving physical shape to the concept created by the Creative Department in the form of final product to be passed on to the client for publication. The staff of the Department includes commercial artists.

Clipping Service

Clipping services, in-house or outside have been used by PR departments for monitoring the impact of any PR campaign. They are also used to monitor environments. Copies or photocopies of what has appeared in the media are collected and put up before relevant executives. This is also a regular exercise in Government PR departments.

Technology has given a new dimension to this service as

well. For example a clipping service vendor is offering, 'We provide you with a customized PowerPoint presentation, showcasing your news announcement as it is republished on various sites throughout the Web. Every slide in the presentation includes a URL linking directly to the mentioned site, allowing you to easily view your news live on the Web. Delivered in a dynamic, user-friendly format, our PowerPoint presentations are an effective accountability tool to be shared with both clients and colleagues alike. After your press release has been distributed to one of our industry-specific channels, our staff will search key websites that would be appropriate publishers of your news. We then capture images of the releases as they appear on these sites and compile them in a PowerPoint presentation. This presentation is e-mailed to you within 24 hours. The PowerPoint presentation will contain at least 10 clippings. This service is also available in Word format.'

Other Monitoring Services

There many other monitoring services on offer from PR agencies, for example:

Trends — Know what is happening today. Add general industry terms such as 'car dealers' or 'biomedical' to stay on top of your industry.

Market Intelligence — Get immediate notification when other industry players merge, launch new products, or open a new call centre. Add the names of your leading competitors and quickly gather insider information so your company can stay one step ahead.

Opinion Monitoring — Be aware of what the press is writing about the general public's reaction to the activities of your company and those in your industry. Press coverage of your CEO or prominent board members can be tracked specifically.

General News and Information — Stay up to date on the actions of the government, private sector or the general economy that will affect your business. Get timely information about legislation and other laws that will impact your business.

In-house PR departments can handle many such monitoring activities. A news agency service, ticker or screen based, could be useful in the PR department and / CEOs office.

Internal Communications

Staff are the primary stakeholders for any organization and good internal communication ensures that they deliver the organization's goals and business objectives. Effective communication helps to drive employees' engagement, ensuring improved delivery for customers.

Good internal communication plays a key role in delivering organizational business objectives and goals. Here are some tips:

- Set clear and achievable objectives, identify target audience(s), prepare strategy, select channel(s), and consider resources.
- Always be clear about the outcome you want your communication to achieve — awareness, understanding, engagement, acceptance or commitment.
- Think carefully about your existing channels and review them regularly. To ensure you are as effective as possible you may need to consider creating new ones.

- Liaise with colleagues in other areas of your communications group, and the wider organization, to ensure you are aware of forthcoming announcements and events.
- Be sure that, as far as possible, staff hear about issues from the department first and the media second.
- Monitor progress, evaluate your success and build in lessons learned when planning future activity.

Every organization should have an internal communications strategy which should take full account of its vision and values, and make clear the role of internal communications in delivering the organization's goals. The strategy should also set out internal communication principles within the organization. One of these principles should be based on the two-way nature of communication. Although there may often be pressure to provide information and 'tell' employees, about initiatives, your strategy should establish the importance of feedback. It should also be based on research among staff and an audit of existing internal communication channels.

Ideally, your strategy should be fully endorsed by your corporate or management board. When approved, it should also be made available to all staff so that they can see the framework that surrounds internal communications and gain insight into the reasoning behind it.

Specific strategies should be produced for individual announcements and policies. These should take into account the overarching strategy and the organization's business/delivery plans. They should highlight a clear objective, segment the internal audience as far as possible, make clear which channels are to be used and outline resources needed, expected outcomes and plans for evaluation.

Your choice of communication channel(s) will depend on the issue at hand. The continuum runs from initial awareness through to commitment. The stages are outlined below, along with suggested channels which can be most appropriate for them. It is vital, however, that you make decisions based on the suitability of the channels in your own organization, for example whether or not your staff magazine is good at raising awareness. Ongoing evaluation of your communication channels to establish how well your audiences respond to them is crucial. Keep up to date with the most effective ways to reach your audiences by asking them what they want.

As with any other communications activity, demonstrating value for money is vital. You should always be able to clearly explain why a particular solution is the most effective and appropriate for your audience.

Intranets

Decide whether you can use an existing intranet to meet your objectives. If you need to set up something new, first decide what you want it to achieve.

A brief should specify:

- your aims and objectives for the intranet;
- your audience and its needs (now and in the near future);
- the appropriate 'look and feel'.

You should also cover:

- the level of technology and platforms on which you want the intranet to run;
- guidelines on what should go onto the intranet;
- how much of the text, photography and videos you

expect your suppliers to create, and how much you will provide;
- who is monitoring/providing content in the long term;
- all services you want (for example, reporting back on access statistics, chat forums, promotion advice);
- a clear description of how a supplier should test and debug programmes; and
- delivery date and other key stages.

Staff Magazines and Newsletters

Most organizations have an in-house magazine, usually published monthly. To maximize its effectiveness staff should be able to trust your magazine.

You should decide upon and set out your magazine's rationale. This states what the objective of the magazine is, how it should communicate with staff, what should (and shouldn't) be covered in it, and its look, feel and tone. Setting out the rationale is particularly important when you have more than one in-house publication.

Generally speaking, magazines can be effective for helping understanding of issues and can, when done well, help bind the organization together. Newsletters can be useful for providing management information and corporate information, along with perhaps more local information.

As long as objectives or a rationale have been set for each magazine or newsletter, you can have a range of regular magazines that work together, each covering a specific territory.

E-mail

E-mail can be used to target specific communities and can promote inclusiveness in multi-site departments. E-mail is active (can direct/alert with links to the intranet) and sign-offs or log-on messages can promote messages and services. The dangers of e-mail are over use (especially messages to all staff) and the possibility of over-reliance, leading to a lack of face-to-face meetings. You will need to decide when to provide all information in an e-mail and when to direct readers to links on your intranet.

Team Briefing

A team briefing is a face-to-face briefing of staff by their managers. Messages are co-ordinated from the centre and briefings work best when staff are given the opportunity to discuss and for feedback (to allow for understanding and engagement), if staff hear messages from someone they know and trust, and can make the information relevant to their local unit. The disadvantages are in managing the message being delivered, and securing buy in from the managers concerned.

The most popular team briefing method is based upon the (former) Industrial Society model that provides core briefing on the four Ps (Progress, People, Policy and Points for action). Any team briefing model used should be tailored to your organization, to ensure it works with and takes advantage of your corporate culture.

Staff Conferences

These can be useful to relay important organizational information to staff on the day it is announced. 'Face-to-face' events with senior management can also be useful for engagement, particularly if staff are allowed the opportunity for a Q & A session. They are also an effective channel for communicating organizational change. The ability to organize a conference for all staff clearly depends upon the size of the organization. A number of smaller sessions could be run over the course of a day if required.

Regular staff conferences can be used to bring staff together to discuss and help to formulate the organization's way forward. For example, a conference could be used to help put together a new vision and values statement and this could be followed up when appropriate.

Lunch-time Seminars

Brief lunch-time talk sessions can be used to update staff on key issues and are often used to give staff the opportunity to find out about each others' work.

Leaflets and Booklets

One-off leaflets and booklets can be produced to support departmental initiatives and announcements.

Display Stands and Electronic Screens

Stands can be produced for reception areas and to support staff conferences or road shows. Electronic screens are also a useful means of keeping staff up to date with 'early morning' messages on the wider organization on their way into work and they provide external visitors with an insight into the organization and its activities.

Timing

The timing of internal communications activity is crucial. It is essential to ensure tie in with external announcements so that staff should pick up information from the organization first, before they see or hear about it in external media.

There may be times when this may not be possible, however the overriding principle should be to provide staff with whatever information is available, as soon as you can, with the promise of further updates when available. As an internal communicator you may need to persuade colleagues that staff should have information ahead of its external release.

Evaluation

As with any communications activity, evaluation is essential. Straightforward quantitative evaluation, such as the number of people who open an e-mail message may be all that is required for some activity. Staff surveys can provide both quantitative and qualitative information and focus groups can be useful if you want qualitative information about employees' views.

Public Relations Ethics

When Western scholars talk about ethics they begin with Socrates, Plato and Aristotle. Indians can easily go back to the Vedas. Those were the times when there was no mass media or Internet. But there was communication. There was speech and ethical principles of communication were established. One finds the essence of the Vedas in the Upanishads. And there we find moral pronouncements like *Satyam vada* (Speak the truth), *Satyat na pramaditavyam* (There should be no inadvertence about truth).[1] There is a related statement in the Mundaka Upanishad, which has been used, in India's national emblem *Satyameva jayate* (Truth alone triumphs).[2] 'Tell the truth. Let the public know what's happening and provide an accurate picture of the company's character, ideals, and practices', is the first of the six Page principles put forth by the Arthur W. Page Society founded in 1983 as a professional organization with a single mission: to strengthen the management

1. Both the phrases are from Taittiriya Upanishad (I-xi-1) as presented in Eight Upanishads, vol. I, translated by Swami Gambhiranand and published by Advaita Ashram, Calcutta, 1957, pp. 283–84.

2. *Satyameva jayate na anrtam* is from Mundaka Upanishad (III-i-6) as presented in Eight Upanishads, vol. II, translated by Swami Gambhiranand and published by Advaita Ashram, Calcutta, 1957, p. 146.

policy role of the chief corporate public relations officer. In this sense ancient Vedas are so contemporary!

Concept of Ethics

It is essential to understand the basic concept of ethics and differentiate this from other related terms and concepts. The closest to it is moral that comes from the Latin word *mos* (plural *mores*), which means 'custom or way of life'.[3] The term ethics is derived from the Greek word *ethos* which means 'custom' or 'character'. Thus the terms 'morals' and 'ethics' are essentially synonyms. However, 'morals' and 'morality' ordinarily refer to the conduct itself while 'ethics' and 'ethical' suggest the study of moral conduct or the system or the code that is followed. For example, we usually speak of an ethical system or code and of a moral act or a moral man.

The moral system under which moral standards are based on customs, which in turn are accepted without reflection is called customary morality and group morality. This system was especially prevalent among kinship groups. As the population increased and society became more complex, it was desirable that the simple customary observances be made more specific. Laws were then formulated. These laws either crystallized previous customs or changed them to some extent.

Ethics attempts to determine what conduct is good or what is bad or what might be approved and what disapproved. It undertakes to furnish a standard for distinguishing between a better character and a worse one. Ethics is a normative study of the principles underlying the desired types

3. The Latin word 'mos' has a twofold meaning, sometimes it means custom and sometimes it means a natural or quasi-natural inclination to perform some particular action.

of human conduct. Ethics is concerned with the value of an activity or a thing. It is the science of what is morally right.[4]

Reflective morality means that stage of moral development in which men formulate moral judgments on the basis of a reflective evaluation of principles and the careful examination of facts in their relation of human life. Men need to ask at times, not what was done in the past, but what the present demands. The growth of intelligence is an integral part of the development of morality. Thus moral life and intelligent life are more or less synonymous.

With the growth of society, regulations expressed themselves outwardly in law and inwardly in conscience. As conflicts arose men searched for standards of judgement and reflective criticism was born. As men became increasingly liberated from blind custom, they tended to direct their conduct more and more on the basis of a distinct philosophy of life. Moral standards grow out of life itself and are related to human feelings and intelligence. As intelligence and experience grow and expand, the requirements of personal and social welfare are taken into account more and more. Human behaviour is never the result of environmental factors alone or of human traits alone: it is always the result of the interaction of the individual and his environment.

It is claimed that there is an inner voice or inner law — a sense of obligation — which must be obeyed. The capacity to feel a moral obligation was called conscience. Conscience is in part the voice of the community within us. It is the result of the training and experience we have had during our impressionable years.

The 'voice' or 'dictates' of conscience consists in the conflict

4. Harold H. Titus, *Ethics for Today*, New York: American Book Company, 1957, pp. 8–9.

between the pull or push of a prescription or a taboo and some contrary impulse. In fact the rule of any code whatsoever is at no time complete or unchallenged. Variations are sometimes allowed, sometimes assert and sometimes operate in secret, but always exist.

Right is the basis of the moral. It is a term of selection. It designates group approval as against group disapproval. Sometimes 'right' is same in all institutions. Occasionally people are described as morally bound but legally free, morally guiltless but legally responsible, moral victors but actual losers, and vice versa.

In ethics we are concerned with questions of right and wrong, duty and obligation and moral responsibility. When moralists use words like good or right to describe a person or action, they generally mean that the person or action has desirable qualities. While moralists often disagree about the nature of these qualities, they all agree that having determined the right thing to do, one must do it and avoid wrong.

Ethics is the organization or criticism of conduct in terms of notions like good, right or welfare. The 'ethical' is the construction or reconstruction of conduct in the light of these rational elements. Contemporary opinion tends to confirm William Graham Sumner (1840–1910)[5] in distinguishing folk-ways and customs as group habits; law as habits found and ordained, but enforced by police power; ethics as a corpus of rules derived by reflection among morals and morals themselves as the sum of taboos and prescriptions in folk-ways by which right conduct is defined.

Ethics should make clear to us why one act is better than another as ethics is the study, which deals with human conduct

5. William Graham Sumner and Albert Galloway Keller, *The Science of Society*, vol. 1, New Haven CT: Yale University Press, 1927, pp. 116–17.

insofar as this conduct may be considered right or wrong. Ethics is especially concerned with the right ways of doing things in the business of living itself and with the principles underlying the realization of these values in all human relationships.

As ethics is a study of human values, it attempts to stimulate the moral sense, to discover the true values of life and to inspire man to join in the quest of these values. Ethics is the secular and critical manner of taking account of the rationalizing process of conduct. Its temper is non-mystical and its orientation is social rather than theological.

The field of ethics, also called moral philosophy, involves systematizing, defending, and recommending concepts of right and wrong behaviour. Philosophers today usually divide ethical theories into three general subject areas: meta-ethics, normative ethics, and applied ethics. *Meta-ethics* investigates where our ethical principles come from, and what they mean. Are they merely social inventions? Do they involve more than expressions of our individual emotions? Meta-ethical answers to these questions focus on the issues of universal truths, the will of God, the role of reason in ethical judgments, and the meaning of ethical terms themselves. *Normative ethics* takes on a more practical task, which is to arrive at moral standards that regulate right and wrong conduct. This may involve articulating the good habits that we should acquire, the duties that we should follow, or the consequences of our behaviour on others. Finally, *Applied ethics* involves examining specific controversial issues. By using the conceptual tools of meta-ethics and normative ethics, discussions in applied ethics try to resolve these controversial issues.

There has been a great revival of applied or practical ethics. It is where media ethics including PR ethics can be located. One possible approach in applied ethics would be to curtail highly abstract philosophical theorizing and attend more closely to the lower level generalization of popular debate. The immediate object of professional service is the welfare of the client. The major problem of professional ethics arises when this objective fails of attainment or when it is incompatible with the public interest. Professional ethics may be distinguished from law not only with reference to different sanctions employed but also by the fact that the legal sanctions apply to all people within a specified territory whereas in professional ethics the incidence is on the members of particular functional groups.

There are many organizations representing PR professionals and the PR business. Most of them have their codes of ethics. It is impossible to deal with all of them but here are some important representative organizations that represent most PR professionals and different sectors of business with significant contributions to ethical codes and principles. There is also a tendency of several organizations joining hands to deal with ethical issues. That is also reflected in this selection.

Public Relations Society of India (PRSI)

International Code of Ethics for Public Relations as adopted by the Public Relations Society of India at the First All India Public Relations Conference, New Delhi, 21 April 1968.

CONSIDERING that all Member countries of the United Nations Organization have agreed to abide by its Charter which reaffirms 'its faith in fundamental human rights, in the dignity and worth of the human person' and that having regard to the very nature of their profession, Public Relations practitioners in these countries should undertake to ascertain and observe the principles set out in this Chapter,

CONSIDERING that, apart from 'rights', human beings have not only physical or material needs but also intellectual, moral and social needs, and that their rights are of real benefits to them only in so far as needs are essentially met,

CONSIDERING that, in the course of their professional duties and depending on how these duties are performed, Public Relations practitioners can substantially help to meet these intellectual, moral and social needs,

And lastly, CONSIDERING that the use of techniques enabling them to come simultaneously into contact with millions of people gives Public Relations practitioners a power that has to be restrained by the observance of a strict moral code,

On all these grounds the Public Relations Society of India hereby declares that it accepts, as its moral charter the principles of the following Code of Ethics, and that if, in the light of evidence submitted to the Society, a member of this Society should be found to have infringed this Code in the course of his professional duties, he will be deemed to be guilty of serious misconduct calling for an appropriate penalty.

Accordingly, each Member of this Society —

SHALL ENDEAVOUR

1. To contribute to the achievement of the moral and cultural conditions enabling human beings to reach their full stature and enjoy the indefeasible rights to which they are entitled under the 'Universal Declaration of Human Rights';
2. To establish communication patterns and channels which, by fostering the free flow of essential information, will make each member of the group feel that he

is being kept informed, and also give him an awareness of his own personal involvement and responsibility and of his solidarity with other members;

3. To conduct himself always and in all circumstances in such a manner as to deserve and secure the confidence of those with whom he comes into contact;
4. To bear in mind that because of the relationship between his profession and the public, his conduct — even in private — will have an impact on the way in which the profession as a whole is appraised.

SHALL UNDERTAKE

5. To observe, in the course of his professional duties, the moral principles and rules of the 'Universal Declaration of Human Rights';
6. To pay due regard to, and uphold, human dignity, and to recognize the right of each individual to judge for himself;
7. To establish the moral, psychological and intellectual conditions for dialogue in its true sense, and to recognize the right of the parties involved to state their case and express their views;
8. To act, in all circumstances in such a manner as to take account of the respective interests of the parties involved: both the interests of the organization which he serves and the interests of the publics concerned;
9. To carry out his undertakings and commitments which shall always be so worded as to avoid any misunderstanding, and to show loyalty and integrity in all circumstances so as to keep the confidence of his clients or employees, past or present and of all the publics that are affected by his actions.

SHALL REFRAIN FROM

10. Subordinating the truth to other requirements;
11. Circulating information, which is not based on established and ascertainable facts;
12. Taking part in any venture or undertaking, which is unethical or dishonest or capable of impairing human dignity and integrity;
13. Using any 'manipulative' methods or techniques designed to create subconscious motivations which the individual cannot control of his own free will and so cannot be held accountable for the action taken on them.

The International Public Relations Association (IPRA)

A group of public relations executives from Britain, the Netherlands, France, Norway and the United States met in Holland in March 1950 under the auspices of the Royal Netherlands International Trade Fair and the Public Relations Society of Holland.[6] Following a review of the needs and challenges entailed in an increasingly international practice of public relations, the participants resolved to set up a provisional committee aimed at promoting exchange of information and co-operation within the profession and eventually establishing an International Public Relations Association (IPRA). The International Public Relations Association (IPRA) was formally established in London on 1 May 1955, with the adoption of a Constitution and the appointment of the first IPRA Council. Throughout its existence IPRA has always sought

6. Before this there was an informal meeting in London.

to provide intellectual leadership for the public relations profession. A key part of this has been the development of Codes to provide an ethical framework for the activities of the profession. Upon joining IPRA all members undertake to uphold these Codes.

The International Code of Ethics or Athens Code[7]

CONSIDERING that all Member countries of the United Nations Organization have agreed to abide by its Charter which reaffirms 'its faith in fundamental human rights, in the dignity and worth of the human person' and that having regard to the very nature of the profession, Public Relations practitioners in these countries should undertake to ascertain and observe the principles set out in this Charter:

CONSIDERING that, apart from 'rights', human beings have not only physical or material needs but also intellectual, moral and social needs, and that their rights are of real benefit to them only insofar as these needs are essentially met;

CONSIDERING that, in the course of their professional duties and depending on how these duties are performed, Public Relations practitioners can substantially help to meet these intellectual, moral and social needs;

And lastly, CONSIDERING that the use of the techniques enabling them to come simultaneously into contact with millions of people gives Public Relations practitioners a power that has to be restrained by the observance of a strict moral code.

On all these grounds, all members of the International Public Relations Association agree to abide by this International Code of Ethics, and that if, in the light of evidence

7. Author: Lucien Matrat, Member Emeritus (France). Adopted by IPRA General Assembly, Athens, May 1965 and modified at Teheran, April 1968.

submitted to the Council, a member should be found to have infringed this Code in the course of his/her professional duties, he/she will be deemed to be guilty of serious misconduct calling for an appropriate penalty.

Accordingly, each member:

SHALL ENDEAVOUR

1. To contribute to the achievement of the moral and cultural conditions enabling human beings to reach their full stature and enjoy the indefeasible rights to which they are entitled under the 'Universal declaration of Human Rights';
2. To establish communications patterns and channels which, by fostering the free flow of essential information, will make each member of the group feel that he/she is being kept informed, and also give him/her an awareness of his/her own personal involvement and responsibility, and of his/her solidarity with other members;
3. To conduct himself/herself always and in all circumstances in such a manner as to deserve and secure the confidence of those with whom he/she comes into contact;
4. To bear in mind that, because of the relationship between his/her profession and the public, his/her conduct — even in private — will have an impact on the way in which the profession as a whole is appraised;

SHALL UNDERTAKE

5. To observe in his/her professional duties, the moral

principles and rules of the 'Universal Declaration of Human Rights';

6. To pay due regard to, and uphold human dignity and to recognize the right of each individual to judge for himself/herself;
7. To establish the moral, psychological and intellectual conditions for dialogue in its true sense, and to recognize the rights of these parties involved to state their case and express their views;
8. To act, in all circumstances, in such a manner as to take account of the respective interests of the parties involved; both the interests of the organization which he/she serves and the interests of the publics concerned;
9. To carry out his/her undertakings and commitments which shall always be so worded as to avoid any misunderstanding, and to show loyalty and integrity in all circumstances so as to keep the confidence or his/her clients or employers, past or present, and all of the publics that are affected by his/her actions;

SHALL REFRAIN FROM

10. Subordinating the truth to other requirements;
11. Circulating information which is not based on established and ascertainable facts;
12. Taking part in any venture or undertaking which is unethical or dishonest or capable of impairing human dignity or integrity;
13. Using any 'manipulative' methods or techniques designed to create subconscious motivations which the individual cannot control of his/her own free will and so cannot be held accountable for the action taken on them.

The IPRA Code of Professional Conduct or Venice Code[8]

A. Personal and Professional Integrity

1. It is understood that by personal integrity is meant the maintenance of both high moral standards and a sound reputation. By professional integrity is meant observance of the Constitution rules and, particularly, the Code as adopted by IPRA.

B. Conduct towards Clients and Employers

1. A member has a general duty of fair dealing towards his/her clients or employers, past and present.
2. A member shall not represent conflicting or competing interests without the express consent of those concerned.
3. A member shall safeguard the confidences of both present and former clients or employers.
4. A member shall not employ methods tending to be derogatory of another member's client or employer.
5. In performing services for a client or employer a member shall not accept fees, commission or any other valuable consideration in connection with those services from anyone other than his/her client or employer without the express consent of his/her client or employer, given after a full disclosure of the facts.
6. A member shall not propose to a prospective client that his/her fees or other compensation be contingent on the achievement of certain results; nor shall he/she enter into any fee agreement to the same effect.

C. Conduct towards the Public and the Media

1. A member shall conduct his/her professional activities

8. Adopted in Venice, May 1961.

with respect to the public interest and for the dignity of the individual.

2. A member shall not engage in practice which tends to corrupt the integrity of channels of public communication.
3. A member shall not intentionally disseminate false or misleading information.
4. A member shall at all times seek to give a faithful representation of the organization which he/she serves.
5. A member shall not create any organization to serve some announced cause but actually to serve an undisclosed special or private interest of a member or his/her client or employer, nor shall he/she make use of it or any such existing organization.

D. Conduct towards Colleagues

1. A member shall not intentionally injure the professional reputation or practice of another member. However, if a member has evidence that another member has been guilty of unethical, illegal or unfair practices, including practices in violation of this Code, he/she should present the information to the Council of IPRA.
2. A member shall not seek to supplant another member with his employer or client.
3. A member shall co-operate with fellow members in upholding and enforcing this Code.

The Charter on Environmental Communications or Environment Code[9]

This code has been prepared as a guide for members of the

9. Adopted by the IPRA Council in Nairobi, November 1991.

International Public Relations Association for areas of practice related to the environment.

1. IPRA Members accept that they have a responsibility to ensure that the information and counsel which they provide, and products or services which they promote, fall within the context of sustainable development.
2. Members shall endeavour to encourage their organizations, companies or clients to adopt policies which recognize that careless use of resources and disregard for the environment can lead to severe limitations for economic growth, grave social disruption and serious health hazards.
3. Members shall, where appropriate, counsel their companies, clients or organizations to undertake regular environmental assessments of products and operations and to produce and communicate environmental codes of practice or guidelines for their employees and other publics.
4. Members shall not publicise or promote products, organizations or services as having environmental benefit unless these benefits are demonstrable in the light of current science and knowledge.
5. Members shall endeavour at all times to promote openness and dialogue which fairly handle both facts and concerns related to the environment and development.
6. Members shall not seek to raise or respond to unrealistic environmental expectations but shall generally support organizations, products or services which are probably taking steps to improve environmental performance in a tie scale which takes account of community concerns and government requirements as well as technological and economic constraints.

7. Members shall seek to develop programmes which counsel and communicate on the benefit of a balanced consideration of environmental, economic and social development factors.
8. Members shall provide a free flow of information within and through IPRA concerning environmental and development issues on an international level.
9. Members should be familiar with, and encourage the organization they work for to support, and abide by, Codes of Practice of other internationally recognized organizations such as the United Nations and the International Chamber of Commerce.

Public Relations Society of America (PRSA)

With the vision to unify, strengthen and advance the profession of public relations, the Public Relations Society of America (PRSA)[10] has established itself as the pre-eminent organization that builds value, demand and global understanding for public relations.

PRSA is the world's largest organization for public relations professionals.[11] Its nearly 20,000 members, organized worldwide in over 100 chapters, represent business and industry, technology, counselling firms, government, associations, hospitals, schools, professional services firms and non-profit organizations.

Chartered in 1947, the PRSA's primary objectives are to advance the standards of the public relations profession and to provide members with professional development opportunities

10. The information is from the website of the society as in November 2005.

11. As it claims.

through continuing education programs, information exchange forums and research projects conducted on the national and local levels

The PRSA Assembly adopted this Code of Ethics in 2000. It replaces the Code of Professional Standards (previously referred to as the Code of Ethics) that was last revised in 1988.

Preamble

Public Relations Society of America Member Code of Ethics 2000

- Professional Values
- Principles of Conduct
- Commitment and Compliance

This Code applies to PRSA members. The Code is designed to be a useful guide for PRSA members as they carry out their ethical responsibilities. This document is designed to anticipate and accommodate, by precedent, ethical challenges that may arise. The scenarios outlined in the Code provision are actual examples of misconduct. More will be added as experience with the Code occurs.

The Public Relations Society of America (PRSA) is committed to ethical practices. The level of public trust PRSA members seek, as we serve the public good, means we have taken on a special obligation to operate ethically.

The value of member reputation depends upon the ethical conduct of everyone affiliated with the Public Relations Society of America. Each of us sets an example for each other — as well as other professionals — by our pursuit of excellence with powerful standards of performance, professionalism, and ethical conduct.

Emphasis on enforcement of the Code has been eliminated. But, the PRSA Board of Directors retains the right to bar from membership or expel from the Society any individual who has been or is sanctioned by a government agency or convicted in a court of law of an action that is in violation of this Code.

Ethical practice is the most important obligation of a PRSA member. We view the Member Code of Ethics as a model for other professions, organizations, and professionals.

PRSA Member Statement of Professional Values

This statement presents the core values of PRSA members and, more broadly, of the public relations profession. These values provide the foundation for the Member Code of Ethics and set the industry standard for the professional practice of public relations. These values are the fundamental beliefs that guide our behaviours and decision-making process. We believe our professional values are vital to the integrity of the profession as a whole.

ADVOCACY

- We serve the public interest by acting as responsible advocates for those we represent.
- We provide a voice in the marketplace of ideas, facts, and viewpoints to aid informed public debate.

HONESTY

- We adhere to the highest standards of accuracy and truth in advancing the interests of those we represent and in communicating with the public.

EXPERTISE

- We acquire and responsibly use specialized knowledge and experience.
- We advance the profession through continued professional development, research, and education.
- We build mutual understanding, credibility, and

relationships among a wide array of institutions and audiences.

INDEPENDENCE

- We provide objective counsel to those we represent.
- We are accountable for our actions.

LOYALTY

- We are faithful to those we represent, while honoring our obligation to serve the public interest.

FAIRNESS

- We deal fairly with clients, employers, competitors, peers, vendors, the media, and the general public.
- We respect all opinions and support the right of free expression.

PRSA Code Provisions

FREE FLOW OF INFORMATION

Core Principle

Protecting and advancing the free flow of accurate and truthful information is essential to serving the public interest and contributing to informed decision-making in a democratic society.

Intent

- To maintain the integrity of relationships with the media, government officials, and the public.
- To aid informed decision-making.

Guidelines

A member shall:

- Preserve the integrity of the process of communication.
- Be honest and accurate in all communications.

- Act promptly to correct erroneous communications for which the practitioner is responsible.
- Preserve the free flow of unprejudiced information when giving or receiving gifts by ensuring that gifts are nominal, legal, and infrequent.

Examples of Improper Conduct under this Provision

- A member representing a ski manufacturer gives a pair of expensive racing skis to a sports magazine columnist, to influence the columnist to write favorable articles about the product.
- A member entertains a government official beyond legal limits and/or in violation of government reporting requirements.

COMPETITION

Core Principle

Promoting healthy and fair competition among professionals preserves an ethical climate while fostering a robust business environment.

Intent

- To promote respect and fair competition among public relations professionals.
- To serve the public interest by providing the widest choice of practitioner options.

Guidelines

A member shall:

- Follow ethical hiring practices designed to respect free and open competition without deliberately undermining a competitor.
- Preserve intellectual property rights in the marketplace.

Examples of Improper Conduct under this Provision

- A member employed by a 'client organization' shares helpful information with a counseling firm that is competing with others for the organization's business.
- A member spreads malicious and unfounded rumors about a competitor in order to alienate the competitor's clients and employees in a ploy to recruit people and business.

DISCLOSURE OF INFORMATION

Core Principle

Open communication fosters informed decision-making in a democratic society.

Intent

- To build trust with the public by revealing all information needed for responsible decision-making.

Guidelines

A member shall:

- Be honest and accurate in all communications.
- Act promptly to correct erroneous communications for which the member is responsible.
- Investigate the truthfulness and accuracy of information released on behalf of those represented.
- Reveal the sponsors for causes and interests represented.
- Disclose financial interest (such as stock ownership) in a client's organization.
- Avoid deceptive practices.

Examples of Improper Conduct under this Provision

- Front groups: A member implements 'grass roots'

campaigns or letter-writing campaigns to legislators on behalf of undisclosed interest groups.
- Lying by omission: A practitioner for a corporation knowingly fails to release financial information, giving a misleading impression of the corporation's performance.
- A member discovers inaccurate information disseminated via a website or media kit and does not correct the information.
- A member deceives the public by employing people to pose as volunteers to speak at public hearings and participate in 'grass roots' campaigns.

SAFEGUARDING CONFIDENCES

Core Principle
Client trust requires appropriate protection of confidential and private information.

Intent
- To protect the privacy rights of clients, organizations, and individuals by safeguarding confidential information.

Guidelines

A member shall:
- Safeguard the confidences and privacy rights of present, former, and prospective clients and employees.
- Protect privileged, confidential, or insider information gained from a client or organization.
- Immediately advise an appropriate authority if a member discovers that confidential information is being divulged by an employee of a client company or organization.

Examples of Improper Conduct under this Provision

- A member changes jobs, takes confidential information, and uses that information in the new position to the detriment of the former employer.
- A member intentionally leaks proprietary information to the detriment of some other party.

CONFLICTS OF INTEREST

Core Principle

Avoiding real, potential or perceived conflicts of interest builds the trust of clients, employers, and the publics.

Intent

- To earn trust and mutual respect with clients or employers.
- To build trust with the public by avoiding or ending situations that put one's personal or professional interests in conflict with society's interests.

Guidelines

A member shall:

- Act in the best interests of the client or employer, even subordinating the member's personal interests.
- Avoid actions and circumstances that may appear to compromise good business judgment or create a conflict between personal and professional interests.
- Disclose promptly any existing or potential conflict of interest to affected clients or organizations.
- Encourage clients and customers to determine if a conflict exists after notifying all affected parties.

Examples of Improper Conduct under this Provision

- The member fails to disclose that he or she has a strong financial interest in a client's chief competitor.

- The member represents a 'competitor company' or a 'conflicting interest' without informing a prospective client.

ENHANCING THE PROFESSION

Core Principle

Public relations professionals work constantly to strengthen the public's trust in the profession.

Intent

- To build respect and credibility with the public for the profession of public relations.
- To improve, adapt and expand professional practices.

Guidelines

A member shall:

- Acknowledge that there is an obligation to protect and enhance the profession.
- Keep informed and educated about practices in the profession to ensure ethical conduct.
- Actively pursue personal professional development.
- Decline representation of clients or organizations that urge or require actions contrary to this Code.
- Accurately define what public relations activities can accomplish.
- Counsel subordinates in proper ethical decision-making.
- Require that subordinates adhere to the ethical requirements of the Code.
- Report ethical violations, whether committed by PRSA members or not, to the appropriate authority.

Examples of Improper Conduct under this Provision

- A PRSA member declares publicly that a product the

client sells is safe, without disclosing evidence to the contrary.

- A member initially assigns some questionable client work to a non-member practitioner to avoid the ethical obligation of PRSA membership.

Council of Public Relations Firms

The Council of Public Relations Firms based in New York, represents the business of public relations of more than 100 main public relations firms as members. Its mission is: To advance the business of public relations by building its value as a strategic business tool, setting industry standards, helping member firms manage successful and profitable businesses, and promoting the benefits of a career in public relations.[12] The following is its Code of Ethics:

> Members of the Council commit to standards of practice that assure clients, the public and media, employees, and business partners and vendors the highest level of professionalism and ethical conduct in every relationship with a Council member. This commitment is a requirement for application and continued membership in the Council.
>
> Member firms will serve their clients by applying their fullest capability to achieve each client's business objectives, and charging a fair price for that service. Members will avoid representing any conflicting or competing client interests without the expressed approval of those concerned. Council firms and their employees will respect clients' confidences and the privacy of client employees, and will refrain from recruiting employees of their clients.

12. From their website as on 8 November 2005.

In communicating with the public and media, member firms will maintain total accuracy and truthfulness. To preserve both the reality and perception of professional integrity, information that is found to be misleading or erroneous will be promptly corrected and the sources of communications and sponsors of activities will not be concealed.

Council members will respect the personal rights of their employees and former employees. They will provide employees the necessary tools to serve their clients and opportunities to develop their professional skills. They will safeguard the privacy and protect the professional reputation of current and former employees.

Commercial relationships with business partners and vendors will be handled in a businesslike manner; credit will be given for ideas and services provided by others.

A special task force comprising Council members created a Statement of Principles in June 2005. This document was created to provide clarity on the industry standards involved with issues such as transparency and PR firm contracts.

Statement of Principles

In their service to clients, public relations firms play a vital role in encouraging public discourse. The professionalism and objectivity of our firms helps clients engage in that discourse, and clients turn to us for our counsel and assistance to vigorously pursue their organizational goals in educating or persuading audiences that matter most to them. Public relations firms help clients as diverse as government agencies, public and private companies, and not-for-profit groups. In a democratic and free-market society, our clients' goals often put us in the sphere of such complex issues as thorny policy debates, intense market competition or critical education needs in areas of public health, safety and well-being.

Our overriding principle is that openness and transparency not only are in the public interest, they are also necessary tools for meeting our clients' objectives.

Members of the Council of Public Relations Firms embrace our responsibilities to open and transparent dialogue. We carry out our business in accordance with the following principles that guide our relationships with clients and the public.

1. *We adhere to the highest standards of ethics in the public relations profession.*
   The employees of public relations firms are members of a profession which has well-established guidelines for ethical behavior. We expect each of our employees to commit themselves to those guidelines, and advise our clients' communications professionals to do so as well.
2. *We are committed to accuracy.*
   Accuracy is fundamental to our business. There may be different points of view about issues and or products, but standards for factual accuracy are clear. We dedicate ourselves to accuracy — the spirit of it as well as the letter of it. We will advise our clients to be transparent and willing to engage in debate and discussion.
3. *We believe that our clients and the public are best served when third-party relationships with spokespeople, partners and allies are open and transparent.*
   Our bias in counseling clients is toward disclosure,

which we believe is appropriate as a principle and effective as a communications tool.

Third-party spokespersons, such as scientists, economists, scholars or celebrities, enrich the public discourse. Third-party organizations such as alliances or coalitions may be created to promote our clients' interests. When a spokesperson or expert is paid for participation we will insist on disclosure of payment.

Our clients and the public are best served when any relationship between third-party organizations and our clients is fully disclosed and when the sponsors of public relations tools such as video news releases are clearly identified.

4. *Working for Federal, state and local governmental entities involves a unique responsibility as it is paid for by taxpayers' dollars and, like the rest of our work, must uphold the public trust at all times. We are conscientious stewards of taxpayer dollars.*

Members of the Council of Public Relations Firms are proud to play a vital role in the development and implementation of these programs.

We recognize and accept this responsibility and act in accordance with the highest degree of ethical and financial conduct.

We strictly adhere to government rules and regulations regarding procurement and execution of government business and maintain the necessary training programs and physical infrastructure necessary to deliver on that commitment.

We believe that the public is entitled to know the identity of our government clients. We encourage government agencies and their communications agency partners to publicly disclose all contractual relationships.

5. *We are committed to agency practices that increase society's confidence in the practice of public relations. When we engage with journalists or other organizations, we disclose who we represent.*

   We respect the opinions of journalists and other spokespeople as their own.

   We do not retain journalists to represent client interests in their media.

   We will implement policies within our firms to carry out these principles, and we will train our employees about the imperative of upholding them and effectively communicating their importance to clients.

Additionally, The Council of Public Relations Firms, as part of its membership in the International Communications Consultancy Organisation (ICCO), participated in the development of the ICCO Stockholm Charter which was adopted in 2003. Firms must adhere to this charter as a part of the criteria of membership into the Council.

The ICCO Stockholm Charter

(Adopted by the International Communications Consultancy Organisation October 2003).

Public Relations consultancies are professional service firms who help clients influence opinions, attitudes and behaviour. Along with this influence comes responsibility to our clients, our people, our profession and society at large.

Objective Counsel and Advocacy — Public relations

consultancies may not have interests that might compromise their role as an independent consultant. They should approach their clients with objectivity, in order to help the client adopt the optimum communications strategy and behaviour.

Society — An open society, freedom of speech and a free press create the context for the profession of public relations. Consultancies operate within the scope of this open society, comply with its rules, and work with clients that have the same approach.

Confidentiality — Trust is at the heart of the relationship between a client and a public relations consultancy. Information that has been provided in confidence by a client and that is not publicly known should not be shared with other parties without the consent of the client.

Integrity of Information — Public relations consultancies should not knowingly mislead an audience about factual information, or about the interests a client represents. Consultancies must make their best efforts to strive for accuracy.

Delivering Promises — Consultancies must work with clients to establish clear expectations in advance about the output of their efforts. They must define specific goals for communications actions and then work to deliver on their promises. Consultancies must not offer guarantees which are not supportable, or which compromise the integrity of the channels of communication.

Conflicts — Consultancies may represent clients with conflicting interests. Work may not commence for a new and conflicting interest without the current client first being offered the opportunity to exercise the rights under any contract between the client and consultancy.

Representation — Consultancies may refuse or accept an assignment based on the personal opinions of the firm's management or the organization's focus.

Governance and Business Practices — Public relations consultancies are committed to ethical behaviour and implementation of best business practices in dealing with all audiences.

Chartered Institute of Public Relations

Institute of Public Relations (IPR), the leading professional body for the UK public relations industry was founded in 1948 and awarded Charter status in 2005 and became the Chartered Institute of Public Relations. The Institute has over 8,000 members. The CIPR is the largest professional body for PR practitioners in Europe. The CIPR is a founding member of the Global Alliance for Public Relations and Communication Management.

The CIPR operates a Code of Professional Conduct and disciplinary powers to which all members agree to adhere. The Professional Practices Committee of the Institute has occasion to handle complaints brought against members of the Institute who are thought to be in breach of the Code. In regard to the supply of public relations services, the Code emphasizes that honest and proper regard for the public interest, reliable and accurate information, and never misleading clients, employers and other professionals about the nature of representation or what can be competently delivered or achieved, are vital components to robust professional practice. Following extensive consultation, and comparison with several codes of other professional and public relations bodies to ensure broad consistency, a revised section A of the Code[13] was ratified at the IPR's October 2000 AGM. Since IPR has got a Royal Charter its name has been changed to Chartered Institute of Public Relations (CIPR):

CIPR Principles

1. Members of the Chartered Institute of Public Relations agree to:
   - i. Maintain the highest standards of professional endeavour, integrity, confidentiality, financial propriety and personal conduct;
   - ii. Deal honestly and fairly in business with employers, employees, clients, fellow professionals, other professions and the public;
   - iii. Respect the customs, practices and codes of clients, employers, colleagues, fellow professionals and other professions in all countries where they practise;
   - iv. Take all reasonable care to ensure employment best practice including giving no cause for complaint of unfair discrimination on any grounds;
   - v. Work within the legal and regulatory frameworks affecting the practice of public relations in all countries where they practise;
   - vi. Encourage professional training and development among members of the profession;
   - vii. Respect and abide by this Code and related Notes of Guidance issued by the Chartered Institute of Public Relations and encourage others to do the same.

13. Section B of the code deals with regulations governing complaints relating to professional conduct and is therefore not so relevant here.

Principles of Good Practice

2. Fundamental to good public relations practice are:

Integrity

- Honest and responsible regard for the public interest;
- Checking the reliability and accuracy of information before dissemination;
- Never knowingly misleading clients, employers, employees, colleagues and fellow professionals about the nature of representation or what can be competently delivered and achieved;
- Supporting the CIPR Principles by bringing to the attention of the IPR examples of malpractice and unprofessional conduct.

Competence

- Being aware of the limitations of professional competence: without limiting realistic scope for development, being willing to accept or delegate only that work for which practitioners are suitably skilled and experienced;
- Where appropriate, collaborating on projects to ensure the necessary skill base;
- Transparency and conflicts of interest;
- Disclosing to employers, clients or potential clients any financial interest in a supplier being recommended or engaged;
- Declaring conflicts of interest (or circumstances which may give rise to them) in writing to clients, potential clients and employers as soon as they arise;
- Ensuring that services provided are costed and accounted for in a manner that conforms to accepted business practice and ethics.

Confidentiality

- Safeguarding the confidences of present and former clients and employers;
- Being careful to avoid using confidential and 'insider' information to the disadvantage or prejudice of clients and employers, or to self-advantage of any kind;
- Not disclosing confidential information unless specific permission has been granted or the public interest is at stake or if required by law.

Maintaining Professional Standards

3. CIPR members are encouraged to spread awareness and pride in the public relations profession where practicable, by for example:

   - Identifying and closing professional skills gaps through the Institute's Continuous Professional Development programme;
   - Offering work experience to students interested in pursuing a career in public relations;
   - Participating in the work of the Institute through the committee structure, special interest and vocational groups, training and networking events;
   - Encouraging employees and colleagues to join and support the IPR;
   - Displaying the CIPR designatory letters on business stationery;
   - Specifying a preference for CIPR applicants for staff positions advertised;
   - Evaluating the practice of public relations through use of the CIPR Research and Evaluation Toolkit and other quality management and quality assurance systems

(e.g. ISO standards); and constantly striving to improve the quality of business performance;

- Sharing information on good practice with members and, equally, referring perceived examples of poor practice to the Institute.

Interpreting the Code

In the interpretation of this code, the Laws of the Land shall apply.

The Global Alliance

The Global Alliance for Public Relations and Communication Management was formally established in Chicago, Illinois, USA, on 25 October 2000 following initial meetings in 1999 at the Institute of Public Relations, London, England. The formation of the Alliance took place after a Public Relations World Congress sponsored by the Public Relations Society of America and the International Public Relations Association. More than 20 national and international associations were actively involved in the founding of this historic framework.

This new entity is an alliance of associations; there are no individual members. However, members of participating associations will benefit in a variety of ways. Interested individuals can access information regarding regional or international conferences and seminars, case studies, awards programs, benchmarking research, and other pertinent communication. The Alliance enhances networking opportunities for professionals and serves as a vehicle for examining ethical standards, universal accreditation options, and other initiatives to strengthen the profession around the world. The Global Alliance for Public

Relations and Communication Management has come up with a global protocol:[14]

Global Protocol on Public Relations (Protocol — Summer 2002)

Declaration of Principles

A profession is distinguished by certain characteristics or attributes, including:

- Mastery of a particular intellectual skill through education and training.
- Acceptance of duties to a broader society than merely one's clients/employers.
- Objectivity.
- High standards of conduct and performance.

We base our professional principles therefore on the fundamental value and dignity of the individual. We believe in and support the free exercise of human rights, especially freedom of speech, freedom of assembly, and freedom of the media, which are essential to the practice of good public relations.

In serving the interest of clients and employers, we dedicate ourselves to the goals of better communication, understanding, and cooperation among diverse individuals, groups, and institutions of society. We also subscribe to and support equal opportunity of employment in the public relations profession and lifelong professional development.

We pledge:

- To conduct ourselves professionally, with integrity,

14. Global Alliance Code of ethics project team: Jean Valin, APR, Fellow CPRS, Canada; Don LaBelle, APR, Fellow CPRS, Canada; Chris Skinner and Gary Mersham, APR, South Africa; Jim Lukaszewski, ABC, APR, Fellow PRSA, United States; Nigel O'Connor, IPR, United Kingdom; Toni Muzi Falconi, Italy, and Ulli Sats, Estonia.

truth, accuracy, fairness, and responsibility to our clients, our client publics, and to an informed society;

- To improve our individual competence and advance the knowledge and proficiency of the profession through continuing education and research and where available, through the pursuit of professional accreditation;
- To adhere to the principles of the Global Protocol on Ethics in Public Relations.

Protocol Standards

We believe it is the duty of every association and every member within that association that is party to the Global Protocol on Ethics in Public Relations to:

- Acknowledge that there is an obligation to protect and enhance the profession.
- Keep informed and educated about practices in the profession that ensure ethical conduct.
- Actively pursue personal professional development.
- Accurately define what public relations activities can and cannot accomplish.
- Counsel its individual members in proper ethical decision-making generally and on a case specific basis.
- Require that individual members observe the ethical recommendations and behavioural requirements of the Protocol.
- We are committed to ethical practices, preservation of public trust, and the pursuit of communication excellence with powerful standards of performance, professionalism, and ethical conduct.

Advocacy

We will serve our client and employer interests by acting as responsible advocates and by providing a voice in the market place of ideas, facts, and viewpoints to aid informed public debate.

Honesty
We will adhere to the highest standards of accuracy and truth in advancing the interests of clients and employers.

Integrity
We will conduct our business with integrity and observe the principles and spirit of the Code in such a way that our own personal reputation and that of our employer and the public relations profession in general is protected.

Expertise
We will encourage members to acquire and responsibly use specialized knowledge and experience to build understanding and client/employer credibility. Furthermore we will actively promote and advance the profession through continued professional development, research, and education.

Loyalty
We will insist that members are faithful to those they represent, while honouring their obligations to serve the interests of society and support the right of free expression.

Advancing the Protocol
We believe it is the responsibility of each member association to draw upon its own member's experiences to expand the number of examples of good and bad practice so as to better inform members' about ethical practices. Experiences should be broadly shared with other members within the association and with the Global Alliance so as to build up case histories that may assist in individual cases throughout the world.

Internet Ethics Code

As the latest communications tool, the Internet presents tremendous opportunities to build positive, productive relationships with a variety of publics. It also presents tremendous challenges to professional standards and ethical practices. The digital world is open and easily accessible to the public at large. Erroneous or misleading information can be posted on the Internet and disseminated instantly and widely. Anonymity on websites can cause irreparable harm. The news media, which increasingly uses the Internet as a source of information, demands accuracy. Public relations practitioners risk losing credibility for themselves and their clients if they violate that trust.

On 13 December 2001 a coalition of eleven public relations organizations agreed on principles that their members would be asked to follow in conducting business on the Internet. 'The coalition members are determined to promote the highest possible professional standards and ethical practices in the digital world,' James E. Murphy, president of the Arthur W. Page Society, the organization which coordinated the development of the principles, said in announcing the new ethics code. 'They want to insure that the information posted on the Internet is accurate and truthful and that the sources for that information are always identified.'

Organizations endorsing the principles included: Arthur W. Page Society, Corporate Communications Institute, Council of Communication Management, Council of Public Relations Firms, The Conference Board's Council on Corporate Communications Strategy, Institute for Public Relations, International Association of Business Communicators, Public Affairs Council, Public Relations Society of America, Public

Relations Society of America Foundation and Women Executives in Public Relations.

This Internet Ethics Code consists of four basic principles:

1. *Present Fact-based Content*: *a.* Tell the truth at all times. *b.* Ensure timely delivery of information. *c.* Tell the full story, adhering to accepted standards for accuracy of information.

2. *Be an Objective Advocate*: *a.* Act as a credible information source, providing round-the-clock access. *b.* Know your subject. *c.* Rely on credible sources for expert advice. *d.* Offer opportunities for dialogue and direct interaction with expert sources. *e.* Reveal the background of experts, disclosing any potential conflicts of interest or anonymous economic support of web content.

3. *Earn the Public's Trust*: *a.* Simultaneously contact multiple stakeholders with relevant and accurate information. *b.* Disclose all participation in online chat rooms and conferences. *c.* Correct information that is online. *d.* Provide counsel on privacy, security and other online trust issues.

4. *Educate the Public Relations Profession on Best Practices*: *a.* Compile case studies on the best use of the new media. *b.* Advance and encourage industry-wide adoption of best practices on the Internet. *c.* Practice principled leadership in the digital world, adhering to the highest standards.

The coalition has no formal mechanism to monitor the use of the Internet principles but is encouraging the members to voluntarily adopt the ethics code they have approved.

Charter on Media Transparency

Six global organizations on 26 July 2004 announced[15] their support for a set of principles designed to foster greater transparency in the dealings between public relations professionals and the media, and to end bribery for media coverage throughout the world. The organizations were the International Press Institute,[16] the International Federation of Journalists,[17] Transparency International,[18] the Global Alliance for Public Relations and Communications Management,[19] the Institute for Public Relations Research and Education,[20] and the International Public Relations Association.[21]

15. Each one of these organizations issued a press release to that effect.

16. The International Press Institute is a global organization with members in 115 countries dedicated to the promotion and protection of press freedom and the improvement of the practices of journalism. IPI's membership is made up of editors, media executives and leading journalists working for some of the world's most respected media outlets.

17. The International Federation of Journalists is the world's largest organization of journalists. The Federation represents around 500,000 members in more than 100 countries and promotes international action to defend press freedom and social justice through strong, free and independent trade unions of journalists.

18. Transparency International, founded in Berlin, Germany, is a non-profit worldwide coalition which is committed exclusively to fighting corruption. It raises public awareness of the damaging impact of corruption on social and economic development, and mobilizes the government, private sector and civil society to work together.

19. The Global Alliance is composed of over 50 member organizations, representing more than 150,000 individuals, with a mission to unify the profession and provide a framework for collaboration among the public relations profession and its practitioners throughout the world.

20. The Institute for Public Relations Research and Education, located at the University of Florida, is dedicated to improving the professional practice of public relations through research, education, measurement and evaluation.

21. The International Public Relations Association is the premier association for senior international public relations professionals, with over 1,000 members worldwide.

The principles, embodied in the *Charter on Media Transparency* developed by the *International Public Relations Association*, are that:

- News material should appear as a result of the news judgement of journalists and editors, and not as a result of any payment in cash or in kind, or any other inducements.
- Material involving payment should be clearly identified as advertising, sponsorship or promotion.
- No journalist or media representative should ever suggest that news coverage will appear for any reason other than its merit.
- When samples or loans of products or services are necessary for a journalist to render an objective opinion, the length of time should be agreed in advance and loaned products should be returned afterward.
- The media should institute written policies regarding the receipt of gifts or discounted products and services, and journalists should be required to sign the policy.

Here are some quotes that came with the announcement:

> 'In too many countries, bribery of the news media robs citizens of truthful information that they need to make individual and community decisions,' said Dr. Donald K. Wright, 2004 President of the International Public Relations Association. 'We started this campaign with the goal of creating greater transparency and eliminating unethical practices in dealings between news sources and the media.'
>
> 'The International Press Institute's General Assembly has endorsed these principles because all attempts to corrupt the media compromise the freedom of expression that protects

all other rights,' said Johann P. Fritz, Director of the International Press Institute.

Peter Eigen, Chairman of the Board of Transparency International, said, 'We have long believed in the power of coalitions to combat corruption in all its forms. The media has an important watchdog role to hold to account those in positions of power. To be credible in this role, it is essential that journalists refuse bribes and the corporate sector desists from offering bribes. It is also crucial that editors, publishers and media owners give journalists all the support they need to implement the media transparency principles announced today.'

'Courageous reporters risk life and limb every day to defend press freedom and human rights,' said Aidan White, General Secretary of the International Federation of Journalists. 'We cannot stand by while bribery mocks those sacrifices, anywhere in the world.'

'We represent professional public relations associations in 53 countries, and we want to bring that grassroots strength to this coalition for media transparency,' said Jean Valin, Chair of the Global Alliance for Public Relations and Communications Management. 'This is closely linked to ethics in organizations, which is a cornerstone of effective and credible communication with the public.'

'Last year the Institute for Public Relations Research and Education joined with the International Public Relations Association to release a comprehensive index that ranks 66 nations[22] for the likelihood that print journalists will seek or

22. Bribery of the media, according to the study, is most likely to occur in China, Saudi Arabia, Vietnam, Bangladesh and Pakistan. By contrast, those countries with the best ratings for avoiding such practices are Finland (first place); Denmark, New Zealand and Switzerland (tied for second place). Germany, Iceland, and the United Kingdom tied for third place, followed by Norway. Austria, Canada, the Netherlands, Sweden, Belgium, and the United States had the fifth best rating. India tied with Kenya for twenty-fifth best.

accept cash for news coverage,' said Frank Ovaitt, President and CEO-Elect of the Institute. 'We continue to believe this is a critical issue that serious journalists and public relations people must address together.'

Further Readings

Agar, Michael. *Language Shock: Understanding the Culture of Conversation*. New York: William Morrow, 1994.

Ali, Moi. *Practical Marketing and Public Relations for the Small Business*. London: Kogan Page, 2002.

Bagdikian, Ben H. *The Media Monopoly*. Boston: Beacon Press, 3d ed., 1990.

Best, Steven and Douglas Kellner. *Postmodern Theory: Critical Interrogations*. New York: Guilford Press, 1991.

Bigge, Morris L. *Positive Relativism: An Emergent Educational Philosophy*. New York: Harper & Row, 1971.

Black, Sam (Ed). *The Practice of Public Relations*. Oxford; Boston: Butterworth-Heinemann, 4th ed., 1995.

——— (Ed.). *International Public Relations*. London: Kogan Page co-published with the International Public Relations Association, 2d ed., 1995.

Carey, James W. *Communication as Culture: Essays on Media and Society*. Boston, MA: Unwin Hyman, 1989.

Center, Allen H. and Patrick Jackson. *Public Relations Practices: Managerial Case Studies and Problems*. Englewood Cliffs, NJ: Prentice-Hall, 4th ed., 1990.

Crable, Richard E. and Steven L. Vibbert. 'Mobil's Epideictic Advocacy: "Observations" of Prometheus Bound'. *Communication Monographs*, 50 (4), 1983, pp. 380–94.

———. 'Managing Issues and Influencing Public Policy'. *Public Relations Review*, 11 (2), 1985, pp. 3–16.

Creedon, P.J. 'Acknowledging the Infrasystem: A Critical Feminist Analysis of Systems of Theory'. *Public Relations Review*, 19 (2), 1993, pp. 157–66.

Conrad, Charles. *Strategic Organizational Communication: An Integrated Perspective*. Ft. Worth, TX: Holt, Rinehart, and Winston, 1990.

Cottone, L.P. 'The Perturbing Worldview of Chaos: Implications for Public Relations'. *Public Relations Review*, 19 (2), 1993, pp. 167–76.

Craig, Robert. 'Communication as a Practical Discipline', in Brenda Dervin, L. Grossberg, B. O'Keefe and E. Wartella (Eds), *Rethinking Communication*, vol. 1: Paradigm issues. New Brunswick, NJ: International Communication Association; Beverly Hills, CA: Sage Publications, 1989, pp. 97–122.

Cutlip, Scott M., Allen H. Center and Glen M. Broom. *Effective Public Relations*. Englewood Cliffs, NJ: Prentice-Hall International, Inc., 6th ed., 1985.

DeFleur, Melvin L. and Sandra J. Ball-Rokeach. *Theories of Mass Communication*. New York: Longman, 5th ed., 1989.

Dervin, Brenda. 'Verbing Communication: Mandate for Disciplinary Invention'. *Journal of Communication*, 43 (3), 1993, pp. 45–54.

Donohue, George A., C.N. Olien, and Phillip J. Tichenor. 'Mass Communication Research: Evolution of a Structural Mode'. *Journalism Quarterly*, 50 (3), 1973, pp. 419–25.

Durkheim, Emile. *The Division of Labor in Society* (Tr. from the French *De la Division du Travail Social* by George Simpson). Glencoe, IL: The Free Press, 1947.

Fine, M.G. 'New Voices in Organizational Communication: A Feminist Commentary and Critique', in Sheryl Perlmutter Bowen and Nancy Wyatt (Eds), *Transforming Visions: Feminist Critiques in Communication Studies*. Cresskill, NJ: Hampton Press, 1993.

Fitzpatrick, M. 'Communication and the New World of Relationships'. *Journal of Communication*, 43 (3), 1993, pp.119–26.

Follett, Mary Parker. *Dynamic Administration: The Collected Papers of Mary Parker Follett*, edited by Henry C. Metcalf and L. Urwick. London; New York: Harper & Brothers, Publishers, 1940.

Giddens, Anthony. *The Constitution of Society: Outline of the Theory of Structuration*. Berkeley: University of California Press, 1984.

Goldhaber, Gerald M. *Organizational Communication*. Dubuque, IA: W.C. Brown, 4th ed.,1986.

Greenwood, John D. *Relations and Representations: An Introduction to the Philosophy of Social Psychological Science*. London; New York: Routledge, 1991.

Grunig, James E. 'Publics, Audiences and Market Segments: Segmentation Principles for Campaigns', in Charles T. Salmon (Ed.), *Information Campaigns: Balancing Social Values and Social Change*. Newbury Park, CA: Sage Publications, 1989, pp. 199–228.

———. 'Symmetrical Presuppositions as a Framework for Public Relations Theory', in Carl H. Botan and Vincent Hazleton, Jr. (Eds), *Public Relations Theory*. Hillsdale, NJ: Lawrence Erlbaum Associates, 1989, pp. 17–44.

——— (Ed.). *Excellence in Public Relations and Communication Management*. Hillsdale, NJ: Lawrence Erlbaum Associates, 1992.

———. 'Implications of Public Relations for Other Domains of Communication'. *Journal of Communication*, 43 (3), 1993, pp. 164–73.

Grunig, James E. and Linda Childers. 'Reconstruction of a Situational Theory of Communication: Internal and External Concepts as Identifiers of Publics for AIDS'. Paper presented at the meeting of the Communication Theory and Methodology Division, Association for Education in Journalism and Mass Communication, Portland, OR, July 1988.

Grunig, James E. and Larissa A. Grunig. 'Models of Public Relations and Communication', in James E. Grunig (Ed.), *Excellence in Public Relations and Communication Management*. Hillsdale, NJ: Lawrence Erlbaum Associates, 1992, pp. 285–326.

Grunig, James E. and Todd Hunt. *Managing Public Relations*. New York; London: Holt, Rinehart and Winston, 1984.

Grunig, Larissa A. 'Toward the Philosophy of Public Relations', in Elizabeth Lance Toth and Robert L. Heath (Eds), *Rhetorical and Critical Approaches to Public Relations*. Hillsdale, NJ: Lawrence Erlbaum Associates, 1992, pp. 65–91.

Guth, David W. and Charles Marsh. *Public Relations: A Values-driven Approach*. Boston: Allyn and Bacon, 2000.

Hall, Edward T. *The Silent Language*, Garden City, NY: Doubleday, 1959.

Haywood, Roger. *All About PR*. London; New York: McGraw-Hill, 1984.

Heath, Robert L. 'The Wrangle in the Marketplace: A Rhetorical Perspective of Public Relations', in Elizabeth Lance Toth and Robert L. Heath (Eds), *Rhetorical and Critical Approaches to Public Relations*. Hillsdale, NJ: Lawrence Erlbaum Associates, 1992, pp. 3–15.

———. 'A Rhetorical Approach to Zones of Meaning and Organizational Prerogatives'. *Public Relations Review*, 19 (2), 1993, pp. 112–55.

Heath, Robert L. and Richard Alan Nelson. *Issues Management: Corporate Public Policymaking in an Information Society*. Beverly Hills, CA: Sage Publications, 1986.

Hiebert, Ray E. *Readings in International Public Relations Theory*. College of Journalism, University of Maryland, College Park, Maryland, 1992.

Holtz, Shel. *Public Relations on the Net: Winning Strategies to Inform and Influence the Media, the Investment Community, the Government, the Public, and More!* New York: American Management Association, 2d ed., 2002.

Hon, L.C. 'Toward a Feminist Theory of Public Relations'. *Journal of Public Relations Research*, 7 (1), 1995, pp. 27–88.

Katz, Daniel and Robert L. Kahn. *The Social Psychology of Organizations*. New York: Wiley, 2d ed., 1978.

Katz, Elihu. 'The Return of the Humanities and Sociology'. *Journal of Communications*, 33 (3), 1983, pp. 51–2.

Kendall, Robert. *Public Relations Campaign Strategies: Planning for Implementation*. New York: HarperCollins College Publishers, 2d ed., 1996.

Kincaid, D. Lawrence. *The Convergence Model of Communication*. Honolulu, HI: East-West Center, 1979.

Kuhn, Thomas S. *The Structure of Scientific Revolutions*. Chicago, IL: University of Chicago Press, 2d ed., 1970.

Laswell, Harold. 'The Structure and Function of Communication in Society', in Lyman Bryson (Ed.), *The Communication of Ideas: A Series of Addresses*. New York: Institute for Religious and

Social Studies; distributed by Harper & Brothers, 1948, pp. 37–51.

Laudan, Larry. *Progress and its Problems: Toward a Theory of Scientific Growth*. Berkeley, CA: University of California Press, 1977.

Lesly, P. 'Coping with Opposition Groups'. *Public Relations Review*, 18 (4), 1992, pp. 325–34.

Levine, Michael. *A Branded World: Adventures in Public Relations and the Creation of Superbrands*. Hoboken, NJ: John Wiley, 2003.

Levy, M.R. and S. Windahl. 'The Concept of Audience Activity' in Karl Erik Rosengren, Lawrence A. Wenner and Philip Palmgreen (Eds), *Media Gratifications Research: Current Perspectives*. Beverly Hills, CA: Sage Publications, 1985, pp. 109–22.

Lowery, Shearon A. and Melvin L. DeFleur. *Milestones in Mass Communication Research*. White Plains, NY: Longman, 2d ed., 1988.

McLeod, J.M, G.M. Kosicki and Pan Zhongdang. 'On Understanding and Misunderstanding of Media Effects', in James Curran and Michael Gurevitch (Eds), *Mass Media and Society*. London: Edward Arnold, 1991, pp. 235–66.

McLuhan, Marshall. *Understanding the Media: The Extensions of Man*. London: Routledge and Kegan Paul, 1964.

McQuail, Denis. *Mass Communication Theory: An Introduction*. London; Newbury Park, CA: Sage Publications, 1987.

Merrill, John Calhoun. *The Imperative of Freedom; A Philosophy of Journalistic Autonomy*. New York: Hastings House, 1974.

Murphy, Priscilla and Juliet Dee. 'Du Pont and Greenpeace: The Dynamics of Conflict Between Corporations and Activists Groups'. *Public Relations Research*, 4 (1), 1992, pp. 3–20.

Mickey, Thomas J. *Deconstructing Public Relations: Public Relations Criticism*. Mahwah, NJ; London: Lawrence Erlbaum, 2003.

Mintzberg, Henry. *Power in and Around Organizations*. Englewood Cliffs, NJ: Prentice-Hall, 1983.

Newcomb, T.M. 'An Approach to the Study of Communicative Acts'. *Psychological Review*, 60, 1953, pp. 394–404.

Newsom, D. 'Conflict: Who gets Media Attention — And Why?' *Public Relations Review*, 9, 1983, pp. 35–39.

Oliver, Sandra M. (Ed.). *Handbook of Corporate Communication and Strategic Public Relations: Pure And Applied*. London; New York: Routledge, 2004.

Prior-Miller, M. 'Four Major Social Scientific Theories and their Value to the Public Relations Research', in Carl H. Botan and Vincent Hazleton, Jr. (Eds), *Public Relations Theory*, Hillsdale, NJ: Lawrence Erlbaum Associates, 1989, pp. 67–81.

Putnam, L.L. and G. Cheney. 'A Critical Review of Research Traditions in Organizational Communication', in Mary S. Mander (Ed.) *Communications in Transition: Issues and Debates in Current Research*. New York: Praeger, 1983, pp. 206–24.

———. 'Organizational Communication: Historical Development and Future Directions', in Thomas W. Benson (Ed.), *Speech Communication in the 20th Century*. Carbondale: Southern Illinois University Press, 1985, pp. 130–56.

Reinharz, S. 'Feminist Distrust: Problems of Context and Content in Sociological Work', in David N. Berg and Kenwyn K. Smith (Eds), *Exploring Clinical Methods for Social Research*. Beverly Hills, CA: Sage, 1985, pp. 63–84.

Robbins, Stephen P. *Organization Theory: Structure, Design and Applications*. Englewood Cliffs, NJ: Prentice-Hall, 3rd ed., 1990.

Rogers, Everett M. *Diffusion of Innovations*. New York: Free Press; London: Collier Macmillan, 1983.

———. *Communication Technology: The New Media in Society*. New York: Free Press; London: Collier Macmillan, 1986.

———. 'The Diffusion of Innovation Perspective' in Neil D. Weinstein (Ed.), *Taking Care: Understanding and Encouraging Self-protective Behavior*. Cambridge: Cambridge University Press, 1987.

Rogers, Everett M. and D. Lawrence Kincaid. *Communication Networks: Toward a New Paradigm for Research*. New York: Free Press; London: Collier Macmillan, 1981.

Rose, Merrill. 'Activism in the 90s: Changing Roles for Public Relations'. *Public Relations Quarterly*, 36, pp. 29, 31–32, 1991.

Rush, R.R. 'Theories and Research to Live By: Communications and Information in the 21st Century'. Paper presented at the Association for Education in Journalism and Mass Communication, August 1993.

Ryan, Michael and David L. Martinson. 'The PR Officer as Corporate Conscience'. *Public Relations Quarterly*, 28 (2), 1983, pp. 20–23.

Sappington, A.A. 'Recent Psychological Approaches to the Free Will versus Determinism Issue'. *Psychological Bulletin*, 108 (1), 1990, pp. 19–29.

Shapere, Dudley. *Reason and the Search for Knowledge: Investigations in the Philosophy of Science*. Dordrecht, Netherlands; Boston: D. Reidel Publishing Co., 1984.

Siebert, Fred S., Theodore Peterson and Wilbur Schramm. *Four Theories of the Press: The Authoritarian, Libertarian, Social Responsibility, and Soviet Communist Concepts of what the Press should Be and Do*. Urbana, IL: University of Illinois Press, 1956.

Strauss, Anselm and Juliet Corbin. *Basics of Qualitative Research: Grounded Theory Procedures and Techniques*. Newbury Park, CA: Sage Publications, 1990.

Suppe, Frederick. *The Semantic Conception of Theories and Scientific Realism*. Chicago: University of Illinois Press, 1989.

Tan, Alexis S. *Mass Communication Theories and Research*. New York; London: Macmillan, 2d ed., 1985.

Toth, Elizabeth Lance. 'The Case of Pluralistic Studies of Public Relations: Rhetorical, Critical, and Systems Perspectives'. In Elizabeth Lance Toth and Robert L. Heath (Eds) *Rhetorical and Critical Approaches to Public Relations*. Hillsdale, NJ: Lawrence Erlbaum Associates, 1992.

Van Zoonen, L. 'Feminist Perspectives on the Media', in James Curran and Michael Gurevitch (Eds), *Mass Media and Society*. London; New York: Edward Arnold, 1991, pp. 235–66.

von Bertalanffy, Ludwig. *General System Theory: Foundations, Development, Applications*. New York: G. Braziller, 2d ed., 1969.

Wagner, Roy. *The Invention of Culture*, Chicago: University of Chicago Press, 1981.

Weaver, D.H. 'Political Issues and Voter Need for Orientation', in Donald L. Shaw and Maxwell E. McCombs (Eds), *The Emergence of American Political Issues: The Agenda-Setting Function of the Press*. St. Paul, MN: West Publishing Co., 1977, pp. 107–19.

Weber, Max. *The Theory of Social and Economic Organization*, (Parsons, Talcott and A.M. Henderson, Trans.), London: Collier-McMillan, 1968.

Windahl, Sven and Benno H. Signitzer, with Jean T. Olson. *Using Communication Theory: An Introduction to Planned Communication*, London; Newbury Park, CA: Sage Publications, 1992.

Wright, D.K. 'Implications of the IPRA "Gold Paper" '. *Public Relations Review*, 9 (2), 1983, pp. 3–6.

Index

MORE TITLES ON HISTORY FROM PILGRIMS PUBLISHING

A History Of Western Tibet One Of The Unknown Empires .... *Rev A H Francke*

Heroes And Builders Of Nepal .... *Rishikesh Shaha*

Benares Illustrated ....
James Prinsep with an Introduction by O. P. Kejariwal

Bhotan And The Story Of The Doar War .... *David Field RenniE*

India & Tibet .... *Francis Younghusband*

The Cultural Heritage Of Central India (Madhya Bharat) ...... *D.R.Patil*

The Life And Contribution Of The Nepalese Princess Brikuti Devi To Tibetan History .... *Min Bahadur Shakya*

Thug Or A Million Murders ....
Colonel James L Sleeman Foreword By Sir William T F Horwood

Tibet Past & Present .... *Sir Charles Bell*

12